"At This Defining Moment"

"At This Defining Moment"

*Barack Obama's Presidential Candidacy
and the New Politics of Race*

Enid Logan

NEW YORK UNIVERSITY PRESS
New York and London

NEW YORK UNIVERSITY PRESS
New York and London
www.nyupress.org

References to Internet websites (URLs) were accurate at the time of writing.
Neither the au thor nor New York University Press is responsible for URLs
that may have expired or changed since the manuscript was prepared.

Library of Congress Cataloging-in-Publication Data

Logan, Enid Lynette.
"At this defining moment" : Barack Obama's presidential candidacy and
the new politics of race / Enid Lynette Logan.
p. cm.
Includes bibliographical references and index.
ISBN 978–0–8147–5297–5 (cloth : alk. paper)
ISBN 978–0–8147–5298–2 (pbk. : alk. paper)
ISBN 978–0–8147–5346–0 (ebk.)
1. Presidents—United States—Election—2008.
2. Race—Political aspects—United States—History—21st century.
3. United States—Race relations—History—21st century. I. Title.
JK5262008 .L64   2011
324.973'0931—dc23   2011020456

New York University Press books are printed on acid-free paper,
and their binding materials are chosen for strength and durability.
We strive to use environmentally responsible suppliers and materials
to the greatest extent possible in publishing our books.

Manufactured in the United States of America

c   10 9 8 7 6 5 4 3 2 1
p   10 9 8 7 6 5 4 3 2 1

Contents

Acknowledgments

It seems hard to believe, but four years have passed since I first conceived this project. Most of the first two were spent thinking, watching the election unfold, and trying to figure out how to explain what was going on, from a sociological point of view—which seemed to me an urgent undertaking. The last two years have been a flurry of writing, revising, and presenting. It has been a long road, but on the way I have benefited from a fantastic support system at home and at work. I have also rediscovered my love of writing and research.

I would like to acknowledge first those who were so instrumental to my life during my graduate school days. Professors Julia Adams, Howard Kimeldorf, and Rebecca Scott at the University of Michigan especially helped to mold my budding sociological mind. Professor Eduardo Bonilla-Silva was around only at the beginning of my graduate school career, but he has been a true scholarly inspiration. I also acknowledge my friends Rochelle Woods, Niki Dickerson, Darcy Leach, Sylvia Orduño, and Tasleem Padamsee. There is something special about your graduate school crew!

My colleagues at the University of Minnesota have helped to make six months of winter per year more than bearable. I especially acknowledge Ron Aminzade, Njeri Githire, Teresa Gowan, Carolyn Liebler, Phyllis Moen, Ann Meier, Joshua Page, Lisa Park, David Pellow, Teresa Swartz, and Chris Uggen. Much gratitude is due as well to our fabulous administrative aide Mary Drew, who makes all things possible in the Sociology Department. Thank you to Ayodele Alofe for the many hours spent proofreading and editing the manuscript, which I'm sure you would have preferred to spend with your kids. I acknowledge my Sociologists for Women in Society mentor, Professor Barbara Trepagnier. It's been nice to know there was another person out there in the sociological universe who had my back. I thank the University of Minnesota for providing me a Grant-in-Aid, Single Semester Leave, and other support toward this research. I also thank my editor at NYU Press, Ilene Kalish, for her excitement about this project from the beginning, and for her work to get it through the stages of review, revision, and copyediting in such a timely manner.

This book is dedicated in part to the curious, thoughtful, lovely students at the University of Minnesota, who have made teaching and learning from them feel like my life's purpose.

To my best friend, Yasmin Holsey, who has been with me since the Sidwell Friends days, I love ya! And thanks to my family: brother, Malcolm; sister-in-law, Youlanda; dad, John; sister, Monica; and mother, Shirley (all Logans). Monica, you are the best wiser sister one could have: I want to be like you one day. Mom (Professor Logan the first), to quote our future president Sarah Palin, you have been a true Mama Grizzly Bear this last year. Thank you for your amazing mother love! Even at my advanced age, it is much appreciated.

I also dedicate this book to my husband, Don Allen, who spent most of the first six months of our marriage watching me sit at my computer and work on this manuscript. Thank you for your love and patience, and for keeping me happy and fed! And thank you for letting me beat you at racquetball several times a week. You and little Jake are my Minnesota miracles.

Introduction

The Landscape of Race in the 21st Century

On February 11, 2007, Senator Barack Obama, who had just the day before in Springfield, Illinois, declared his intention to run for the U.S. presidency, gave an interview with the *60 Minutes* reporter Steve Kroft. Shortly into that interview, they had the following exchange:

> KROFT: Your mother was white. Your father was African.
> OBAMA: Right.
> KROFT: You spent most of your life in a white household.
> OBAMA: Yeah.
> KROFT: I mean, you grew up white.

Obama's response to this statement was quite interesting:

> I'm not sure that would be true. I think what would be true is that I don't have the typical background of African Americans. Not just because my mother was white, but because I grew up in Hawaii; I've spent time in Indonesia. There [were] all sorts of ethnicities and cultures that were swirling around my head as I was growing up. . . .
>
> There were times where that was difficult. One of the things that helped me to resolve a lot of these issues is the realization that the African American community, which I'm now very much feel a part of, is itself a hybrid community. . . .
>
> What I also realized is that the American experience is, by definition, a hybrid experience. I mean, you know, one of the strengths of this country is that we have these people coming from, you know, all four corners of the globe converging . . . sometimes in conflict . . . to create this tapestry that is incredibly strong. And so, in that sense, I

feel that my background, ironically, because it's unusual, is quintes-
sentially American.

Undaunted by Obama's attempts to explain his hybridity, and the hybridity of the American people in general, Kroft continued:

KROFT: You were raised in a white household?
OBAMA: Right.
KROFT: Yet, at some point, you decided that you were black?

Obama responded:

OBAMA: Well, I'm not sure I decided it.[1]

The present book is about this exchange, and the thousands of others
like it that took place in the public sphere during the 2007–2008 presidential campaign. It is about the nation's journey toward electing its first
non-white president in its history, a time period spanning more than two
centuries. It is about the awkward, fraught, and determined questionings
of the nature, meaning, and authenticity of Obama's blackness. And it
is about the responses of the multiracial electorate to the narratives of
national triumph, racial redemption, and post-racialism that were spun
by the media and by the Obama campaign.

The key issue that is explored in this book is how Barack Obama's presidential candidacy served to reflect and shape the dynamics of race in the
contemporary United States. The study is timely and important, because
the present moment constitutes a pivotal juncture in the sociopolitical life
of our nation. Obama's election will have a lasting impact on race relations
in this country, and it is perceived to have ushered in a "new age" in American racial politics. Thus the conclusions that are reached concerning the
meaning of race at this particular juncture are likely to set the parameters
for teaching, activism, and scholarship about race for decades to come.

Theoretical Concerns

A number of prominent theorists have claimed that with regard to the
issue of race, we find ourselves in a period of profound uncertainty and
instability. As we move forward into the post–civil rights, post-feminist,

and ever more global age, they ask, what institutional, experiential, and ideological contours will the social construct of race take on?

This question has acquired even more urgency, uncertainty, and interest with the recent election of a man socially identified as black as the president of the United States. For the last several years, scholars, pundits, and laypeople alike have furiously debated what the Obama phenomenon says about the current state of race relations in the United States, and what it portends for our future. I conceive of this project as a case study in U.S. race relations that takes the candidacy of Barack Obama as its object. The power of this particular case is that it allows for a close exploration of a number of the most pressing questions in the field of race relations at this time, including the following:

❖ How do we adequately capture the complexity of race in the 21st-century United States?[2]

❖ How does racism most often manifest itself in the United States today? What fundamental differences are there in how whites and non-whites understand race?[3]

❖ To what extent are race and gender parallel constructs, and in what ways do they differ?[4]

❖ Is the black/white binary still the primary axis around which race relations in this country revolve? Or has the racial map been fundamentally altered by the mass influx of immigrants from Latin America and Asia in the last several decades?[5]

❖ Does it make sense to speak of "a" black community, or "the" black experience? Or have differences in socioeconomic status among African Americans led to markedly divergent worldviews, experiences, and identities?[6]

❖ Will the "browning of America" result in a peaceable redefinition and expansion of national identity? Or will it provoke a culture war over what it really means to be an American?[7]

❖ Is the United States on the verge of overcoming its legacy of racial exclusion? Or will racism in the 21st century simply become more covert, insidious, and entrenched?[8]

Barack Obama's presidential bid brought each of these issues sharply into focus. From the moment he declared his candidacy in February 2007, the nation was forced to undergo a thorough reexamination of its core beliefs, subconscious fears, and highest ideals concerning the concept of race—and the place of African Americans, in particular.

Data, Methods, and Study Design

The vigorous debates about the election found in the print and online media constitute particularly fertile ground for a study of the changing politics of race in the 21st century. Thus articles, postings, and commentary gathered from the mainstream media and the blogosphere constitute the chief source of primary data used in this book.

The most frequently referenced sources include newspapers (*Wall Street Journal, New York Times, Washington Times, Washington Post, Los Angeles Times, Chicago Tribune, Boston Globe, Atlanta Journal-Constitution*), newsmagazines (*Time, Newsweek, National Review, The Atlantic, Weekly Standard, New Republic, Monthly Review, The Nation, American Prospect*), political blogs (Townhall.com, *Michelle Malkin, Daily Kos, AlterNet*, Salon.com, *Huffington Post, RealClearPolitics*, Politico.com, *Drudge Report, The Root, Jack & Jill Politics, Black Agenda Report, Jezebel, Feministing*), and other major media outlets (Associated Press, Reuters, Fox News, National Public Radio, CNN, CBS News, ABC News, MSNBC).

The arguments developed in the book are based on my analysis of some 1,500 articles published or posted over an approximately three-year period. I began collecting data in earnest in November 2006, about three months before Obama declared his candidacy. That month saw the publication of the article "What Obama Isn't: Black Like Me on Race" by the cultural critic Stanley Crouch, which was one of the first questionings of Obama's blackness. That month the *Washington Post* also printed Benjamin Wallace-Wells's influential "Is America Too Racist for Barack? Too Sexist for Hillary?" This was an early attempt to parse the differing ways that race and gender would likely play out in the election. My analysis extends well into the first three years of Obama's presidency, during which observers continued to take stock of the historical and cultural import of Obama's victory, and during which new controversies over race, politics, and nation would erupt.[9]

At each stage of reporting on the election, I focused on the ways that race figured into the stories and reports that were offered. I examined the frames—both positive and negative—used to interpret Obama's life history, his relationship to the social construct of blackness, his appeal to voters across racial lines, and his political beliefs and affiliations. I studied the ways that ideas about race circulated through debates about the economy, gender, religion, patriotism, and foreign policy. I was particularly interested in assessments of the broader role of race in the election, and the significance of Obama's candidacy for the nation at large. After identifying key themes found in discussions of the election, I linked these themes to wider discourses about race in American society.

One of the unique contributions of this book lies in its intersectional approach. Scholars of intersectionality have argued that in order to understand how race works in any given context, we must consider the role of other social variables as well. Race, gender, class, and sexuality do not act independently of one another, but rather interrelate and are experienced simultaneously. One of the most fascinating aspects of the 2008 presidential election was that as race came ever more to the fore, questions of gender, religion, class, age, and nation were dragged right into the middle as well. Thus, while two chapters of this book focus primarily on the variable of race, others examine race in relationship to gender and to nation.[10]

The Landscape of Race in the 21st Century

To set the stage for this study, we must consider the racial conditions that established the context for Barack Obama's presidential bid. I begin with the observation that racial dynamics at present are contradictory, complicated, and in flux. The sociologist Charles Gallagher has stated that we live in a racially "schizophrenic" time. Similarly, Eduardo Bonilla-Silva writes of "the strange enigma of race in contemporary America."[11] And as Howard Winant has observed, "The contemporary United States faces a pervasive crisis of race, a crisis no less severe than those the country has confronted in the past. . . . The cultural and political meaning of race, its significance in shaping the social structure, and its experiential or existential dimensions all remain profoundly unresolved as the United States approaches the end of the twentieth century. As a result, the society as a whole, and the population as individuals, suffer from confusion and anxiety about the issue (or complex of issues) we call race."[12]

The predominant features of the contemporary racial landscape include the following:

Persistent inequality. The important but partial gains of the civil rights movement. The contradiction, or irony, of formal legal equality and a widespread commitment to racial equality in the abstract, contrasted with profound, and in many cases deepening, inequality in education, housing, wealth, income, employment, life expectancy, child welfare, and criminal justice.[13]

New immigrants of color. Mass immigration from Asia, Latin America, and Africa following the elimination of national origins quotas in 1965. The development of "new racial subjects" and the emergence of Asian American and Latino pan-ethnicity. The new immigrants complicate, but do not displace, the black/white binary understanding of racial dynamics. And as Ngai writes, the new demographics "have both enhanced the politics of diversity and multiculturalism and provoked nativist sentiment and campaigns." In the 2008 campaign, fears about immigration were especially relevant to the larger discourses of race and nation that emerged from the political right. (Among liberals however, the conversation about race was primarily a discussion about black and white.)[14]

Black identities. The emergence of plural black identities and complicated meanings of blackness. Of chief importance is the growing class divide among black Americans, leading to differences in identity, experience, and political ideology. Dominant understandings of blackness today are further challenged by the increasing visibility of multiracial Americans, and the presence of black immigrants from the Caribbean, Latin America, and Africa.[15] Of particular relevance to the issues addressed in this book is the emergence of a highly successful cohort of "post-racial" black figures in music, sports, movies, television, and politics.

Crisis in white identity. As a number of scholars have written, the post–civil rights United States is characterized by considerable anxiety and insecurity associated with the social construct of whiteness. As whites have themselves become "racialized," whiteness is no longer a transparent or taken-for-granted category of identity. But what it *means* to be white is far from clear. The anxieties of whiteness have been provoked by the demands of the racial justice movements of the 1960s, mass immigration from developing countries, the decline of American international hegemony, and shifts in popular culture toward a valorization of "diversity."[16]

These changes, scholars claim, have led to a pervasive sense of white marginalization, disadvantage, and victimization.[17] The range of current responses to the crisis of whiteness includes looking to one's ethnic roots for sources of "tradition," seeking authenticity in the cultures of others, embracing multiculturalism, rejecting multiculturalism, adopting an identity as a member of a "beleaguered minority," or seeking to affirm the roots of the "real America" in Christianity, "small-town America," and conservative values.[18] One of the central arguments of this book is that the racial politics of both Obama's supporters *and* his detractors were formulated in response to the anxieties associated with whiteness and with race in the contemporary United States.

Globalization and the construct of nation. The global dimensions of the anxieties of race must be considered as well. They stem first from the demographic and cultural shifts accompanying mass immigration from developing countries, as referenced above. The second most important factor in the production of racialized anxieties of nation is the threat of global terrorism. Questions that have been asked anew include: Who is an American? Do whites even have a place in their "own land" anymore? Or does the current wave of immigration in fact constitute a dangerous "immigrant invasion"?

Colorblind individualism. The landscape of race is also very much shaped by the predominance of the ideology of colorblind individualism. This ideology holds that racial discrimination against non-whites is largely of a thing of the past, that it is better not to speak about racial matters, and that policy initiatives designed to remedy racial inequality are themselves discriminatory and unfair.[19] The Obama presidency could lead to the consolidation of this ideology, by seeming to "prove" that race is no longer a significant barrier to achievement. Alternately, this or other 21st-century racial realities could lead to cracks in the hegemony of racial colorblindness.

Post-racialism and the new politics of race. The 2008 presidential election brought to the fore discussions of post-racialism and new racial politics. Currently the new race politics is an elaboration of the ideology of colorblind individualism, articulated as a set of racialized expectations of black Americans and other non-whites. It holds the potential, however, to develop into a more inclusive, empowering politics.

As the discussion above suggests, this book engages with the theories of scholars who have made broad predictions about race relations in the coming decades. The authors I am in dialogue with include (but are not limited to) Howard Winant, Charles Gallagher, Michael Omi, Joe Feagin, Eduardo Bonilla-Silva, Eileen O'Brien, Claire Jean Kim, George Yancey, and Andra Gillespie.[20] I draw especially on theoretical insights concerning the nature of contemporary race relations found in Winant's *The New Politics of Race* and Bonilla-Silva's *Racism without Racists*. The central theoretical concepts I work with, and expand on, in this book include colorblind individualism, post-racialism, "new race politics," and white racial anxiety.

Elements of the Argument

We heard from many corners in the 2008 election that race was largely irrelevant to the majority of Americans. Whites in particular did not "see" Obama's color, they just saw Obama the man. And having elected a black president, the logic went, we were on the verge of achieving a truly post-racial society, where race no longer significantly affected one's opportunities or life chances.

Social indicators, on the other hand, would seem to demonstrate the opposite. In terms of average wealth, income, educational achievement, rates of death, disease, arrest, incarceration, infant mortality, single parenthood, voter participation, and home ownership, the United States remains profoundly racially stratified. While immigrants from certain parts of the globe have become fairly well integrated into the economic and cultural life of the nation, lower-income African Americans in particular seem to remain the insoluble, indigestible "other." And despite claims that race mattered little to Americans choosing a president, a review of the evidence reveals that the mainstream media and the blogosphere were *saturated* with race talk in 2007/2008. So how do we make sense of these apparent paradoxes?

It is my argument that race played a central role in the 2008 campaign, though in ways different than in the past. Blackness did not figure here as an automatic disqualifier for political office, but it was hardly irrelevant either. Obama won not in spite of race, but because he offered an appealing, carefully mediated version of blackness that a majority of the electorate readily consumed. Crucially, this model of blackness provided a powerful "rebuke" to more problematic versions of black politics understood to be embodied by leaders such as Jesse Jackson, Al Sharpton, and Jeremiah Wright. Obama's election was said to herald the dawn of a "new politics of race."

The central narrative of the election crafted by the press was in many ways the story of America's definitive "triumph" over racism. Obama was seen to offer the nation, and whites in particular, redemption and absolution for the sins of the past. Supporting the Obama campaign was presented as a revolutionary act that would bring about meaningful and definitive social change. This was so despite the fact that Obama was clearly most comfortable in the middle of the political spectrum. Further, while Obama invited Americans to believe that his campaign was a movement for racial justice, he was clear that he would neither make substantive demands of whites nor fundamentally disrupt the racial order.

Obama's win has already influenced U.S. racial politics by bringing certain trends to the forefront while decreasing the likelihood that others will take root. In the former category are the expansion of black public identities and the ascendance of the 21st-century racial etiquette that I identify as the "new politics of race." Obama's win also means that a renewal of white support for race-based affirmative action is very unlikely. The racial controversies of the first years of the Obama administration (the Sotomayor nomination, the Henry Louis Gates arrest, the racially inflected backlash politics of the "Tea Party") further suggest that racial dynamics under the regime of the new race politics may be shifting to the right.[21]

The election has particularly important ramifications for internal and external conceptions of American national identity. The person selected as president is the symbolic embodiment of a certain vision of our national past and present. With the election of Barack Obama, the "we" that we are is now potentially conceived of as red, white, blue, and brown. Obama won the 2008 election while claiming an impressive 43% of the white vote. But post-electoral developments—such as the vocal protests of "birthers" claiming that he is not a U.S. citizen, the attempts of certain members of the Tea Party movement to reestablish whiteness as a criterion of national identity, and the proposals to revise the 14th Amendment to restrict citizenship rights—suggest that contentious debates over race and national belonging will continue well into the 21st century.

Organization of the Book

In chapter 2, I turn to the weeks immediately following November 4, 2008. I identify and critically evaluate the predominant interpretation of the meaning of Obama's victory, which I call the "triumphalist narrative of post-race America." It is my argument that this ostensibly celebratory narrative encoded a series of deeply problematic assumptions about black Americans, the course of American history, and the roots of social inequality. Its assertion that the nation had been proved to be officially race-blind ignored the crucial, if complicated, ways that race *did* play into the presidential race. Most fundamentally, this narrative strongly supported the conservative, "colorblind individualist" perspective on race—

one that masks and defends entrenched racial inequality while paradoxically claiming to champion racial justice. But in the absence of a vigorous critique—or even better, an alternative, critical, and empowering analysis of the significance of Obama's win—this narrative is likely to take root in the American psyche and become the new "common sense" about race in the United States today.

Chapter 3 discusses the so-called new politics of race that the age of Obama is said to herald. The highly celebrated "new politics of race" is an outgrowth, or elaboration, of the ideology of colorblind individualism. The new politics focuses on the responsibilities of blacks (and other non-whites) in achieving a society free of racial strife. In the new politics, blacks are called to "get over" race by ceasing to talk about it, leaving behind identity politics, and viewing racism not as systematic or structural but as episodic and rare. Reasonable blacks should agree that most whites are well intentioned and colorblind, that whites and blacks can be *equally* racist, and that blacks must pull themselves up by their bootstraps and solve their own problems.

There were many moments in the 2008 election in which the "new" politics of race were juxtaposed against the "old." Obama's careful presentation of himself as a next-generation black politician, fundamentally different from previous African American leaders, was, and continues to be, crucial to his ability to garner white support. I contend that the new politics of race as presently formulated constitute a form of colorblindness in the defense of white racial privilege. But I suggest that the concept of new race politics may hold some promise, as the social and political realities of the 21st century do demand new ways of thinking about and dealing with race.

In chapter 4, I discuss and compare the ways that race and gender figured into the democratic primary. Here I rely on evidence from the print and online media, as well as quotes from a subsample of a large set of in-depth interviews I conducted with college students in the weeks preceding the election.[22] In the first part of the chapter, I discuss the impassioned, often angry debates about race and gender that the contest occasioned, and the deep divides that were revealed to exist between women to the left of center. Among other things, the debates demonstrated that despite decades of discussion about multiculturalism and inclusiveness, conceptions of "womanhood" among many prominent feminist activists and white female members of the rank and file remained tied to notions of whiteness. They also entailed an increasing sense of victimization vis-à-vis non-whites, a key characteristic of the contemporary construct of whiteness.[23]

Chapter 5 analyzes the relationship between race and nation in the discourse of Obama's campaign. Though many pundits argued that Obama ran a largely "deracialized" campaign, it is my contention that race was a central, if implicit, element in Obama's core narrative. Obama positioned himself as heir to both the civil rights struggle and the American Revolution, and implied that through his candidacy, the highest ideals of the nation would be fulfilled. Having triumphantly lived up to its creed, the nation would be absolved of the sins of past and present.

While the archetype of national identity that Obama presented was very different from the racially bounded, exclusionary forms of nationalism to emerge from the right, I argue, it was not without its own shortcomings. National unity was to be achieved in part by glossing over historical and contemporary manifestations of racial injustice, and by promoting a vision of national "diversity" largely devoid of an agenda for social justice.[24]

In chapter 6, I discuss racial politics among Asian and Latino voters in the 2008 contest. The chapter is motivated in part by a series of theoretical questions pertaining to the racialization of non-black non-whites in the 21st century. Specifically, I assess the usefulness of a black/white understanding of race relations for understanding the experiences of non-black populations of color, and I explore Claire Jean Kim's concept of "racial triangulation." I look both at portrayals of Latino and Asian American communities found in the mainstream media, and I consider the politics of race from the perspective of those in the "racial middle" themselves.[25]

I find first that the national discussions about race that took place during the 2008 presidential campaign were overwhelmingly framed in terms of black and white. The members of the racial middle, while not entirely absent from the discourse about race, were mostly peripheral to it. To the extent that Latino and Asian voters were discussed in the mainstream media at all, they were most often presented as the racial antagonists of African Americans. Their early, overwhelming support for Hillary Clinton was taken as a manifestation of deeply held anti-black prejudices, and as confirmation of the raging antipathies said to exist between blacks and other non-whites. I argue that this characterization of Latino and Asian voters had a functional role in the larger narrative of the election, as it served to verify whites' own triumph over race.

The seventh chapter of the book critically examines the racial politics of the right. I argue that the "real America" narrative forwarded by the McCain/Palin campaign was rooted in the racially coded populist discourse that the right has aggressively forwarded since the late 1970s. According to the architects of this discourse, the nation is profoundly imperiled by cultural and demographic trends characteristic of the present age. At the top of the list are non-white immigration, secular liberalism, gay rights, feminism, "black racism," political correctness, and Islamic terrorism. Obama was figured as the embodiment of these threats, a foreign other who stood in opposition to the interests of "everyday Americans" and the nation itself. A vote for the Republican ticket, we were told, was a vote to uphold the sanctity and security of conservative, white, Christian America.

In the concluding chapter, I discuss how developments since the election relate to the larger arguments that I have presented in the book. In particular, I focus on the birther and Tea Party movements. In the last section of the chapter, I consider the legacy of the 2008 election for the politics of race and nation in the future.

What we saw in 2008, I argue, was neither that race no longer matters in American politics nor that the United States is irredeemably racist. Rather, we learned that a certain kind of black candidate, relying on a specific deployment of blackness, could in fact make it to the presidency. Obama won for many reasons—because he appeared to be an antidote to the Bush years, because he had an excellent team of advisers, because the economic meltdown made McCain look out of touch, and, in part, because of his race. Making scholarly sense of this fact is crucial to addressing the puzzle of race in the 21st century. I attempt to do so in this book.

Post-race American Triumphalism and the Entrenchment of Colorblind Racial Ideology

On January 20, 2009, Barack Obama became the 44th president of the United States. In the weeks following the election, as in the months that preceded it, countless social observers from across the ideological spectrum offered commentary concerning the cultural, social, and political significance of the Obama phenomenon. They especially discussed what Obama's successful campaign said about the state of our democracy and the role of race in the saga of the nation.

While the voices were not monolithic, a sort of consensus emerged in the public sphere. The pundits spoke, triumphantly, of the "major transformation" that had taken place in the life of the nation. Obama's win was said to be the realization of our national ideals and evidence of the maturation of our democracy. Observers from across the political spectrum proclaimed that we stood on the verge of a new, post-racial age, in which people would be judged by character and not by color. With the victory, the narrative went, the old politics of race, focusing on black grievance, victimhood, and protest, were vanquished, leaving in their place newer, more effective ways of getting things done. Obama's success was said to prove that if racism was not dead, surely it was on its way out. And while the election held many lessons for the country as a whole, the ones it offered to blacks were said to be among the most important: there are no longer any "excuses" for your failure.

In this chapter I identify and critically evaluate the predominant narrative interpretation of Obama's victory, which I call the "triumphalist narrative of post-race America." It is my argument that this ostensibly celebratory narrative encodes a series of deeply problematic assumptions about black Americans, the course of American history, and the roots of social inequality. Its assertion that the nation has been proved to be officially race-blind ignores the crucial, if complicated, ways that race did play into the presidential race. Most fundamentally, this narrative strongly supports the conservative, colorblind individualist perspective on race—a perspective that masks and defends entrenched racial inequality while paradoxically claiming to champion racial justice.[1]

The statements that are referred to in this chapter come primarily from journalists, bloggers, and other writers whose work appears in the mainstream and online media. I draw on approximately 150 articles appearing in the months immediately before and after the election. I analyze writing found in major newspapers, newsmagazines, widely read political blogs, and other large media outlets, from across the political spectrum.[2]

The objects of my analysis, therefore, are the interpretative frames pertaining to the election presented in the American media. It is vital that scholars critically engage with these discourses, because the interpretations of Obama's victory that they encapsulate constitute the very grounds on which hegemonic understandings of the meaning of race in American society are being renegotiated. As one young black writer stated during the election, "at night the cable talk shows are filled with trifling gibberish that either extols Obama's 'postracialism' or cautions him against being branded the 'black presidential candidate'. . . . These pronouncements are almost always made by men who would most likely be hard-pressed to recall the last time they sat down to dinner with a black family." Speaking of the pundit class itself, he continued, "I can't think of a group more ill equipped to bear witness to humanity, much less a phenomenon as intricate and complicated as race in America."

Similarly, just after Obama's win, one political scientist wrote, "Nowhere are promises of the 'end of race' better represented than in pro-Obama postelectoral celebrations in corporate media outlets . . . . It has become commonplace in media debates to refer to segregation and racism as ancient history. . . . The intent is clear enough: the message is sent that Americans are finally transcending, or have transcended race." Taken together, these statements underscore the necessity of our challenging the outsized role that the media has played in shaping the national conversation on race.[3]

Triumphalism and Colorblind Individualism in the 2008 Election

The narrative of post-race America is a 21st-century version of American triumphalism. The political scientist Claire Jean Kim writes that American triumphalist narratives present the U.S. as "a uniquely great nation" that has "overcome all obstacles [in a] march towards the perfect fulfillment of its founding ideals." "A hallmark of triumphalist narratives," she continues, "is their transformation of national vices into virtues, and their citation of the putative overcoming of these vices as proof of the nation's dynamic progress towards the fulfillment of its creed."[4] Each of these elements was present in the dominant narrative of the 2008 presidential race. Once tarnished by a history of racial strife, and more recently disgraced by our participation in an unpopular war in the Middle East, we were said to have emerged from the election a nation redeemed. According to the pundits, Obama's victory proved that we had left the era of racial oppression solidly behind us and were a nation for the world to again admire.

The basic understanding of racial matters on which the myth of post-race America is built is the ideology of colorblind individualism. Sociologists have identified colorblind racial ideology as the dominant racial paradigm of the post–civil rights era.[5] While there are liberal and conservative variants of this ideology, the differences between them at this juncture are fairly small. For example, while antidiscrimination legislation, voting rights, school integration, welfare rights, and affirmative action were once pillars of liberalism, these initiatives are now only weakly defended by mainstream liberal politicians.[6] The overall terms of debate about race in this country have moved significantly to the right in the last several decades, as the neoconservative perspective has won over the more left-leaning framings of racial politics.[7]

The central axiom of colorblind individualism is that we have already achieved an essentially colorblind society, one in which race is largely irrelevant to the life chances of non-whites. While most whites hold that they and others like them simply do not see race, non-whites are understood to be irrationally preoccupied with color. Acts of discrimination against people of color are viewed as infrequent, unlikely, and overreported. Under this paradigm, persistent racial inequality (in areas such as education, income, wealth, housing, and employment) is viewed as natural and inevitable, or explained as being due to the cultural deficiencies of people of color. Blacks, in particular, are therefore called to get over their victim mentality, stop looking for increasingly rare instances of racism, and pull themselves up by their bootstraps.[8]

As sociologists have demonstrated, colorblind individualism has many pitfalls. It enforces blindness to the historically accumulated advantages that whites receive in this society, as well as to the covert, routine mechanisms of discrimination that are in place today. This perspective naturalizes inequality and allows strong anti-black views (i.e., they are lazy, sexually irresponsible, "ghetto," prone to crime) to flourish under the cover of supposed race-blindness. Increasingly, colorblind racial ideology positions whites either as exempt from racial matters or as victims of reverse racism. The onus for solving the problems of race therefore lies squarely on the shoulders of people of color. Further, in this model, the achievement of abstract equality before the law, or "race-neutrality," entirely supplants the goal of substantive equality. Thus efforts to achieve representative parity in education or employment, for example, are characterized as illegitimate, anti-American, and unfair to whites.[9]

Colorblind individualism emerged as a racial project of neoconservatives and members of the New Right who sought to halt or reverse the gains of the racial justice movements of the 1960s. Howard Winant argues, convincingly, that colorblind individualism attained hegemonic status because it responds to the manifold anxieties—cultural, demographic, and economic—associated with whiteness in the late 20th century. Charles Gallagher further claims that colorblind individualism is appealing because "it removes from personal thought and public discussion any taint or suggestion of white supremacy or white guilt, while legitimating the existing social, political, and economic arrangements which privilege whites."[10]

Dominant interpretations of the significance of Barack Obama's victory found in the press strongly reflected the ideology of colorblind individualism—in its more conservative and reactionary formulations. An emergent theme of the coverage of the presidential election was that race was largely a problem of people of color, as whites—having supported Obama in large numbers—had proved themselves to be truly colorblind. The news media especially forwarded the idea that reverse racism (à la Jeremiah Wright) was the most serious and prevalent form of racism today. Those who talk about racism were widely characterized as "race-baiters" and "agitators," and identified as the true source of our racial problems; thus, following Obama's example, we were told that it was best to discuss race very little, if at all. Race itself was said to have factored very little in the election. But to the extent that it did, the pundits wrote, it was largely to Obama's *benefit*—confirming the notion that blacks as a group tended to be racially advantaged in today's society. Further, our new president's success was said to prove that affirmative action was unnecessary and unfair, and that blacks who were struggling to make it were largely to blame for their own problems—because they would not get over their obsession with race, because they preferred handouts to hard work, and because they tended to be poor parents (especially fathers) to their children.

The ideology undergirding the triumphalist electoral narrative thus instructed us to turn our attention away from the mechanisms that continue to sustain black marginalization, and firmly toward the deficiencies of the marginalized themselves. Rather than leading to a broad, critical dialogue about race, the kinds of arguments detailed above tend to foreclose the possibilities for meaningful dialogue altogether. An irony of the election of our first black president, then, is that the narrative forwarded in celebration of his victory may serve to "stall transformation of the racial order in the direction of greater equality."[11]

Three interrelated claims formed the cornerstones of the narrative of post-race America: first, that Obama's victory redeemed the United States by proving that we were truly blind to color; second, that it demonstrated that we had officially solved the problem of race; and third, that all it would take for black Americans to be fully integrated into the American mainstream was a solid work ethic, family values, and a willingness to get over their victim mentality. These claims are explored, and then interrogated, below.

A Nation Redeemed

A particularly triumphal tone was found in discussions of the meaning of the election for the country as a whole. Like other national events, such as the emancipation of the slaves, apologies for the Japanese internment, or the "liberation" of Iraq, the 2008 presidential election figured as a moment where American benevolence was said to shine triumphant.[12] A nearly universal claim of the pundit class was that Obama's victory demonstrated the greatness of our country, and stood as an affirmation of our most cherished ideals. In the *Wall Street Journal*, for example, the black conservative Shelby Steele described the win as "documentation of the moral evolution we have gone through in the past 40 years." And on *RealClearMarkets*, former U.S. civil rights commissioner Russell Redenbaugh declared Obama's climb to the presidency to be "the definition of the American dream."[13]

So widespread was the implication that Obama's victory made the United States a better place that the conservative news analyst Tucker

Carlson bitterly argued on November 4 that the media had framed the choice between Obama and McCain "as a referendum on the goodness of America." Carlson was not far off the mark. In a February 2007 segment of NBC's *Meet the Press*, for example, the Politico.com chief political analyst Roger Simon had stated, "If America actually nominates him and then votes for him for president and elects him, this will be a sign that we are a good and decent country that has healed its racial wounds."[14]

Pundits especially emphasized Obama's purported power to redeem the United States in the eyes of the world. Whereas the "disgraceful" years of the Bush administration had led international leaders to regard the United States with condescension and scorn, our selection of Obama was said to have led to renewed appreciation. As Garrison Keillor wrote on Salon.com, "We are being admired by Swedes! We don't have to pretend we're Canadians. We elected Barack Obama!" And as Bruce Cain declared in the *Los Angeles Times* on November 5, "If the U.S. can overcome its racial past, it gives hope to other democracies as well."[15]

Post–Civil Rights and Nearly Post-Race

The press also forwarded the notion that Obama's victory meant that we had definitively turned the page on the problem of race. For the pop sociologist Michael Dyson, the election represented "a quantum leap" in our nation's racial progress. And according to James Bacon in the *Richmond Times-Dispatch*, Obama's win "gave Americans the opportunity to put the grievous demon" of black oppression solidly "behind them."[16]

Obama's ascent was said to prove that racism in the United States was no longer systematic or institutionalized. As Ward Connerly, black America's most prominent affirmative action foe, asked in the *Boston Globe*, "How can you say there is institutional racism when people in Nebraska vote for . . . a self-identified black man?" In the *Chicago Tribune*, the liberal African American columnist Clarence Page echoed these sentiments, stating, "It's hard to argue that our society is irredeemably racist when our multiracial electorate just elected a man with African roots and an Arabic-sounding name to be commander-in-chief."[17]

Still others claimed that with the election the U.S. had solved the problem of race entirely. According to the black columnist Phillip Morris, on November 4 "the nation unburdened itself of the albatross of race" and "completed its evolution into a racial meritocracy."[18] In the *Philadelphia*

Daily News, Stu Bykofsky declared that with Obama's victory, "America got the race monkey off its back."[19] And on the day after the election, the *Wall Street Journal* declared, "One promise of [the] victory is that perhaps we can put to rest the myth of racism as a barrier to achievement in this splendid country. Mr. Obama has a special obligation to help do so."[20] While right-wing advocates of colorblind ideology had long forwarded similar arguments about the end of racism, the 2008 election encouraged many political liberals to join the chorus.

Some commentators took their arguments even further. For them, Obama's success served as a strong and decisive rebuke to those "obsessed" with race and racism, proving that they had been wrong all along. Such misguided individuals included "professional fear-mongers" and "race-baiters" (such as Jesse Jackson and Al Sharpton), race-conscious liberals, "victimologist" professors on campuses all over the country, and most of the black rank and file. On the night of Obama's unexpected January 3, 2008, Iowa primary win, the conservative commentator George Will declared triumphantly on ABC News, "The big losers, two big losers tonight are probably Jesse Jackson and Al Sharpton." The *New Republic* chief editor Martin Peretz opined in April 2008 that "race hustlers" like Cornel West were "afraid that Obama has so deeply touched a nerve among white Americans that they will soon be out of work forever."[21]

From early in the democratic primary, journalists discussing the kind of change that was coming claimed that with Obama's rise to power, the "old politics of race"—focusing on victimhood, grievance, and confrontation—had been vanquished, giving way to a politics that downplayed race while emphasizing interracial unity and self-help. As they triumphantly slammed the door on the old black politics, pundits displayed special zeal in shoving the "old black politicians" out the door with them. Obama's ascent was repeatedly cast as the final verdict on the tactics and careers of Jesse Jackson and Al Sharpton, whom many in the pundit class consistently discussed in terms betraying their disgust and irritation. In a 2007 *Atlantic* article titled "The Great Black-White Hope," Stuart Taylor triumphantly proclaimed that with Obama's rise, the United States could "relegate to the dustbin of history the snake-oil salesmen who have been anointed by the media as the leaders of black America, even as they have used their prominence to poison race relations while (in many cases) living high on the hog."

The black conservative Larry Elder predicted on Townhall.com that whether Obama won or lost, "Jackson and Sharpton and the rest of the like-minded traveling circus [would] remain in the business of ferreting out, exploiting and often exaggerating allegations of racism for face time on TV and continued relevance." And Juan Williams wrote on November 10 in the *Wall Street Journal*, "The market has irrevocably shrunk for Sharpton-style tirades against 'the man' and 'the system.' The emphasis on racial threats and extortion-like demands—all aimed at maximizing white guilt as leverage for getting government and corporate money—has lost its moment."[22]

The Jeremiah Wright episode was a pivotal moment in the 2008 presidential campaign, in which the old politics of race were juxtaposed against the new. Wright, who had been Obama's pastor for more than 20 years, strongly condemned the racism and imperialism of the United States in a series of fiery sermons between 2001 and 2003. When tapes of the sermons surfaced amid the Democratic primary and were looped repeatedly across the 24-hour cable news cycle, the Obama campaign was thrown into a state of crisis. Conservatives excoriated Obama, denouncing him as a false prophet of post-racialism.[23] Moderate and liberal commentators were taken aback by the sermons, at best. The Wright revelations threatened to derail Obama's campaign by undermining its core, implicit promise—to unite the nation through racial reconciliation.

In his widely acclaimed "race speech" of March 18, 2008, Obama at first defended Reverend Wright, claiming that he could "no more disown him" than he could disown the larger black community. But he also characterized Wright as a relic of a past era, an individual who held a "profoundly distorted view" of American history. In the weeks following the speech, Obama was forced to renounce Wright entirely, as his subsequent statements proved to be too incendiary for the candidate to explain away.[24] The *New York Times* wrote of Wright's April appearance at the National Press Club, "It required a powerful, unambiguous denunciation—and Mr. Obama gave it."[25] As a next-generation black politician, Senator Obama could not afford to be associated with the divisive, polarizing politics of the "past."

Thus the old and new racial politics theme was an important—and particularly powerful—component of the postelection narrative. In essence, it was the final verdict on the progressive/liberal platform for racial justice, which was disparaged as having wastefully siphoned money away from white taxpayers while encouraging black dependency and victimhood. The conservative, colorblind framing of racial politics, which the post-race America narrative powerfully advanced, not only advocated wholesale abandonment of the left/liberal racial agenda—it forcefully demanded it.

We've Done Our Part, Black America, Now It's Up to You

The last aspect of the post-race triumphalist narrative that I highlight in this chapter concerns the meaning of the election for black people. While different observers claimed that Obama's victory offered hope to African Americans and gave them a fuller sense of citizenship, one argument resonated above all: a black president meant that the days of complaining about white racism were over. It was time for African Americans to give up their crippling sense of victimhood and claim full responsibility for their own lives.

It was the candidate himself who introduced the personal responsibility theme into the discussion. During the 21 months of his campaign, Obama garnered both praise and scorn for repeatedly calling on low-income black males to become better fathers and more responsible citizens.[26] Black and white pundits alike seized on this message with relish. A week after the election, the retired African American columnist William Raspberry (a 40-year veteran of the *Washington Post*) wrote that blacks must start to "see life as a series of problems and possibilities" rather than "just a list of grievances." The conservative writer Stuart Taylor claimed that Obama's success "should tell black children everywhere that they, too, can succeed, and they do not need handouts or reparations." And Juan Williams argued in the *Wall Street Journal* that "the onus now falls on individuals to take advantage of opportunities," beginning with "keeping families together and taking responsibility for the twisted 'gangsta' culture that celebrates jail time instead of schooling."[27]

The top personal responsibility buzz phrase in the weeks after the election was that in the age of Obama, there would be "no more excuses" for black failure.[28] In the days following the election, major media outlets circulated numerous stories filled with quotes from ordinary citizens who held such sentiments. In one November 10 article from the *Wall Street Journal*, a black college student was cited as saying, "Obama strips us as African Americans of every excuse, every 'ism,' every schism we've tried to hide behind. . . . We can't hold the government responsible for our failings." In a *Washington Post* story, a Harlem actor argued, "Barack Obama represents no more excuses. Like Booker T. Washington said, throw your buckets down and get busy." And in a November 6 *Boston Globe* piece, appropriately titled "Closing the Door on Victimhood," the Reverend Eugene Rivers (a frequent Fox News contributor) was quoted as triumphantly proclaiming, "With [Obama's election] the theory of white racism is off the table. . . . Black people don't want to hear it. White people don't want to hear it. . . . The old school is over."[29]

The sociologist Howard Winant has identified such arguments as central components of the discourse of colorblind individualism. For years, he claims, those on the right and the left "have ceaselessly instructed racially defined minorities to pull themselves up by their own bootstraps . . . and exhorted them to accept the content of their character as the basic social value of the country . . . in callous distortion of the message of Martin Luther King."[30]

Post-race Triumphalism Interrupted

While the arguments detailed above are highly reductive and problematic, I also recognize that they have a certain appeal. In the United States after November 4, there was a deep desire to celebrate Obama's victory, to make sense of it, and to take stock of where we were as a nation. Obama came to prominence at a time when many middle-class African Americans were frustrated and embarrassed by the stalled progress of the black poor, the stale rhetoric and tactics of self-appointed black leaders, and the persistent, if subtle, presence of discrimination in their own lives.[31] Americans of all races were drawn to Obama by the sense of *redemption* that he seemed to offer, and by a desire to feel good about the United States again.[32] In this context, the story the pundits offered—that the United States was still a land of opportunity, and that blacks who worked hard could rise to the highest of heights—was a powerful one.

The danger of this narrative, however, is that while it was superficially cloaked in the language of triumph and possibility, it was also firmly grounded in notions of white racial innocence and widespread black cultural pathology. Utterly failing to grasp the complex, multidimensional nature of the social construct of race, this narrative is nevertheless poised to become the new common sense about race in the United States today. Thus, in the section below, I offer a much-needed critique.

On National Redemption

First, despite the claims that Obama's victory redeemed the nation by proving us to be beyond concern with the issue of race, it is clear that the election was thoroughly saturated with racial meaning. For one, many of the attacks on the candidate relied on veiled or explicit references to race. But even more important, I submit, Obama's *appeal* to many voters was linked to his color as well.[33]

It was, after all, largely *from* his blackness, and *through* his blackness, that Obama was thought to derive his redemptive abilities. Though Hillary Clinton's bid for the presidency was equally historic, there was, from the beginning, a presumption that an Obama presidency would be somehow more significant and more transformative for the nation. As Benjamin Wallace-Wells wrote in a November 2006 *Washington Post* article, "There is the sense that, by electing a female president, the nation would be meeting a standard set by other liberal democracies; the election of a black man, by contrast, would be a particularly American achievement, an affirmation of American ideals and a celebration of American circumstances."[34]

Obama's attempt to portray himself as the embodiment of hope and change during the Democratic primary was astoundingly successful, despite the fact that his policies differed very little from those of his opponent. Obama's tremendous appeal to many voters stemmed in part from his personal charm and relative youth, but it was also certainly due to his race. To quote the black conservative Shelby Steele in the *Los Angeles Times*, "Obama's special charisma . . . always came much more from the racial idealism he embodied than from his political ideas. In fact, this was his only true political originality. . . . This worked politically for Obama because it tapped into a deep longing in American life—the longing on the part of whites to escape the stigma of racism." Steele made a similar point, a bit more cynically, in a *Wall Street Journal* article in March 2008:

> Bargainers make the subliminal promise to whites not to shame them with America's history of racism, on the condition that they will not hold the bargainer's race against him. And whites love this bargain—and feel affection for the bargainer—because it gives them racial innocence in a society where whites live under constant threat of being stigmatized as racist. So the bargainer presents himself as an *opportunity* for whites to experience racial innocence. This is how Mr. Obama has turned his blackness into his great political advantage, and also into a kind of personal charisma.[35]

Thus Barack Obama was not just any black man, nor was he in any way a "civil rights–style" black politician. An icon of post-racialism, Obama stressed personal responsibility and self-help, and hardly ever spoke about racism. He was careful to not appear angry and to not be overly identified with black issues. Further, he presented his blackness to white voters as a kind of offering—a source of authenticity, innocence, rebirth, and redemption.[36]

It should be noted that just underneath the claim that Obama's victory said something great about the nation was the real message—that it said something great about *white people*.[37] Though Obama won 95% of the black vote, little praise was heaped on the shoulders of blacks for voting for him in such large numbers; in fact, much more common was the implication that African Americans supported him out of blind, unthinking racial chauvinism.[38] Obama's victory was portrayed as a special sort of victory for whites, who proved themselves to be more tolerant, more colorblind, and more jubilantly egalitarian than anyone had suspected. In this classic triumphalist formulation, Obama's victory transformed vice into virtue, and reaffirmed the greatness of white America.[39]

America, Post-Race

We must particularly interrogate the claim that the country has largely solved the problem of race. While Obama's victory was an important milestone, it cannot alone erase the systematic and institutionalized nature of racial inequality in our society. Much sociological research has revealed the distance that we have yet to travel in this regard.

We can begin by looking at the criminal justice system. Though African Americans constitute just over 12% of the general population, they are nearly half the prison population and 42% of those on death row. In our supposedly race-blind society, white felons are more likely to be called back for a job interview than blacks with no criminal record. Persistent residential segregation means that African Americans across the socioeconomic spectrum are far more likely to live in areas of super-concentrated poverty, thus exposing them to higher levels of violence, social isolation, and chronic unemployment. Recent research has further shown that the extension of subprime loans to low-income borrowers of color in the 1990s not only made these homeowners especially vulnerable to foreclosure, but also increased the rate of residential segregation in many areas.[40]

Inequality in the area of public education is particularly glaring. In the last decade and a half, courts around the country have reversed integration orders from the 1960s and 1970s, sending black and Latino students back to schools that are more than 90% non-white. Such high indices of segregation make it likely that the funding received in majority-white and majority-non-white school districts will continue to be vastly unequal, due to the greater political and economic power of white parents compared to parents of color. History has shown us that "separate" is inherently unequal, and the effects today are devastating. In a number of major American cities, fewer than one in three black males graduates from high school, and most of these young men are eventually incarcerated.[41]

Sociologists have determined that one of the most important explanations for the persistence of racial inequality is the racial wealth gap. While the gap in income between whites and non-whites is considerable, the racial gap in wealth is far more substantial. The median net worth of the average white family in the United States is estimated to be *10 times* that of the average African American family, and more than 60% of blacks have no net worth to speak of. Scholars have also found that the wealth gap transcends class and education. The highest-educated blacks, for example, have less than 25% the average net worth of similarly educated whites.[42]

The ideology of racial colorblindness implies that the wealth gap must be due to racial differences in drive and initiative—that whites have more because they have worked harder. But a review of the historical record reveals that the wealth gap was created by generations of government programs and other policies that systematically favored whites. Among the most important mechanisms for the perpetuation of the racial wealth gap today is the intergenerational transfer of wealth. Asset-poor blacks are not able to pass on to their children the financial launching pad that is available to the offspring of relatively asset-rich whites. This means that younger whites are much more likely to be able to purchase a home, finance higher education, pay off or stay out of debt, and further grow their savings. It has been further shown that racial differences in wealth have a substantial impact on other dimensions of racial inequality, including the likelihood of employment, years of education completed, marital stability, and out-of-wedlock birth. Thus, some scholars argue, unless there is a leveling of the mechanisms of wealth accumulation, it will be virtually impossible for blacks to achieve parity with whites.[43]

Racial inequality also transcends considerations of class. People of color are underrepresented in the upper ranks of corporations, universities, and law firms. Blacks currently hold 2% of all elected offices in this country, and since the Reconstruction era, only three black senators have been elected to the U.S. Congress (one of them being Barack Obama in

2004). Studies have also found that blacks with the highest levels of education report the highest levels of workforce discrimination.[44]

We must also keep in mind that the significance of race in the United States cannot be fully captured in statistics. Race pertains also to the domains of culture and ideas. In the 2008 election, pundits were obsessed with the question of race even before Obama officially declared his candidacy. Commentators asked, Is Obama really black? Is he black enough? What kind of black person is he?[45] Questions about Obama's racial identity were clearly embedded with myriad others, such as, Will Obama seek to make white Americans feel uncomfortable about race, or will he just let the issue go? Is he like or unlike Al Sharpton and Jeremiah Wright? How did such a mild-mannered guy end up married to such an angry, bitter black woman? Just how patriotic is Obama? Is he, in fact, American at all? Race may have mattered in the election in ways that were surprising—more complicated and perhaps less predictable than we may have imagined—but to say that it did not matter at all is manifestly false.

No More Excuses

Lastly, I want to address the assertion that Obama's victory proves that all blacks have an equal chance of making it in this society, so long as they work hard, improve their attitudes, and give up their victim mentality. In evaluating this claim, it is vital to note that Barack Obama was, in many ways, an exceptional black man.

As the son of an East African immigrant, he had no ancestral ties to the histories of slavery or state-mandated segregation in this country. He was light-skinned and biracial, raised by his white mother and grandparents in Hawaii and Indonesia. And as repeatedly emphasized during the campaign, he came to politics with an Ivy League education, having served as president of the prestigious *Harvard Law Review* and, later, as a law professor at the University of Chicago.

This all matters in many different ways. High indices of school segregation, attacks on affirmative action in higher education, and a funding structure that ensures that the children of the poorest Americans will continue to receive the lowest-quality public education mean that the chances that the "average" black child will matriculate to the Ivy League are very slim. Thus Obama entered the race with educational qualifications that were far beyond the reach of most African Americans.[46]

Second, sociological research suggests that when whites perceive differences between black immigrants and native-born black Americans, they tend to prefer the former.[47] In her 1999 study of West Indians in New York, for example, Mary Waters found that white employers readily expressed a willingness to discriminate in favor of West Indians, whom they saw as more hardworking, trustworthy, and honest than African Americans. In 2004, the journalist Noam Scheiber suggested that Obama's nontraditional name had worked in his favor during his political career, because it marked him as something other than "stereotypically African American." Similarly, the sociologists Eduardo Bonilla-Silva and Victor Ray noted that newspaper articles discussing Obama's popularity among whites often focused on his Kenyan ancestry in order "to show how his racial background [was] different from that of the 'traditional' black candidate."[48]

Obama's background mattered in other ways as well. Being biracial and light-skinned, he was phenotypically much closer to whites than were many other African Americans. Numerous studies of "colorism" have found that light skin has long offered myriad advantages to those socially categorized as black in the United States. Based on a survey of more than 2,000 African Americans, Verna Keith and Cedric Herring wrote in their 1991 *American Journal of Sociology* article that light skin was a stronger predictor of high education, employment, and income than parental socioeconomic status. In a recent *Social Forces* piece, Jennifer Hochschild and Vesla Weaver noted that lighter-skinned blacks were perceived as more attractive, intelligent, and pleasing by blacks and non-blacks alike. And since 1865, lighter-skinned blacks have been vastly overrepresented among the ranks of those holding political office. As Hochschild and Weaver write, "Colorism operates in the political realm in much the same way that it does in [the] socioeconomic realm; dark skin amplifies racial inequality."[49]

The findings of these studies are especially relevant to the 2008 presidential election. Obama was regularly described in the press as handsome, dashing, cool, and "swoon-worthy." As a light-skinned, biracial man, Obama's appearance offered him a presumption of intelligence, trustworthiness, safety, and attractiveness not available to the majority of African Americans, whose skin color, hair texture, and facial features make them more "stereotypically" and problematically black. (It has also not gone without notice that many of the other "next-generation" or "post-racial" black leaders—such as Cory Booker, Adrian Fenty, and Harold Ford, Jr.—are also very light-skinned.)[50]

The last, and perhaps most important, aspect of Obama's exceptionalism is related, again, to his ancestry. It was not just that he was the son of an immigrant, but that he was not the descendant of American slaves. Critical observers claimed from early in the race that Obama's appeal to whites stemmed in large part from the fact that his biography (and how he spun it) allowed them to sidestep or ignore the realities of our racial history. As the MSNBC commentator Chris Matthews declared in January 2007, "No history of Jim Crow, no history of anger, no history of slavery. . . . All the bad stuff in our history ain't there with this guy."[51] This particular point of view was one that Obama himself reinforced. From his speech at the 2004 Democratic National Convention forward, Obama repeatedly declared that "only in America is my story possible." Thus, through Obama, the slave was transformed into a voluntary migrant—and, further, one who had achieved the American dream.

I do not in any way mean to imply that Obama was "not really black," or that he was less "authentically" black than are other African Americans. But it must be noted that his experiences and background made him far from the "average" black man, and thus mean that it was profoundly illogical to argue that his victory proved that all blacks could achieve the American dream if they just stopped making excuses. As James Grossman of Chicago's Newberry Library asked the day after the election, "As we congratulate ourselves for overcoming four centuries of racial oppression, we need to recognize the extent to which Barack Obama also stands outside of that history. . . . He has no roots in American slavery, the era of Jim Crow, or urban ghettos. . . . Is it possible that the only African-American who could cross the fragile bridge across the racial divide was a man unassociated with the great crucibles of African-American life?"[52]

Conclusions

This chapter has identified and critiqued elements of the post-racial narrative of American triumphalism forwarded in celebration of Obama's victory. This narrative was firmly grounded in the tradition of colorblind individualism, and thus inherited the dangers and ideological blind spots of this paradigm.

Far from proving that the nation was "beyond" the issue of race, the 2008 presidential election was thoroughly saturated with racial meaning—for Obama's supporters as well as his opponents. Obama did not win a majority of the white electorate in 2008, but he won a larger share (43%) of whites than had Kerry, Gore, Dukakis, or Mondale; and Clinton tied him only in 1996.[53] Obama attained a larger slice of the popular vote than any other Democratic candidate since Lyndon B. Johnson. And as the first black man to be elected president, he shattered a barrier that many thought would never be broken in their lifetimes. Obama achieved this victory in part because he was seen as a "post-racial" candidate who might unify and redeem the nation *through the vehicle* of his race.

The pundits hailed the age of Obama as the dawn of a new era in racial politics, and as evidence of the nation's definitive triumph over the problem of race. But the supposition that the United States had largely solved its racial problems may be disproved by a consideration of the deep and in many cases widening indices of racial inequality. Though there were those who asserted that Obama's story proved that the failure of poor blacks to rise from the bottom of the socioeconomic hierarchy was best explained by their cultural deficiencies, it was in fact the exceptional, atypical, "post-racial" nature of Obama's blackness that was crucial to his all-American success.

Despite the power of this problematic post-race narrative, we do find ourselves in a moment of possibility. We have a president with a mandate for "change," which is related in some way to his race. After several years of race talk accompanying Obama's meteoric ascent, hegemonic conceptions of the ways that race operates in this society may be in a period of relative flux and renegotiation.

Race is a powerful, multivalent cultural signifier, with complicated and contradictory meanings.[54] In this country, racial symbols—especially those related to the constructs of black and white—have for centuries deeply influenced our economic, cultural, and political life. Further exploration of the complex ways race figured into the 2008 presidential election is found in the next chapter of the book, as I discuss post-racial black identities and the promises and pitfalls of the "new politics of race."

3

Rooted in the Black Community but Not Limited to It

The Perils and Promises of the New Politics of Race

The idea of the "new black politics" or the "new politics of race" gained tremendous currency during the 2008 American presidential election. According to the triumphal narrative spun by the pundits, Barack Obama's ascendance signaled that the "old" politics of race, focusing on black grievance, victimhood, and protest, were vanquished, leaving in their place newer, more effective ways of getting things done.

Referencing the differences between himself and those who had come before, Obama claimed that he was "rooted in the black community" but "not limited to it."[1] The senator was widely described as a member of a new cohort of black politicians whose style, tactics, and rhetoric differed markedly from those of their civil rights–era predecessors. Among those identified as fellow members of the next generation were Newark, New Jersey, Mayor Cory Booker, Massachusetts Governor Deval Patrick, former Washington, DC, mayor Adrian Fenty, former Tennessee representative Harold Ford, Jr., and former Republican Party chairman Michael Steele.[2]

While the term has been used primarily in reference to blacks in electoral politics, the "new politics of race" are part of the broader politics of post-racialism. The concept of post-racialism has been used in reference to African Americans in television, music, sports, and film for a number of years. Exemplars of post-racialism outside the field of politics include Oprah Winfrey, Will Smith, Michael Jackson, Michael Jordan, Tyra Banks, and Tiger Woods. In this chapter, I use the phrases new politics of race, new black politics, and politics of post-racialism more or less interchangeably.

It is my argument that the so-called new politics of race is an outgrowth of the ideology of colorblind individualism. It is a set of proscriptions for handling racial matters in the 21st-century United States with both discursive and practical dimensions. The new race politics focuses on the responsibilities of blacks and other non-whites in achieving a society free of racial strife. Blacks are called to "get over" race by ceasing to talk about it, leaving behind identity politics, and viewing racism not as systematic or structural but as episodic and rare. Reasonable blacks should agree that most whites are well intentioned and colorblind, that whites and blacks can be *equally* racist, and that blacks must take sole responsibility for their own lives. The highly lauded new politics of race thus place the burden of solving the nation's racial problems primarily on the shoulders of people of color, while declaring whites to be largely absolved of responsibility.

There were many moments in the 2008 election in which the "new" politics of race were juxtaposed against the "old." One the one hand, we had Jesse Jackson's criticism of Obama for "talking down to black people," Cornel West's anger that he did not attend the State of the Black Union summit, and Jeremiah Wright's fiery sermons. Contrast these with Obama's repeated calls for black personal responsibility, his implied preference for class-based affirmative action, and his tendency to avoid explicit discussion of the issue of race.

Though Obama played the new politics of race to win, he certainly did not establish the rules of the game himself. Obama's careful presentation of himself as a next-generation black politician, fundamentally different from (if partially indebted to) previous African American leaders, was, and continues to be, crucial to his ability to garner white support. In the few instances in which Obama has been seen as crossing over into "old" race politics—by speaking too openly about racism, or evidencing too much color consciousness—he has been rebuked by the mainstream media and the general public.

The present chapter constitutes a theoretical exploration of the dimensions of the new politics of race. Though the term has thus far not entered into the lexicon of social scientists in the sense used here, it is nevertheless crucial that scholars of race consider its political and social implications. Pundits, journalists, and other commentators from across the political spectrum now regularly refer to the "new racial calculus" or "new race politics" in seeking to describe, and influence, racial dynamics in the age of Obama. Further, while there may be certain promises in the idea of a new race politics, in its present formulation, the perils of the discourse are far more numerous. Thus insight into the so-called new politics of race is a vital point of entry for scholars who wish to engage the wider discussions of race taking place in the United States today.

Questions, Concerns, and Context

My discussion of the new politics of race is based on a careful review of the discourses that emerged from the media coverage of the 2008 presidential election. I considered writings, speeches, and other public statements made by conservative and liberal observers. I examined several hundred articles and blog posts over a two-year period, from the opening months of Obama's candidacy to well into the first year of his presidency. My focus in this particular chapter is on the conceptual frameworks used by political observers in seeking to explain their own excitement about Obama's way of dealing with issues of race. Why did it seem to so many that Obama alone might finally take us beyond the "stale" and "exhausted" racial politics of the last several decades?[3] (As the subtitle of one article breathlessly asserted, "Obama Shakes Up America's Cultural Landscape with His Unprecedented Ability to Bridge the Color Divide.")[4] And why was this so important in the 2008 presidential race?

I became specifically attuned to the concept of "new race politics" via the numerous articles that appeared on the subject. As writer after writer claimed that Obama was a part of a "new generation" of black leaders who had rejected the "divisive" and "confrontational" methods of their forbears, I detected a note of joy in these pronouncements.[5] Eventually, it appeared that rather than simply chronicling Obama's words and deeds, political discourse in the presidential race had begun to articulate a set of expectations, or demands, of Obama, and of other African Americans by extension. If Obama was striking a bargain with white America in his quest for the White House, I wondered, what exactly did this bargain entail? And what would be the longer-term implications of this bargain for the rest of black America?

I thus began to regard the new black politics discourse with a very critical eye. In some ways it seemed that the eagerness to move beyond our decades-old "racial stalemate" was in fact an eagerness to put an end to affirmative action, to condemn the black poor, and to sweep discussions of racial inequality under the rug. Was Obama really helping to open up a vibrant new dialogue about race in America, as he had suggested? Or was he (unwittingly?) helping to shut down the voices of racial progressives, and to shift the terms of debate about race even further to the right?[6]

The issues that I explore in this chapter are similar to ones that have been discussed in the field of political science. Since the mid-1990s, political scientists have especially inquired into the changing dynamics of black electoral politics.[7] One particular topic of study has been the degree to which black candidates have garnered the support of an increasing number of white voters. In a pivotal essay from 1993, Joseph McCormick and Charles Jones argued that many successful African American candidates had begun to rely on a strategy of "deracialization," or the attempt to "diffus[e] the polarizing effects of race" by "eschewing explicit reference to race-specific issues."[8] Candidates pursuing this strategy avoid the impression that they will specifically cater to blacks by "emphasizing those issues that are perceived as racially transcendent." Deracialized politicians of color are careful not to associate "with people that white voters will view as racial partisans," and make sure to project a "nonthreatening," "reassuring image to the white electorate."[9]

I identify many of these same elements in my analysis of the new politics of race. But I depart from McCormick and Jones in at least two key respects. First, the concept of deracialization in my view is overly dichotomizing. While Obama and other contemporary black politicians do tend to de-emphasize the issue of race, the new black politics does not involve a complete disavowal of racial themes, but rather it implies a particular *orientation* toward issues of race. As I argue further in chapter 5, *implicit* racial appeals were very significant to the core messaging of Obama's campaign. Though numerous pundits described Obama as having "transcended" race entirely, I argue that his particular presentation of blackness was actually key to his electoral success. As a post-racial black candidate (i.e., *through* his magical blackness), Obama could (a) serve as the antidote to Jesse Jackson and Al Sharpton, (b) grant whites absolution for the racial sins of the past, and (c) redeem the nation by demonstrating the United States to be again a shining beacon of democracy and progress.

This particular critique of the deracialization thesis (that it is overly black and white) is widely found in the most recent wave of political science literature.[10] I depart still further from this literature, however, in that the black politics I refer to transcends the electoral realm. The new politics of race in my view is not only a set of expectations that voters have of black political candidates, it is a set of expectations of African Americans as a whole. Consider the many "lessons" that Obama's November 4 victory was said to have for the black community (discussed in chapter 2): that there were no more excuses for black failure, that the days of complaining about white racism were over, and that the notion of racism still being a significant barrier to achievement was a myth that had been definitively disproved.[11] Thus another key reason for scholars to grapple with the concept of the "new politics of race" is that the discourse potentially establishes parameters of acceptable or desirable behavior for all blacks in the 21st century.

The Racial Pact

It should be apparent from the paragraphs above that my use of the term "new politics of race" differs from other usages found in the social science literature. Howard Winant, for example, published a book by the same name in 2004. For Winant, the new politics of race refers to the broad range of conditions characterizing race relations in the contemporary era. Here, however, the new politics of race is more narrowly defined.

I use the term as it was applied in the 2008 presidential election—to draw distinctions between the rhetoric and tactics of leaders such as Barack Obama, and those of figures such as Jesse Jackson and Al Sharpton. My dichotomy between new- and old-style black politics is similar to the distinction made by the African American conservative Shelby Steele, though my analysis of the significance of this distinction is completely different.[12]

The key concepts in Steele's typology are "bargaining" and "challenging," which he defines as "two of the masks" that blacks commonly assume in dealing with whites. Bargainers, Steele writes, "make a deal with white Americans that gives [them] the benefit of the doubt: I will not rub America's history of racism in your face, if you will not hold my race against me."[13] In exchange, he claims, whites respond with "gratitude, warmth, and even affection." While Barack Obama, for Steele, is a classic bargainer, Jesse Jackson is a prototypical challenger. Challengers, Steele writes, try to "manipulate" or "shame" whites into giving them "some form of racial preference." They "use the moral authority of their race's historic grievance to muscle for preferential treatment," which makes whites "quietly seethe." "Mr. Obama," on the other hand, "has been loved precisely because he was an anti-Jackson," Steele claims. He is "a bargainer who grants [whites] innocence before asking for their support."[14]

There are several useful elements of this argument, which I will discuss below. But first, I must point out what is wrong with it. The fundamental flaw in Steele's formulation, in my view, is that it analyzes racial dynamics entirely outside the context of the material relations in which they are embedded. Steele implies that racial politics is a game devised and manipulated entirely by African Americans. Blacks deploy historical grievances against innocent and well-intentioned whites who are eager—or even desperate—to please them. In this perspective, whites in their "natural state" stand apart from the issue of race. They only become involved in racial matters to the extent that they are drawn in by blacks who play on their guilt. Whites do not systematically benefit from racial privilege, they harbor no discriminatory sentiments, and in fact they would not notice race at all if it were not thrust into their faces. Such an argument could make sense only in a vacuum—if there were no actual existing racial hierarchy, no gaping racial disparities in wealth and in health, no entrenched patterns of residential segregation, under-employment, or over-imprisonment, or if the nation's political and economic systems were not still largely under the control of whites.

What Steele gets right, I believe, is the notion that the politics of race today involve a sort of negotiation or exchange, and that in today's society whites are eager to be absolved of responsibility for the issue of race. But the locus of power in Steele's exchange is fundamentally wrong. Racial dynamics today may involve a negotiation, but blacks as a group simply do not have the power to entirely determine the terms of the negotiation themselves. Further, a far more basic, and less nefarious, end than special treatment or unfair advantage that non-whites would seek in any such exchange is *access*: access to the goods, services, wealth, esteem, influence, and opportunities that are for the most part, again, largely controlled by whites. Concretely, these ends may include safer neighborhoods, better schools, higher-paying jobs, or positions of political power. Most broadly, they amount to fuller integration and acceptance into American society.

Colorblind Ideological Roots

To understand the new politics of race, it is crucial to understand the central ideology from which it is derived. Colorblind individualism has been identified as the predominant ideological framework through which most Americans understand racial matters today.[15] The basic premise of this ideology is that we have already achieved a largely colorblind, race-neutral society, one in which race has little impact on the life chances of non-whites. Thus, in this view, policies such as affirmative action are unfair to whites and probably unconstitutional.[16] Acts of anti-black discrimination are viewed as infrequent and unlikely, while "reverse racism" is seen as a far more serious concern.

Many whites today hold that they, like the nation's laws and institutions, are largely colorblind. But non-whites, by contrast, are often perceived to be irrationally preoccupied with race.[17] In making sense of the many ills that plague low-income communities of color, a colorblind individualist perspective holds that such problems are either natural and inevitable (i.e., there have to be some poor people, so why not them?) or due primarily to the personal failings of non-whites.[18] Poor blacks are seen as especially troubling members of the polity. Colorblind individualism holds that if blacks would simply learn to take responsibility for their own lives and free themselves of the self-limiting ideologies of victimhood and failure, then no barriers could stand in their way.[19]

The new politics of race is an elaboration, or outgrowth, of the ideology of colorblind individualism, formulated as a set of expectations of African American political candidates and other blacks by extension. As stated earlier, the new race politics focuses on the responsibilities of blacks and other non-whites in achieving a society free of racial strife. In many ways, the new race politics is a kind of 21st-century racial etiquette. It is a contract, a pact, or a bargain made between white Americans and upwardly mobile blacks.[20] In exchange for full integration into the American mainstream, and in the name of racial harmony, the new politics of race calls on African Americans to do the following:

1. Adopt an open, friendly manner.
2. Give up the language of "grievance" and "victimhood."
3. Play down the significance of racism.
4. Distance yourself from divisive, angry, or otherwise problematic black public figures.
5. Repudiate the choices and lifestyles of the black poor.
6. Focus on self-help and self-reliance. Avoid being overly identified with "black issues."
7. Reaffirm your love of country. Emphasize your Americanness above all, leaving behind identity politics and separatism.[21]

In the section below, I elaborate on these principles and place them in the context of the 2008 presidential election.

Dimensions of the New Politics of Race

1. Adopt an open, friendly, nonthreatening manner in order to counter the unease or discomfort that other blacks have caused whites to feel. The first dictum of the new race politics has to do with tone or style. Having a distinctly friendly, nonthreatening persona is strongly characteristic of each of the major icons of post-racialism (Oprah Winfrey, Tyra Banks, Will Smith, etc.). As Massachusetts Governor Deval Patrick said in 2007, "In so much of the work I've done, I've found that you had to put people at ease on the question of race before you could even start to talk about what you were doing."[22] Barack Obama referred often to the "core goodness" and "essential decency" of (white) Americans during the presidential race. Commentators were particularly enthralled with his "megawatt smile," affable manner, and apparent inability to display anger.

The *New York Times* discussed the importance of Mr. Obama's seeming aversion to anger in an article titled "Color Test: Where Whites Draw the Line."[23] The conservative Abigail Thernstrom argued in the *National Review* that "anger and alienation are arguably the most worrisome aspects of black urban life and culture."[24] Thus it was clear from early on that there would be no tolerance for an angry black man in the White House. Obama's upbeat, approachable nature was a prerequisite of the new racial contract.

2. Give up the language of grievance, victimhood, and confrontation. Agree that protest and anger are tactics that are unhelpful and unwarranted, and should thus be abandoned. Calls for the black community to give up the politics of "grievance" and "victimhood" echoed loudly throughout the presidential race.[25] The consensus was that the general public was tired of hearing blacks complain about racism, and further, that such complaints—characterized as "perverse," "pathological," and "self-defeating"—were major barriers to black success.[26]

Barack Obama was celebrated as the harbinger of a new era in which black grievance would be a thing of the past. *Reason Magazine* associate editor Michael Moynihan wrote in November 2008 that Obama had "disowned the ossified policies of the post-King civil rights movement"— which included "paranoia about the actions of whites" and a obsession with "racial authenticity." In his November 10 *Wall Street Journal* article, the African American journalist Juan Williams stated triumphantly, "The idea of black politics now tilts away from leadership based on voicing grievance, and identity politics based on victimization and anger." "How does anyone waste time on racial fantasies like reparations for slavery," he asked, "when there is a black man who earned his way into the White House?" Calls for blacks to give up victimhood continued well into the first year of Obama's presidency. In early 2009, a writer at the *National Review* declared that while "the grievance/victimhood industry" had taken "a major hit with the election of President Obama," it was "not out of business."[27]

Several black journalists pointed out that this discourse tended to imply that pessimism, grievance, and self-defeating behaviors were not only major parts of black culture, but in fact the essence of contemporary black culture (especially among the black poor). As Ta-Nehisi Coates states, "One thing I do know, the . . . definition of blackness [as] 'a sense of black grievance' . . . is a joke. . . . That sort of flat rendering of black America, keeps up this false idea that the most unifying factor of black culture is the ability to make white people feel guilty." "Look, I know this is tough to believe," he continued, "but black people aren't nearly as obsessed with white people, as the media would have you think."[28]

3. *Play down the significance of racism. Acknowledge how little racism there is in the United States today compared to the pre–civil rights era. Affirm that the past is the past and that today things are far different.* Obama did this at several key moments during the election. In his March 2007 speech in Selma, Alabama, for example, he stated that the United States had come 90% of the way toward achieving racial equality.[29] And in his highly praised race speech of March 2008, Obama argued that his former pastor Jeremiah Wright had a "profoundly distorted view" of race relations that "elevates what is wrong with America above all that we know is right with America." In the 2008 presidential race, even more important than minimizing the significance of racism, however, was the story of the United States' *triumph* over race. A central element of the narrative of the campaign was that Obama's ascent represented the final march toward the achievement of racial equality. As the president-elect stated in his November 4 victory night speech, "If there is anyone out there who still doubts that America is a place where all things are possible . . . tonight is your answer."[30]

Almost never speak about racism, even when pressured to do so. Obama and his advisers have been generally careful to abide by this dictum. In fact, they have at several points declared as invalid the allegations of racism made by his allies. The White House was quick to disagree with former president Jimmy Carter's September 2009 assertion that opponents of Obama's health care plan were motivated by racism.[31] And in October 2009, Obama "chided" Attorney General Eric Holder for stating that the United States was a "nation of cowards" when it came to dealing with the issue of race.[32]

If you must speak about racism, however, agree that it is a two-way street, and that whites and blacks can be equally racist. (Neoconservative version) In fact, you will probably find yourself focusing on *black* racism most of the time. Blacks, after all, tend to be more racist than whites, because their constant focus on race and overblown racial paranoia leads them to engage in racist thinking, speech, and behavior on a regular basis.[33] In 2008, conservatives latched onto the notion that Obama's former pastor, the Reverend Jeremiah Wright, was a racist (and a nutcase)— and so was Obama, by association.

(Liberal version) If you must discuss white racism, talk about it not as systematic, institutional, or implicating white Americans as a group (e.g., unearned advantages that accrue regardless of whether they are desired; pervasive but unacknowledged anti-black stereotypes). Racism is to be understood as the kind of overt actions, speech, and ideas characteristic of the pre–civil rights era, now generally committed only by Archie Bunker types and members of hate groups—the old-style racism that most Americans easily identify and eagerly condemn.[34] Talking about racism in this sense (every once in a while) in the liberal paradigm is not only tolerable but is in fact a social good. In condemning old-style racism, Americans are afforded the opportunity to affirm that they are anti-racist, colorblind, and thus morally upstanding people.[35]

When Obama has directly or even indirectly addressed contemporary manifestations of racism in a more spontaneous manner, he has found himself in hot water. His August 2008 remark that he did not look like "all the presidents on the dollar bills" led to a sharp decline in his approval rating among whites.[36] As the title of one article read, "More Voters Think Obama Played Race Card Than McCain in Recent Political Mini-Firestorms."[37] Similarly, President Obama's July 2009 statement that the arrest of the Harvard professor Henry Louis Gates, Jr. was part of a legacy of U.S. racial profiling provoked another slide in his approval rating and weeks of debate in the press.[38] One reporter warned that the comment constituted Obama's second major "race mistake" (the first being his association with his controversial former pastor). The Fox News commentator Glenn Beck infamously claimed that the statement proved that Obama was "a racist" who had "a deep-seated hatred for white people or the white culture." More than a year later, the *Wall Street Journal* published an article again denouncing Obama's Gates statements as divisive and polarizing.[39]

4. *Distance yourself from divisive, angry, or otherwise problematic black public figures. (Liberal version)* The "old guard" should be avoided because they are from a past era, fighting a battle to end widespread racial discrimination that has already been won.[40] *(Conservative version)* The problem with the Sharptons and the Jacksons is that they are "hate-mongers" and "race peddlers" who stir up racial conflict simply to advance their careers.[41]

In their 1993 article, McCormick and Jones identified achieving distance from racial partisans as one of the pillars of deracialization. This strategy was a particularly important component of Barack Obama's presidential campaign. As Peter Beinart wrote in the *New Republic*, "In U.S. politics . . . there are no 'good' blacks without 'bad' blacks. . . . For many white Americans, it's a twofer. Elect Obama, and you not only dethrone George W. Bush, you dethrone Sharpton, too."[42] In addition to Al Sharpton, the problematically black figures of the 2008 electoral season were Jesse Jackson, Reverend Wright, and sometimes Michelle Obama.

There were numerous moments in 2007/2008 in which Obama drew clear distinctions between himself and the architects of the old race politics. In response to Jesse Jackson's July 2008 statement that he wanted to "cut [Obama's] nuts off" for "talking down to black people," Obama pledged to keep speaking out about the problem of absentee fathers. In an address delivered in Selma, Alabama, during the Democratic primary (while rival Hillary Clinton spoke at a neighboring church), Obama spoke at length about the "Moses" and "Joshua" generations. The former leaders, he claimed, had taken the black community most of the way toward the promised land.[43] Now it was time for the Joshua generation and ordinary blacks to do their parts.

The press eagerly emphasized the distinctions between Obama and his predecessors as well. Andrew Sullivan of *The Atlantic* regarded Jesse Jackson's highly publicized frustration with Obama as a "very encouraging sign" that would "help illustrate one of the game-changing features of the Obama candidacy." After all, he wrote, Obama "is not only running against Clinton and her well-oiled machine. He's also running against the failed past in racial politics."[44] For Terence Samuel, Obama represented a generation of black leaders who were "determined to move beyond both the mood and the methods of their forebears." Obama, Samuel wrote, represented "the full flowering of a strain of up-tempo, non-grievance, American-Dream-In-Color politics."[45] Jonetta Rose Barras declared in the *Washington Post* that "Obama's arrival in the White House underscores the reality that the post–civil rights era is in full swing in American politics"—even if many black Americans were not yet ready to acknowledge that fact.[46] In summing up this sentiment, the black writer Gary Younge noted in *The Nation* that "the emergence of this cohort has filled the commentariat with joy. . . . They have been hailed not just as a development in black American politics but as a repudiation of black American politics [itself]."[47]

5. *Repudiate the choices and lifestyles of the black poor.* For political conservatives, highlighting the failures of the black poor is a particularly salient component of the new politics of race. In the paradigm of colorblind individualism, the economic and social ills that plague the racially marginalized are viewed as being due to their own cultural deficits, rather than to structural or institutional barriers.[48] Such deficits include irresponsible sexuality, poor family structure, a preference for handouts over hard work, a failure to value education, a "victim" mentality, and a propensity toward crime.[49]

Obama's willingness to repeatedly speak about the failings of low-income black men was a key dimension of his campaign. In speech after speech, he called on "Ray Ray," "Cousin Pookie," and other mythical low-income black males to get up off the couch, go vote, and be responsible fathers to their children.[50] Obama adopted his most strident tone in his June 15, 2008, Father's Day address before a black congregation in his home city of Chicago. In one of many similar passages, he declared, "If we are honest with ourselves, we'll admit that what too many fathers also are is missing—missing from too many lives and too many homes. They have abandoned their responsibilities, acting like boys instead of men."[51]

Obama received high marks from both conservatives and centrist liberals for such language. As a June 16 headline in *New York Magazine* stated, "Obama's Tough Talk on African-American Fathers Wins Big Points with Pundits." The *New Republic* described Obama's Father's Day address on the crisis of black fatherhood as "pathbreaking," brave, and necessary.[52] Critiques of Obama's personal responsibility rhetoric came only from those on the far left of the political spectrum. On the *Black Agenda Report*, Kevin Alexander Gray argued that Obama's "'bash the black man' game passes on one of the lowest of all the smears and stereotypes: the lie that black men have no morals." The political scientist

Adolph Reed declared Obama to be a "vacuous opportunist" who talked "through" African Americans in order to score points with whites.[53]

Whatever its intent, the political utility of Obama's rhetoric was clear. In a climate characterized by generalized disdain for the black poor, Obama positioned himself not so much as a champion of lower-income blacks but as a moral and social reformer.[54] The electorate was made to understand that Obama would not encourage the victimhood, irresponsibility, and dependency believed to be rampant in the black community.

6. *Focus on individual achievement, self-help, and self-reliance. Avoid being overly identified with "black issues" or appearing to have a civil rights agenda.* The sixth axiom of the new race politics is that blacks must downplay discussion of external or institutional barriers to equality—not just those facing the black poor, but also those that confront blacks in boardrooms, courtrooms, and classrooms as well. It is expected that next-generation black politicians will not forward policies that would be seen as primarily benefitting people of color, nor will they advocate a strong racial justice platform.[55] Advocacy of race-based affirmative action should therefore be downplayed or abandoned. In the liberal formulation, universalist or class-based programs that target all Americans are acceptable substitutes.[56] For conservatives, however, any government programs or interventions are suspect in general.[57]

In the 2008 presidential race, there was much discussion of what Obama would mean for affirmative action. As the conservative writer Dennis Byrne asked in the *Chicago Tribune*, "If one of the signs that we should be moving [toward the elimination of affirmative action] isn't the election of an African-American president, then what is?" For Ward Connerly, black America's most prominent affirmative action opponent, Obama's success proved "that affirmative action is an idea whose time has passed."[58]

Obama himself avoided openly defending affirmative action, and in a May 2007 interview with George Stephanopoulos he implied a preference for class-based policies. In March 2008, Dahlia Lithwick wrote admiringly on the liberal website Slate.com that Obama's opaqueness on the issue was evidence of his "fresh thinking," "skill at projecting empathy," and desire to "get beyond race as a singular, defining category in America." The article's subtitle encapsulated her point: "Barack Obama Has Gotten Past Affirmative Action. Have We?"[59]

The fact that the turn away from affirmative action is part of the new race politics under both conservative and liberal paradigms is evidence of the increasing rightward shift in American racial politics over the last several decades. Whereas affirmative action in employment and education, welfare rights, school integration, and voting rights were once cornerstones of liberalism, such programs are now only meekly defended, if at all, and affirmative action is widely seen as a form of reverse racism that unfairly victimizes whites.[60]

There were numerous other "black issues" concerning which Obama pointedly did not take a stand. These included the controversy over statements by the radio host Don Imus (who referred to the members of the Rutgers women's basketball team as "nappy-headed hos"), the arrest and detention of six black teenagers in Jena, Louisiana, and the April 2008 acquittal of the New York City police officers who fatally shot a twenty-three-year-old African American, Sean Bell.[61]

Obama's propensity toward "race-neutrality" was met with mixed reviews. Civil rights activists were at first highly critical of the presidential candidate. His absence from the 2007 State of the Black Union summit, for example, led to an angry denunciation by the activist and scholar Cornel West.[62] Conservatives, on the other hand, were clearly overjoyed. George Will praised Obama as "a model of blacks' possibilities when they are emancipated from ideologies of blackness." And after Obama's Iowa primary win, former education secretary Bill Bennett stated excitedly, "He never brings race into it. He never plays the race card." "Talk about the black community," Bennett continued, "he has taught the black community you don't have to act like Jesse Jackson, you don't have to act like Al Sharpton. You can talk about the issues. Great dignity. And this is a breakthrough."[63]

Many blacks regarded Obama with a mixture of excitement and pained ambivalence. As Amina Luqman wrote in the *Washington Post* following a July 2007 forum at Howard University:

> The average black American onlooker can't help feeling proud but also just a little hurt watching Obama. . . . During the debate, black Americans in the audience sat, hands poised, yearning to applaud a black candidate able to articulate our passions and sense of injustice. We wanted to hear that he understood and loved us—not in the general, "we the people" sense but in the specific. Yet we know that with each utterance about injustice, each puff of anger or frustration about racism, we lose the very thing we seek: a viable black candidate. The closer Obama comes to us, the further he would be from winning the nomination and the presidency.[64]

7. *On the nation, emphasize your Americanness above all, leaving behind identity politics and separatism. Present your own life history as evidence of the greatness of the nation. Reaffirm your love of country, and avoid the appearance of grievance or ingratitude.* This pillar of new race politics is especially relevant for blacks running for political office.[65]

(*Neoconservative version*) Many conservatives are profoundly critical of African American perspectives on the nation, considering blacks to be deeply ungrateful to a country that has given them so much.[66] In 2007/2008, Obama was forced to counter numerous accusations that he was unpatriotic, particularly in light of controversies surrounding statements made by his former pastor and by his wife.[67] The neoconservative paradigm of national identity calls for the reaffirmation of traditional "American" values—symbolized by baseball, apple pie, small towns, and pickup trucks.[68] This America (or the "real America," as Sarah Palin called it in the 2008 race) is an essentially white, Christian nation at its core, in which ethnic, racial, and religious diversity is to be kept at a minimum.[69]

(*Liberal version*) Occasionally, Barack Obama attempted to present himself as traditionally or typically all-American.[70] But more often, his campaign emphasized the diverse elements of his biography (his immigrant background, biracial heritage, Indonesian stepfather), suggesting that together they made him uniquely qualified to lead the nation.[71] Obama spoke of himself as a sort of black Horatio Alger, one whose story demonstrated the United States to be a "magical place" of opportunity and tolerance. And he emphasized that national unity transcended racial divides, such as in his oft-cited quote from the 2004 Democratic National Convention: "There's not a black America and white America and Latino America and Asian America; there's the United States of America."[72] Here Obama articulated a liberal, multicultural vision of the nation. In this America, diversity was celebrated, but the nation stood above all.

In the post-racial United States, the cultural forms of people of color are understood to be artifacts that anyone may consume, appropriate, or claim as their own.[73] Blacks are called to offer their blackness to the wider society, rather than regarding it as part of an oppositional, minority culture. Obama's bounded performances of blackness in 2007/2008 included such things as his affectionate fist bumps with his wife, Michelle, occasional references to rap lyrics, serious basketball habit, ability to slip into (and out of) black forms of speech, generally "cool" demeanor, and evocation of the timbre and tone of civil rights–era discourse.[74] In the 2008 race, it seemed that Obama's blackness—bounded, limited, and largely depoliticized—might serve as the foundation for a revitalized, newly authentic American identity.

The Race Speech

In many ways, Obama's March 18, 2008, "A More Perfect Union" speech represented new race politics par excellence. It was delivered in response to the firestorm of controversy surrounding Obama's relationship with the Reverend Jeremiah Wright.[75] In my view, the speech embodied both the perils and the promise of the new race politics. In it, Obama was careful to empathize with the frustrations of both whites and non-whites, including white resentment over affirmative action. He emphasized loyalties of nation above those of color. And, as stated above, he characterized Wright as a relic of the past, one whose views on race were "profoundly distorted."

Some observers have been very critical of the address, seeing in it only classic colorblindness and racial denial.[76] But I believe that it is also important to note the degree to which Obama attempted to defend Wright here. As he said, "As imperfect as he may be, he has been like family to me. He strengthened my faith, officiated my wedding, and baptized my children. . . . He contains within him the contradictions—the good and the bad—of the community that he has served diligently for so many years. I can no more disown him than I can disown the black community. . . . These people are a part of me. And they are a part of America, this country that I love."[77]

Obama attempted to explain the black church tradition without reducing it to caricature, and black frustration without reducing it to pathology. While black anger was not always productive, he argued, "it is real; it is powerful; and to simply wish it away, to condemn it without understanding its roots, only serves to widen the chasm of misunderstanding that exists between the races." Thus he asked that white Americans listen to, and validate, the legitimate concerns of black Americans. Further, he argued that the poverty and violence witnessed in many urban areas were primarily due to years of institutional discrimination and neglect, rather than to the failings of black people themselves.

In other speeches (such as his Father's Day address), Obama would back away from these kinds of statements. And ultimately he did renounce Reverend Wright, whose appearance at the National Press Club in April 2008 proved to be too incendiary for Obama to explain away.[78] In the March 18 speech, however, Obama demonstrated a kind of courage on race that he has arguably not often demonstrated since. The positive reception of the speech suggested, most importantly, that the new politics of race had the potential to develop into a genuine racial dialogue, rather than serving largely as a series of dictates for African Americans.

New Politics, Right and Left

In my reading, blacks who play the new politics of race are accepted or tolerated by political conservatives. Unlike many others (angry blacks, ungrateful blacks, racist blacks, welfare cheats, teen mothers, gang-bangers, and the "victimologist" white college professors who serve as their allies), "post-racial" African Americans are not objectionable to members of the right. Those who focus on black hypocrisy, black racism, and black cultural pathologies (e.g., Juan Williams, Thomas Sewell, John McWhorter, Larry Elder, and Shelby Steele) may be viewed as fellow freedom fighters and patriots.[79]

Under the liberal paradigm, however, blacks who abide by the new politics of race are more than tolerated; they may be loved, adored, or—as in Obama's case—exalted.[80] Post-racial blacks offer to liberal whites psychic or cultural goods that they need, want, or crave, including "authenticity," identity, acceptance, redemption, innocence, and a sense of being good and moral people.[81] Obama's formulation of new race politics, in which he presented his blackness as a source of national redemption and rebirth, was very powerful, in part because it spoke directly to the anxieties and insecurities associated with whiteness in the contemporary era.[82] As Gary Kamiya writes, "Obama's charisma, which is his unique political strength, is real, but it cannot be separated from the fact that he's black. When Obama speaks of change and hope and healing divisions, his words carry an electric charge because of who he is: *He embodies his own message*, the very definition of charisma. As a black man offering reconciliation, he is making a deeply personal connection with whites, not merely a rhetorical one."[83]

These points aside, there is currently much agreement between liberal and conservative versions of the new politics of race. With the rightward turn of the last several decades, the neoconservative framing of racial politics has come to predominate over more progressive or left-leaning variants. The new race politics has its grounding in the ideology of colorblind individualism, which emerged as a conservative response to the gains of the movements for racial equality. It therefore shares this ideology's basic assumptions about the nature of racial inequality and what should, and should not, be done about it.[84]

Consider, again, the move away from group rights and identity politics signaled by post-racialism. While such a move is clearly demanded by conservatives, is it also, I suggest, deeply comforting to many liberals (hence the "Obama love"). Though many liberal whites doubtlessly believe that they should support affirmative action and strong expressions of racial pride, it is likely that in today's political climate few are sure they actually do.[85] Post-racialism takes the pressure off, allowing whites to participate in (consume, laugh at, explore, appropriate) blackness while making no group-based racial demands.

The Future: Perils and Promises

Racial politics in the coming decades will be shaped by a number of factors, which comprise the landscape of race in the contemporary United States. These include the crisis in white identity, the growing class divide among blacks, the emergence of Asian and Latino pan-ethnicity, and the contested relationship of black immigrants and biracial Americans to the social construct of blackness.[86] "Non-racial" factors such as the pressures of globalization, U.S. foreign policy, the strength or weakness of the economy, and the agency of the icons of post-racialism themselves will also strongly influence racial dynamics.

Though the ideology of colorblind individualism is fairly solidified (and rightward leaning) at this point, the new politics of race are still in relative flux and negotiation. Thus they hold both peril and promise. In my view, the perils are considerable indeed. In the United States and elsewhere, the ideology of colorblind individualism has served "to [stall] the transformation of the racial order in the direction of greater substantive equality."[87] Attempts to achieve representative parity are rendered illegitimate under this paradigm. In 2009, for example, an article in the *Wall Street*

Journal complained that Obama's nomination of Sonia Sotomayor to join the Supreme Court "commits the cardinal sin of identity politics," in seeking "to elevate people more for the political currency of their gender and ethnicity than for their individual merit."[88] Further, the new politics of race asks the black middle class to abandon or condemn lower-income African Americans in exchange for a seat at the table. Thus the inclusion of non-whites envisioned by the new politics may be limited to "happy diversity"—a "celebration" of traditions and cultures that ignores real differences in power and opportunity, and is entirely absent an agenda for racial justice.[89]

As long as it remains grounded in the assumptions of the ideology of colorblindness, the new politics of race will put all the emphasis for solving the nation's racial problems squarely on the shoulders of the racially marginalized. As described in the pages above, in the 2008 presidential election the new race politics were articulated as a set of demands for African Americans. A central component of the dominant narrative that emerged to explain Obama's success was that in selecting the Illinois senator as president, white Americans had been absolved of the issue of race and "done their part" to address racial inequality. Now, the story went, it was up to black Americans to "get over" race and help themselves.

Some may argue that Obama's deployment of the new race politics should be viewed as primarily tactical. Perhaps progressive, justice-oriented social ends can be achieved if he and other leaders simply avoid calling attention to them, or reframe them in a way that is less likely to be perceived as unfair or objectionable. It is my argument that this is not the case; in fact, one of the chief "perils" of new race politics as presently formulated is that it closes off the possibility of achieving or even discussing certain ends. As Obama had declared, repeatedly, that racism was no longer serious a problem in the United States, his (few) attempts to address contemporary manifestations of racism did not sit well with the public, which responded with both outrage and accusations that Obama was a false prophet of post-racialism.[90] During the opening years of his presidency, Obama seemed to become increasingly timid in dealing with racial matters, and at times he appeared to be simply capitulating to the demands of the far right rather than taking a principled stand.[91]

There is some evidence that the space for addressing problems of racism under the current regime of new race politics is in fact shrinking. In the last several years, we have seen a number of instances in which direct or even implied allegations of racism in politics have led to immediate accusations (usually by conservatives) that the accusers are themselves racist. These are often followed by denunciations of the original charge of racism by others who are seen as their allies, and sometimes by swift retractions (or "clarifications") by the accusers themselves.[92] Increasingly, charging that an individual or institution is racist is viewed as an act of anti-white racial aggression itself, more odious, perhaps, than the supposed racism that was being called out in the first place.[93] This is color-blind logic taken to the extreme.

Despite its very substantial drawbacks, the new race politics may hold some promise. The realities of the 21st century do call for new ways of thinking about race, more diversity of thought and opinion among African Americans, and new modalities of public blackness. Not everyone can be Jesse Jackson, Al Sharpton, or Barack Obama (and even Sharpton has adopted a much more accommodating political stance as of late).[94] I believe it is true that racial dialogue in this country has reached a kind of stalemate. There are many new developments (demographic, cultural, and political) that we do not even have the language to critically explain. And in debates over issues such as affirmative action, institutional racism, proportional representation, and immigration, the nation is increasingly polarized, with neither side particularly willing to listen to the other. I do not wish to argue that all perspectives are equally valid. But as a practical matter, if you are right but no one will listen to you anymore, it may be impossible to get your point of view across or to get anything done.

It seems to me that the United States urgently needs a *new* new politics of race. At its best, the new race politics would involve a genuine dialogue on racial issues. It would facilitate unity across racial divides without demanding silence around issues of injustice and inequity. This "insurgent" new race politics would be multiculturalist and pluralist in orientation, envisioning a particularly valued role for people of color in American society. And the most progressive envisionings of new race politics would respond to the profound demographic and cultural shifts that the United States is currently undergoing by promoting a truly expanded, inclusive vision of nation, rather than one driven by the racial backlash politics, Islamophobia, and immigration hysteria that we have witnessed over the past several years.[95]

4

Contesting Gender and Race in the 2008 Democratic Primary

During and immediately after the Democratic primary, commentators offered a number of explanations as to why Obama fared better with voters than did Clinton. It was variously argued that Obama won because he was a man, and it was "impossible" to be a powerful woman in politics; because Obama was a sexist who actively encouraged stereotypes about Clinton; or because while racism is universally regarded as taboo, no one takes sexism seriously. Others claimed that it could be historically demonstrated that "blacks" always get their rights before "women" get theirs, or that blacks as a group receive more advantages than whites in the wider society. Still others wrote that Obama's success was simply due to the fact that he was better organized than Clinton; that he represented change whereas she represented the status quo; or that while Obama was a "likeable" person, Hillary Clinton was not.

I take on these arguments and others in this chapter, as I discuss and compare the ways that race and gender figured into the 2008 Democratic primary. In the last several decades, feminist and other critical scholars have insisted that we must consider how constructs such as race, class, and gender articulate in relationship to one another. There is no generic "woman" or generic "black person"—people live the various dimensions of their identity simultaneously. This is the concept of intersectionality. Despite the fact that intersectionality represents an important theoretical advance, few social scientists have systematically applied it in their work. The 2008 Democratic primary, however, presents an ideal case study for an exploration of intersectionality. Senator Barack Obama's matchup against Senator Hillary Clinton raised important questions about the contrasting ways that both race *and* gender function in the post–civil rights, post-feminist United States.

In the first part of this chapter, I discuss the impassioned, often angry debates that were occasioned by the contest, and the deep divides that were revealed to exist between women to the left of center. I focus on statements, found in the mainstream press and the blogosphere, from three main groups of women: powerful "second wave," white feminists who supported Clinton, the mostly younger white female supporters of Obama, and progressive women of color both inside and outside academia.

I find that the arguments voiced for and against each of the candidates presupposed fundamental disagreements about what it means to be a feminist in the 21st century, and about the salience of gender relative to other social divides. The debates further show that despite decades of discussion about multiculturalism and inclusiveness, conceptions of "womanhood" among many prominent feminist activists and white female members of the rank and file remain tied to notions of whiteness. They also entail an increasing sense of victimization vis-à-vis non-whites, which is a dominant characteristic of the contemporary construct of whiteness.[1]

In the second part of the chapter, I consider the roles that race and gender played in the outcome of the primary. Here I especially explore the strategic deployment of ideas about race and gender by each of the candidates. I use both evidence from the print and online media and quotes from a subsample of the approximately 125 in-depth interviews I conducted with college students in the weeks preceding the election. I argue that though Clinton was subject to constant sexist disparagement by the press, her seeming ambivalence regarding her presentation of gender, and her use of tactics that many viewed as patriarchal and racist, alienated her from voters who might otherwise have come to her defense. As for the issue of race, I find that the Clinton camp attempted to mobilize the construct of whiteness in her favor, through the use of racial code words and innuendo—aka "dog-whistle racism"—that would highlight Obama's racial "otherness." Yet, I argue, these maneuvers ultimately backfired, because Obama was able to neutralize the potentially "problematic" aspects of blackness in his campaign (by escaping associations with the "old race politics") and frame the 2008 race as an opportunity for racial and national redemption.

I believe that gender did work in Obama's favor, both because of the supposed naturalness of the link between masculinity and leadership, and because of his "movie-star good looks." But in the end, I claim, it was not so much Obama's reliance on his gender privilege, as it was his self-presentation as a "post-racial" black candidate, and his successful mobilization of the powerful trope of race—as redemptive and as revolutionary—that were the keys to his victory. Ultimately, I conclude, in order to make sense of the ways that race and gender played out in the 2008 primary, we must move beyond static conceptions of how each "operates" in American society, to consider the specific ways that Clinton and Obama positioned themselves in relationship to the social constructs that so defined their candidacies.

Divided Sisterhood

The 2008 primary might have been a moment of shared euphoria that the Democratic Party had put forth its first serious female and black candidates in the same election. But instead it led liberals to become sharply polarized around the issues of race and gender. The divide was particularly acute, and painful, among women. As Bella English wrote in the *Boston Globe* in February, "There's a delicious irony in the 2008 Democratic presidential campaign: Liberal women who usually vote as a bloc are split. It has come down to a black man and a white woman, and no less than history hangs in the balance. The race has pitted friends against friends, sisters against sisters, and mothers against daughters, with many feeling they have to justify their votes."[2] The intense infighting that the contest occasioned among feminists received substantial coverage in the press. While women under 40 tended to throw their enthusiasm behind Obama, many older, second-wave feminists ferociously supported Hillary Clinton. As the race progressed and Clinton's lock on the nomination began to appear less than secure, numerous accusations were hurled from the pages of newsprint editorials and blogs across the ideological and generational divides.

Prominent Clinton feminists took special aim at women they felt were betraying the cause. Those who sided with Obama were variously accused of being fickle, naive, elitist, and romantically infatuated. The most serious charge was that they had capitulated to the patriarchal status quo. Gloria Steinem argued in the *New York Times* that some of Obama's female supporters "hope to deny or escape the sexual caste system." Robin Morgan, publisher of the classic 1970s feminist anthology *Sisterhood Is Powerful*, charged that many of those who supported Obama were "eager to win male approval by showing [that] they're not feminists." They would not say anything positive about Clinton, she charged, for "fear that their boyfriends might look at them funny." These women were unable to identify with the New York senator, she wrote, "because she is unafraid of eeueweeeu yucky power." Former Planned Parenthood president Gloria Feldt wrote in the *Huffington Post* that while women had the right to vote for whichever candidate they liked, their historic "responsibility," as women, was to vote for Clinton.[3]

Many of the accused responded with anger. As Adele M. Stan wrote in the *Washington Post*, "I take no issue with the feminism of women who disagree with my choice [to back Obama]. I do, however, take issue with those who disparage my character as their explanation for my choice." Some rejected the implication that they should back Hillary Clinton simply because of gender. As Donna Darko blogged, "Clinton's feminist contingent is not pleased that all of us vagina owners will not vote for the vagina candidate. Seriously, see if any of them mention any other reason why we should vote for Clinton." The self-identified "Obama feminist" Courtney Martin claimed in the *American Prospect* that she'd "been chastised, dismissed, lectured, and humiliated by older women" who supported Clinton. But, she argued, "I've also been respectfully challenged, constructively criticized, moved, and celebrated. And the differences between those types of treatment shed light on larger dynamics playing out across the feminist movement."[4]

Numerous Obama feminists claimed that supporting Clinton did nothing to advance the cause of feminism. In an article titled "Death of a Saleswoman: How Hillary Clinton Lost Me—and a Generation of Young Voters," Megan O'Rourke stated; "The more Clinton's campaign floundered . . . the more masculine and hard-nosed she made herself out to be." On Salon.com, the 1960s feminist Frances Kissling claimed that Clinton had "run as a stereotypical male and represents the same old cowardly Clintonian politics." In the *Huffington Post*, Ellen Bravo claimed that many feminists had turned away from Clinton when she began to treat Obama "as women are treated—patronizing him as merely a 'good speaker,' trivializing his accomplishments . . . and using surrogates to demonize his morality." And, in an article titled "Why Women Hate Hillary," University of Michigan professor Susan J. Douglas wrote that "for many of us feminism did not mean trying to be more like men. It meant challenging patriarchy." Yet "Hillary, by contrast, seems to want to be more like a man in her demeanor and politics . . . leaving some of the basic tenets of feminism in the dust." In truth, she argued, "[Clinton] is like patriarchy in sheep's clothing."[5]

Though they chafed at the scolding of the Clintonistas, Obama's feminist supporters were alarmed by the misogynistic overtones of the criticism directed at Hillary Clinton. In a piece called "Hey, Obama Boys: Back Off Already!," the self-described "longtime Clinton skeptic" Rebecca Traister wrote, "I [began to get] e-mails from men I didn't know well who approached me as a go-to feminist to whom they could express their hatred of Hillary and their anger at her. . . . One of my closest girlfriends, an Obama voter, told me of a drink she'd had with a politically progressive man who made a series of legitimate complaints about Clinton's policies before adding that when he hears the senator's voice, he's overcome by an urge to punch her in the face."[6] Similarly, in a June 2008 article titled "Dear Hillary: A Letter from an Obama Feminist," Courtney Martin thanked Clinton "for weathering this storm of anxious masculinity and outright sabotage, but even more, for creating a moment where the kind of subtle sexism that women experience every day . . . was brought to undeniable light."[7]

Again Invisible: Women of Color and the Oppression Sweepstakes

In addition to reviving intergenerational and ideological tensions within the predominantly white, middle-class feminist movement, the election also battered the tenuous alliance between mainstream feminists and progressive women of color. The feminist "third wave" was launched by women seeking to revive the feminist movement and to address its most serious tactical and ideological shortcomings. From the 1980s onward, dozens of essays have been written promulgating the following ideas: that feminism must be inclusive and multicultural, that opposing race and class injustice should be central to its mission, that domestic and international women of color should not be marginalized, and that movement leaders should cease to write and speak as if "all the women are white and all the blacks are men." In fact, these have been defining principles of the third wave, widely proclaimed to be part of the painful but necessary evolution of the movement.[8]

From the start of the Democratic primary, however, it seemed that these working consensuses had been all but abandoned. Academics, journalists, and bloggers of color were alternately amazed and infuriated to see Clinton's feminist supporters render their points of view and experiences as tangential distractions to the "core" or "true" women's issues. This tendency was often found implicitly in discussions of how "women" felt about Hillary Clinton that excluded the possibly very different feelings of women of color.[9] On the *XX Factor* blog, Kim McLarin wrote that after being "confused" that "so many white women could be so shocked that sexism still exists," she finally figured out that the angry debate among feminists was "a family fight between older white women and their daughters," and "me and my mother and my sisters are not even in the conversation." "What a relief," she concluded. "Ya'll carry on."[10]

A more explicit claim that race and class justice were not feminist issues was found in the June 8 *Washington Post* article "Looking Forward, Feminism Needs to Focus." There, Linda Hirshman called for feminists to unite around the singular cause of gender oppression, leaving distractions like intersectionality aside: "The Clinton campaign has, perhaps unwittingly, revealed what many in the movement know—that if feminism is a social-justice-for-everyone (with the possible exception of middle-class white women) movement, then gender is just one commitment among many. And when the other causes call, the movement will dissolve."[11]

Numerous young feminists—black, brown, and white—were offended by Hirshman's article. Jill, a blogger at *Feministe*, protested Hirshman's separation of "authentic 'feminist' issues" from "those 'other' issues that those 'other' women are trying to integrate into feminism." She wrote, "It's a question of who feminism belongs to, and who is entitled to set out its goals and concerns." One Latina blogger argued on *La Chola*, "This is not a movement. I repeat, this is not a movement. It's an exclusive networking club. And no woman, of color or otherwise, owes her allegiance to an exclusive networking club simply because she has a vagina and the exclusive networking club members have vaginas."[12]

In addition to taking issue with what they saw as renewed calls for their marginalization, many women of color were particularly disappointed by the resolute blindness of mainstream feminists to what they perceived to be the numerous racial insults issued by the Clinton campaign. As the black feminist scholar Patricia Hill Collins (then president of the American Sociological Association) was quoted as saying in *The Nation*, "It is such a distressing, ugly period. Clinton has manipulated ideas about race, but Obama has not manipulated similar ideas about gender."[13]

Black women complained in particularly bitter terms about the deafening silence of white feminists, who failed to rally to the defense of Michelle Obama during the months she faced widespread attacks from the conservative media. As the blogger Rikyrah wrote on *Jack & Jill Politics*, "One has to wonder, as Michelle Obama is being labeled unpatriotic, bitter, mean, angry. Where are those feminists who saw sexism lurking around every corner with Hillary Clinton? Why is [Michelle Obama] not worthy of defense by the feminist establishment?"[14]

Very soon into the primary, debates about the election seemed to have devolved into an "oppression sweepstakes." In a May 2008 interview with the *Washington Post*, Senator Clinton herself stated, "You can go to places in the world where there are no racial distinctions, [but] everyone is joined together in their oppression of women. The treatment of women is the single biggest problem we have politically and socially in the world." Lynette Long argued that one of the painful lessons that "women" had learned from the primary was that "in the world of presidential politics, race trumps gender." And Gloria Steinem, in her January 2008 *New York Times* op-ed, claimed that though "the sex barrier [is] not taken as seriously as the racial one" in our society, "gender is probably the most restricting force in American life."[15]

Women of color responded to these arguments with particular frustration. As the self-identified "angry Asian-American woman" Jennifer Fang wrote on the blog *Reappropriate*, "Is it no wonder, then, that women of colour have long felt alienated by feminists like Steinem? Where do we fit when we're being asked to choose between Obama and Clinton as a metaphor for race versus gender?" "The juxtaposition [of race and gender]," she continued, "is disingenuous, divisive, overly simplistic, and ultimately harmful. . . . We all compete to see both who's more oppressed, and who will make it out of that 'Oppression Box' first."[16]

Seeking to bridge the growing, acrimonious divide, a coalition of black and white feminists met over breakfast in February 2008. Present at the meeting were Beverly Guy-Sheftall, Johnnetta B. Cole, Kimberlé Crenshaw, Patricia Williams, Carol Jenkins, Eleanor Smeal, Mab Segrest, Laura Flanders, Gloria Steinem, and others. Reflecting on the bitterness of the previous months, they asked, "How . . . did a historic breakthrough moment for which we have all longed and worked hard, suddenly risk becoming marred by having to choose between 'race cards' and 'gender cards'? By petty competitiveness about who endures more slings and arrows? . . . What happened . . . to the last four decades of discussion about tokenism and multiple identities and the complex intersections of race, gender, sexuality, ethnicity, and class?"[17]

Despite these and other statements from feminists urging unity, the debate over "who has it worse" continued throughout the summer.[18] During the final weeks of the primary, cable news stations projected the images of crowds of angry white women, swearing that they would either sit out the general election or vote for McCain in the fall. In response to this specter, the white anti-racist activist Tim Wise declared, "It is high irony, bordering on the outright farcical, to believe that electorally bonding with white men, so as to elect McCain, is a rational strategy for promoting feminism and challenging patriarchy." "Voting against Senator Obama," he continued, "is not about gender solidarity. It is an act of white racial bonding, and it is grotesque."[19]

A Black President: A Uniquely American Achievement

Analyses of the 2008 election that pit "women" against "blacks" are counterproductive, and tend to erase women of color from the equation altogether. Yet it is clear that, for a number of reasons, race worked for Obama in a way that gender did not work for Hillary Clinton. First, while pundits were fascinated by the idea that the country might select a man classified as black to be president, much less discussion was devoted to what it would mean for the United States to choose a woman. There was a clear sense, from the beginning, that Obama's candidacy was somehow more potentially transformative for the nation than was Clinton's.

Such sentiments were reflected in many of the interviews I conducted with college students in the weeks before the general election.[20] When asked which would be more meaningful, historic, or significant for the country, most of the students we spoke to chose the election of a black president. Consider, for example, Scott, a 20-year-old white male, who stated, "I'd be more inclined to say African American just because . . . I don't know, I just feel like African American people are more substantial for some reason?" Or as Aileen, a 22-year-old white female, said more concretely, "I think it would be more historic if it would be our first black president, because I don't know . . . obviously we started off as a country with . . . really horrible race relations and we had black people enslaved and now we have the potential for a black man to be running things. So I think, you know, it's kind of come full circle, not in every way, but historically we've come full circle."

As the quote above suggests, the explanation for the difference lies in the subconsciously understood role of race in our nation's history. It is the line between blacks and whites that most acknowledge to be the country's deepest divide and most enduring symbol of shame. As Howard Winant writes, "Racial conflict is the very archetype of discord in North America; the primordial conflict that has in many ways structured all others."[21] And as Benjamin Wallace-Wells wrote in late 2006, "Even if race is more socially crippling than gender, race can work better . . . for Barack than gender for Hillary, because most Americans want to believe that the culture has moved past its racial problems. . . . There is the sense that, by electing a female president, the nation would be meeting a standard set by other liberal democracies; the election of a black man, by contrast, would be a particularly American achievement, an affirmation of American ideals."[22] For a nation seeking to restore its honor in the aftermath of an unpopular and seemingly unending war, the prospect of choosing a black president was especially appealing. Further, in the post–civil rights United States, thinking of oneself as anti-racist, and being perceived by others as anti-racist, is much more central to the self-concept of liberal Americans than is opposition to sexism.[23]

While blackness worked in Obama's favor in many respects, it was his specific deployment of blackness that was key. Obama positioned himself as a "next-generation" or "post-racial" black candidate, carefully avoiding the appearance of anger, protest, victimhood, or "grievance." At a number of key moments in the election, he crucially differentiated himself from the styles and tactics of other black public figures that many whites (and non-whites) had come to strongly dislike. Thus he was able to neutralize the "problematic" aspects of blackness while highlighting the redemptive ones.[24] As one young white female (Fiona, age 19) said to my interviewer, the genius of Obama was that he "uses the motivation and excitement" of men like Jesse Jackson and Malcolm X in ways that seem "less harmful, aggressive," and "offensive." Another stated that Obama "seems like he could be your friend."

Through speeches declaring that "only in America is my story possible," Obama forwarded the notion that in voting for him, whites demonstrated their "core goodness" and the United States proved itself to be a place of opportunity and tolerance. As Gary Kamiya notes, the Clinton campaign found this message hard to counter: "Unable to directly challenge Democratic voters' race-driven enthusiasm for Obama because that would make her look racially insensitive, Clinton's attacks on Obama as a false messiah covertly echo this theme. 'Now I could stand up here and say, "Let's get everybody together, let's get unified, the sky will open, the light will come down, celestial choirs will be singing,"' she said sarcastically one Sunday in Rhode Island. 'And everyone will know we should do the right thing, and the world will be perfect.'"[25] The promises of racial rebirth and renewal were also strongly reinforced via Obama's characterization of himself as the candidate representing "change" rather than the status quo. Voting for Clinton, who ran on a platform of "experience," offered no redemptive blackness or psychological payoff regarding gender, about which she seemed ambivalent.

Say What? Sexism?

Given these observations, it is perhaps unsurprising that the racial innuendoes designed to undermine Obama received much more analysis and condemnation from the press than the often more blatantly sexist rhetoric directed at Clinton. Let us begin with the conservative talk show host Rush Limbaugh. He argued in December 2007 that Clinton would not make a suitable president because no one would "want to watch a woman get older before their eyes on a daily basis." In April 2008, he also took a swipe at Clinton's female supporters: "They've been married two or three times; they've had two or three abortions; they've done everything that feminism asked them to do. They have cut men out of their lives; they have devoted themselves to causes and careers. And this—the candidacy of Hillary Clinton—is the culmination of all of these women's efforts."[26] In July 2007, the *Washington Post* ran a story on Clinton's "plunging neckline." Her cleavage was said to "stir up the same kind of discomfort that might be churned up after spotting Rudy Giuliani with his shirt unbuttoned." Like "catching a man with his fly unzipped," the author continued, it is best to "just look away!"[27]

In addition to her looks, writers often disparaged Clinton's voice. Her laugh was repeatedly referred to a "cackle," as in "hens cackle. So do witches. And, so does the front-runner in the Democratic presidential contest" (and this from a relatively flattering article about Clinton in the *Boston Globe*). One *Washington Post* writer argued in January 2008 that Clinton "needs a radio-controlled shock collar so that aides can zap her when she starts to get screechy." That same month, a Fox News commentator stated that "when Barack Obama speaks men hear 'Take off for the future.' And when Hillary Clinton speaks, men hear 'Take out the garbage.'"[28]

During the campaign, Hillary Clinton nutcrackers "with stainless steel thighs" were sold in gift shops throughout the country. The *New York Post* (gleefully) reported on the brisk sales of the item in the story "Nut Buster: Wacky Hillary Gizmo Is a Real Easy Shell." In July 2007, MSNBC's Tucker Carlson stated, "When she comes on television, I involuntarily cross my legs." And in February of the following year, Carlson hosted on his program Roger Stone, founder of the anti-Clinton group Citizens United Not Timid (or CUNT).[29]

Such facts were discussed very little in the mainstream media. They provoked no angry rants from Keith Olbermann. Feminists bloggers were incensed, but few others seemed to notice. The students I interviewed, in fact, confessed to being scarcely aware of insults directed at Clinton because of her gender. And even for those who described themselves as feminists, the notion that sexism had anything to do with why Clinton lost held little weight. Consider this exchange with Avery, a 25-year-old self-described "black feminist":

> INTERVIEWER: Some Clinton supporters say that she could possibly have lost because of sexism. What do you think of that?
>
> AVERY: That's ridiculous. You're less likely to lose from sexism than racism. Just historically, I mean, it's very funny. . . . I remember being irritated when her campaign started talking about sexism.

Students were especially unsympathetic to reports that Clinton had become teary-eyed in a speech before the New Hampshire primary. In the words of Dwayne, a 22-year-old Caribbean American male who had initially supported Clinton, "I think that she is a little too sensitive to run the country. . . . I mean, maybe she's not built for it. That's what I would say. She has some great ideas . . . [but] she's not 'Built Ford Tough' to be president . . . not at all." When Julia, a 20-year-old female was asked why she thought Clinton had lost the primary, she stated, "Umm, I remember hearing a lot of talk about her crying during a speech or something like that. . . . I think she needs to have better control of her emotions." Another female student stated, "I personally sometimes didn't like [Hillary] 'cause of how she acted. Like, um, when was it that she cried or something? That was my—that's why I was kind of iffy about her."[30]

Clinton's failure (until late in the primary) to address the issue of gender, and her use of tactics that many considered to be "masculine," likely caused her to lose the support of younger feminist-identified women who might have otherwise come to her defense. As one interviewee (Alyssa, age 21) stated, "I think if Hillary Clinton had given a speech on gender, you know, the way Barack Obama gave a really honest speech on race, that would have been huge for her, but she never did." The author Rebecca Traister writes that "years of putting her (female) humanity in deep freeze to preserve an aura of (male) impermeability was a seemingly unbreakable habit" that came to "cripple" Clinton in the primary: "She was unable to simply be herself in public."[31]

Dog-Whistle Racism and Black Anger

Clinton's reliance on what several writers have referred to as "dog whistle" racism—designed to appeal to the latent racism of "downscale" whites—alienated her from another core constituency: black Americans.[32] Throughout the primary, Clinton and her surrogates used code words and innuendo to cast Obama as the *problematically* (rather than redemptively) "black candidate."[33]

We were told, variously, that Obama could only get black votes (claims that may be attributed to the Clinton pollster Sergio Bendixen, Bill Clinton, and Hillary Clinton herself), that he was anti-white by association (the Reverend Wright controversy), anti-patriotic (the flag pin controversy), a drug user (to cite the New Hampshire Clinton campaign cochair Bill Shaheen), possibly a drug seller (the BET cofounder Bob Johnson), and married to an angry, ungrateful black woman (that Michelle!). Though he had managed to "shuck and jive" his way through the primary (to quote Andrew Cuomo), Hillary had to stay in the race in case he was assassinated (like RFK, JFK, MLK, and Malcolm X).[34] Like other affirmative action babies, Obama only got where he was because of his race (Geraldine Ferraro), and yet, being a latte-sipping elitist ("Bittergate"), he deigned to look down on "hardworking white Americans." Far from being post-racial, Clinton and her supporters hammered home the point that Obama was in fact overdetermined by his race.

While such messaging may have gained Clinton some white votes, it also contributed to the perception that her campaign was actively seeking to stir up white racial resentment. A particularly interesting perspective on this issue was offered by the former Bill Clinton adviser and current Republican strategist Dick Morris. In a January 2008 *RealClearPolitics* article, he argued that the ex-president had deliberately raised the issue of race before the South Carolina primary in order to provoke a back-lash against Obama. He wrote, "Why is he making such a fuss over a contest he knows he's going to lose? . . . Precisely because he is going to lose it. If Hillary loses South Carolina and the defeat serves to demonstrate Obama's ability to attract a bloc vote among black Democrats, the message will go out loud and clear to white voters that this is a racial fight. . . . That will trigger a massive white backlash against Obama and will drive white voters to Hillary Clinton."[35]

In response, many African Americans, who had once warmly referred to Bill Clinton as America's "first black president, "came to express a mixture of "seething, barely-contained rage" and "revulsion" when discussing the Clintons.[36] As Terence Samuel wrote in April:

> The Clintons do not seem to understand that the kind of revulsion they are generating in what was once the heart of their base is not your garden-variety political frustration. It is born out of a historical anger that requires 25 minutes in the supermarket aisle or 900 words on the op-ed page of the *New York Times* to explain. The idea that Obama, having played by all the rules and won by all the traditional measures, could lose the nomination because of Clinton's argument that he is unelectable because he is black, is profoundly revolting to many black people.[37]

In the end, the kinds of racial innuendoes utilized by the Clinton campaign gained her little mileage. Obama had succeeded in defining the 2008 campaign as a referendum on the goodness-cum-racial tolerance of white Americans, and of the nation by extension. In this context, the extra-vigilant liberal media, many white Democrats, and most African Americans were repelled by what they perceived to be clear attempts by the Clintons to appeal to the baser, more racist instincts of the general population.

The Obama Crush

In addition to analyzing the role that whiteness played in Clinton's campaign, we must also consider the ways that gender helped, or hurt, Barack Obama. While he has been primarily described in terms of his race, it is also crucial to remember that Obama was running for president as a man.

And as a man, Obama automatically commanded a kind of authority and legitimacy in his quest to become the president of the United States that a woman could not.[38]

But the senator's masculine appeal went deeper, as sexuality and "celebrity" factored into the equation as well. Obama was uncommonly attractive and known for his (white-collar) masculine swagger. Regularly described as handsome, dashing, cool, and "swoon-worthy," the American press corps and women everywhere were said be to "in love" with Obama. And in a way they were. See, for example, this quote from the *Washingtonian Magazine*: "When Barack Obama speaks, people listen. But we're also taken by his movie-star looks. With his megawatt smile and soulful eyes, it's no wonder he got everyone's attention at the 2004 Democratic convention. He's got a great physique, too. . . . This past summer, HottestUSSenator.com ran an online contest for the 'Hottest U.S. Senator Not Counting Obama.' Obama was omitted before the voting even began because of his 'extreme hotness.'"[39] John McCain's infamous July 2008 "Obama Love" campaign ad ridiculed the media's "obsession" with the junior senator. And conservative women gleefully mocked their Democratic counterparts. The "proud conservative" Kyle-Anne Shiver, for example, wrote in the *American Thinker*, "Liberal women are leading the Obama Crush pack. *It's wonderful; it's delicious; it's positively grand.*" In the *Washington Post*, the anti-feminist writer Charlotte Allen claimed that reading about women "swooning and gushing" over Obama made her think that perhaps their brains had been "permanently occluded by random emotions, psychosomatic flailings and distraction by the superficial."[40]

But the Obama crush was not limited to the female gender. In July, the writer Jewel Woods commented, "Sure, women swoon, but have you ever noticed that guys, too, seem almost weak-kneed over the senator with mad skills and a million-dollar smile?" He continued, "[Men] as diverse as Colin Powell, Michael Eric Dyson, Andrew Sullivan, Tom Joyner, Ted Kennedy, Bill Richardson, Christopher Hitchens, and numerous others, appear to have . . . a 'man crush' on Sen. Obama." The August 2008 cover of *Ebony Magazine* described Obama as one of the "Coolest Brothers of All Time." And during coverage of the Potomac primary, the MSNBC anchor Chris Matthews famously stated that after hearing Obama speak, "I felt this thrill going up my leg." He continued, "I don't have that too often."[41]

Even Obama's detractors commented on his cool factor. As part of the Clinton/GOP characterization of Obama as an arrogant elitist, Karl Rove stated in June 2008, "Even if you never met him, you know this guy. . . .

He's the guy at the country club with the beautiful date, holding a martini and a cigarette that stands against the wall and makes snide comments about everyone who passes by."[42]

Sidebar on Sarah Palin

Gender scholars have argued that women in politics often feel pressured to be as much like men as possible in order to succeed.[43] But the example of the Republican vice presidential nominee Sarah Palin, whose clever quips (at the RNC), physical beauty, and "sexy hockey mom" persona catapulted her to instant celebrity, suggests that gender and sexuality might also be harnessed to the benefit of a female candidate, depending on how these factors are deployed.

It is unclear, however, how far these attributes could have taken Palin, or any woman in politics. Fairly soon after Palin's "sensational" appearance at the Republican National Convention, she became a national laughingstock. Following a series of disastrous television news interviews, Palin was parodied on *Saturday Night Live*, torn apart in the tabloid press, and widely derided as a bimbo, an idiot, and an airhead (to quote some terms used by my student interviewees). Many of her initial GOP defenders seemed clearly embarrassed to have once supported her. Liberal feminists reviled her. And though Palin was regarded as a generally likeable, "relatable" person, many voters nevertheless came to view her as completely incompetent to hold the office to which she aspired.[44]

I will note that Palin has manage to resuscitate her "brand" somewhat post-election, becoming the biggest "celebrity" on the political right. Whether this means that voters will find her to be electable, however, is an open question. It remains to be seen, therefore, if another woman can crack the 21st-century gender code in 2012, and become the revolutionary, powerful, "post-feminist" candidate that neither Clinton nor Palin could in 2008.

Lessons from the 2008 Race

Views about the role of sexism in Hillary's loss, and about her legacy for women, are widely contradictory. Though some held Clinton to be a feminist hero, others found her political maneuvers to be repugnant and anti-feminist at their core.[45] And though Clinton's camp did seem to try to manipulate racial stereotypes in her favor during the primary, it is also true that she was continually subjected to an undercurrent of sexism from the conservative and liberal press. How, we must ask, do we disentangle "simple dislike" for Hillary Clinton from hatred directed at her specifically because she was a woman stepping outside her socially ascribed place?[46] How do we parse the role of sexism from the other factors that led to her loss? Jonathan, a 19-year-old Latino male, told one of my interviewers, "A lot of people were turned off by her . . . because she was too shrewd, manipulative, you know . . . I'm trying to not use curse words, but you know, the *B* word." In the end, he opined, what hurt Clinton was not her gender but "the fact that she was Hillary."

Obama likely benefitted from both the positive associations between masculinity and leadership, and from the many ways that Clinton was disparaged because of her gender. Yet it does not logically follow—as some have argued—that his gender privilege simply "cancelled out" or "trumped" the issue of race in the campaign. In the end, I argue, the 2008 primary was less about Obama relying on sexism "to get over," and more about him "doing race right." As a new-millennium, "post-racial" candidate, Obama deployed the concept of race more appealingly, and more strategically, than Clinton did gender. While she was the candidate of the status quo (who could be just as tough as the boys), he was "your cool black friend"—and the candidate of change.[47] Capitalizing on the fervent desire in this country to say that we have overcome our racial problems, and deploying the tropes of renewal, redemption, and rebirth, Obama tapped into the revolutionary potential of his candidacy in a way that Clinton simply did not. As Alyssa E., a 21-year-old women's studies major, said to an interviewer: "I definitely loved Hillary Clinton. But I don't think it was because of sexism that she lost. I think there were some really ugly, really sexist things that happened. But she was very far ahead at one point, and I don't think that *suddenly* we became sexist. I think that she could have had this really revolutionary candidacy; but it wasn't quite right. She wasn't talking about change."

5

The Trope of Race in Obama's America

As the French philosopher Etienne Balibar has written, "The discourses of race and nation are never very far apart."[1] The relationship between these discourses, however, has long been fraught with tension and contradiction. The pretense of nationalism is that it is an ideology of profound inclusion—the nation is "always conceived as a deep, horizontal comradeship" of citizens who are posited to be equals.[2] Yet as many scholars have argued, nation building has always included practices of both inclusion and exclusion, articulated, most prominently, around the axes of race, class, gender, and sexuality. Further, we are reminded, exclusions and hierarchies are not tangential or accidental to the form and formation of nation-states, but have in fact been integral to them.[3]

Scholars have especially studied the ironies and contradictions of nation in the Americas.[4] The United States, for example, was founded on both the ideals of liberty and equality, and the practices of racial slavery, conquest, and genocide.[5] This central contradiction has complicated notions of identity and belonging in the nation since its birth. The founding documents declared all men to be created equal but constructed those tainted by the condition of enslavement as three-fifths of a full human being. The indigenous people of America, on the other hand, were viewed as outside the nation-state entirely.[6]

The rights movements of the mid-to-late 20th century drew attention to these contradictions, demanding that the United States live up to its creed. The denial of full citizenship and the violent subjugation of blacks in the Jim Crow era became a "source of embarrassment" to the United States, which "jeopardiz[ed] the effective maintenance of our moral leadership of the free and democratic nations of the world."[7] More than half a century later, the course of American history continues to be characterized by competing paradigms of national identity, organized around principles of inclusion and exclusion. And the persistent marginalization of African Americans, despite important but partial gains, is alternately seen as a source of shame, frustration, and recrimination. In some ways blacks seem to be the most American of Americans, and in some ways they seem the least. More than a decade into the 21st century, the black/white relationship remains the central organizing metaphor for race relations in this country. It is also the basic point of reference for all other social divides.[8] As I demonstrate below, these realities were crucial in shaping the discourses pertaining to race and nation that emerged in the 2008 presidential election.

21st-Century Anxieties of Race and Nation

As in the past, the constructs of race and nation today are dynamically and conflictually intertwined. In the 21st century, the politics and anxieties of race have clear national and global referents. In the last several decades, the terrain of race in this country has been dramatically reshaped by the high numbers of immigrants entering from Latin America, Africa, and Asia. The newcomers have complicated, but not displaced, the black/white lens through which race has long been understood. And they have occasioned a demographic shift according to which whites will soon become a numerical minority for the first time since the country's founding.

Since the 1960s, the demographic and cultural import of African Americans has expanded as well. The nation has witnessed the development of a sizeable black middle class, increasing (though still low) rates of black/non-black intermarriage, and the emergence of black super-celebrities in sports, television, music, and now politics. Hip-hop has transitioned from an "urban subculture" to American youth culture writ large, performed and consumed as a means of expressing rebellion, "cool," and masculinity around the world.[9] The cultural and demographic "browning of America" means that the construct of American nationhood—long tied firmly to notions of whiteness—has been thrown into question. This has led to a quest for new answers to questions such as, Who are we as a people? What does it mean to be an American? Are there not some parts of the United States, and some people, that are more American than others? Where will whites fit in a country in which they are no longer numerically and culturally dominant?

The crisis dimension of this national questioning has also been heightened by the decline of the United States as a global superpower. The idea of American superiority in virtually all areas—military, political, economic, scientific, ethical, and so on—is an established tenet of national identity. But recent events—such as the dramatic growth of the economies of China and India, the strength of the euro over the dollar, the Abu Ghraib prisoner torture scandal, and the ten years it took to capture Osama Bin Laden—have profoundly shaken the idea of American preeminence.[10]

The attacks of 9/11 and the subsequent war on terror have certainly been among the most defining factors in the production of contemporary racialized anxieties of nation. Since late 2001, there has been the sense that the United States was attacked because it was seen as an enemy of the Arab world and as an arrogant, imperial, white, Christian nation. Over the last decade, a parade of brown-skinned men from the Middle East, Latin America, and Africa has appeared across our television screens as the face of terror, having plotted to kill Americans and their allies here and abroad. In some ways, at some times, it seems like a race war. At the very least, it has been perceived to be a clash of civilizations.[11]

The conservative response to what are seen as severe threats to the American way of life (or as a hostile takeover by the third world) has been to reaffirm "traditional" American values. This tendency has been reflected on right-wing websites, cable television programs, and radio broadcasts, and in the writing of authors such as Patrick Buchanan and Peter Brimelow. The 2008 presidential race was often framed as a battle to defend the interests and integrity of the nation. Obama's opponents challenged him both as a black man (i.e., inferior, incompetent to stand for the nation) and as a foreign other (i.e., dangerous to, or having no right to stand for, the nation). Obama, the narrative went, was a terrorist sympathizer, a man who hated the United States, someone that could not be trusted.[12] We were told that a vote for the Republican ticket was a vote for the "real America"—an America delimited as nonurban, Christian, conservative, and white.[13]

A substantial part of Obama's campaign was directed toward addressing the anxieties of race and nation. At some points, he played to the traditionalist/neoconservative paradigm of national identity. Consider, for example, his frequent references to his mother's Kansas roots, his speeches on patriotism, and his intermittent attempts to "establish his American cultural normalcy."[14] But Obama's strength lay in his elaboration of a multicultural, cosmopolitan vision of nation. It was here that he was by far the most dynamic, authentic, and visionary.

In the pages below, I analyze the relationship between race and nation in Obama's campaign for the White House. Rather than being race-neutral or deracialized, I argue, race was a central, if implicit, element in the core narrative of Obama's campaign. Obama subtly deployed the trope of race to construct a nation that was triumphal and ascendant. He positioned himself as heir to both the civil rights struggle and the American Revolution. Uniting several continents through his biography, he was a citizen of the world and a black Horatio Alger. Through his candidacy, the imagery of the campaign implied, the wound of race, and by extension all others, would be healed. And having triumphantly lived up to its creed, the nation would be absolved of the sins of the past and present. Articulated squarely within the framework of the "new politics of race" (see chapter 3), Obama's nation was the nation that "had overcome."

Ultimately, I conclude, the paradigm of national identity that Obama presented was inclusive, globally oriented, and forward-thinking in several important respects. Certainly it was a far cry from the circumscribed, white, conservative nation (the real America) forwarded by the McCain/Palin camp, or the reactionary white nationalism (Tea Party nation) that emerged in response to Obama's victory. Obama's America was not without its limitations, however, stemming in large part from the color-blind racial liberalism in which it was grounded. The nation achieved its unity in large part by silencing histories of racial injustice, and by ignoring ongoing, entrenched practices of racial discrimination. It rested on a notion of cultural diversity that was grounded in "happy talk" rather than in substantive justice.[15] And while it proclaimed itself broadly inclusive, it was fundamentally organized around black-and-white metaphors of race. The campaign implied that voting for Obama was a revolutionary act that would bring about fundamental social change, obscuring the fact that Obama was a centrist-liberal politician at best.[16] Support for the senator was presented as a form of anti-racist activism, sufficient for whites to be able to say that they had done their part and could now definitively leave the problem of race behind. These issues and others are discussed below.

The Candidate and His Wife: As American as Apple Pie?

Obama's unconventional background was potentially a source of profound electoral discomfort. He was not only black, but also biracial. The one-term senator had been raised in Hawaii and in Indonesia, attended

Ivy League schools, and married a tall, outspoken black woman from the South Side of Chicago. His middle name was shared with the Iraqi dictator that the United States had recently hunted down, and his last name rhymed with that of the mastermind of 9/11. How might the campaign convince the public that Obama was the best person to lead, and moreover to *represent*, the nation?

One strategy was to try to neutralize Obama's "difference" by presenting him as the "guy next door."[17] This was an especially important maneuver at the start of the general election, as Obama faced off against the all-American war hero John McCain. Shortly after accepting the Democratic nomination, Obama's strategists launched a campaign to reintroduce him to the white working class. He would become "as American as apple pie." In a television ad released on June 19, 2008, Senator Obama stated, "I was raised by a single mom and my grandparents. We didn't have much money, but they taught me values straight from the Kansas heartland where they grew up." Absent were references to his Kenyan father or to his childhood years outside the U.S. mainland. Obama was pictured in several frames surrounded not by multiracial representatives of the new America, but by groups of "ordinary-looking white people." As Jonathan Martin and Ben Smith wrote on Politico.com, "Touching down in heavily-white communities in Missouri, Ohio, Colorado, and North Dakota last week, Obama paid homage to [the national touchstones of] patriotism, faith . . . and military service." They continued, "Obama's campaign at present is mostly an exercise in assurance. . . . Many voters need to be convinced that they can relate to Obama and feel comfortable with him in the White House."[18]

The push to frame Barack Obama as an exemplar of solid, white, American values extended to his wife as well. In late June, Michelle Obama appeared as a cohost on the daytime talk show *The View*. She discussed the importance of being at home with the kids and her preference for bare legs over panty hose. When asked what the Obamas ate for breakfast, Michelle emphasized that bacon was regularly on the menu—thus signaling that they were neither latte-sipping elitists nor secret Muslims.[19]

The new emphasis on Michelle Obama's domesticity and "mommyness" was part of a broader effort to modify her own public persona. Michelle Obama had been subject to relentless attacks by opponents of the campaign, many of which were articulated around racialized fears. Rumors that she had been caught on tape "ranting and raving about whitey" flooded right-wing websites. Conservatives expressed particular outrage over Mrs. Obama's claim that "for the first time in my adult lifetime, I am really proud of my country." In response, a writer on Townhall.com went so far as to refer to Michelle Obama as a "nasty, bitter, openly racist ingrate." While Mr. Obama was to be seen as more American by becoming less exotic, his wife would appear more reassuringly American by becoming less feminist and less black. The image of the pleasant, supportive homemaker would suppress more disparaging characterizations of Michelle as an aggressive career woman or an "angry black harridan."[20]

The public was vaguely familiar with Michelle Obama's credentials. She held a law degree from Harvard, had served on six boards of directors, and had recently held a post as vice president of a Chicago hospital. At the close of the primary, however, polls revealed that many white voters viewed Michelle Obama in decidedly negative terms.[21] An all-American presidential candidate needed an anti-Hillary *and* an anti-Farrakhan by his side. Michelle's successful image makeover de-emphasized her career, degrees, and Chicago upbringing. Further, her opinions on policy issues other than those relating to children were downplayed. In the first year of Obama's presidency, Michelle became very popular, known as an American fashion icon and as the "mom in chief." As she said in an April 2009 interview, "I've worked in corporate America, I've worked for non-profits, and I consider this a very important job. . . . I wake up every morning, first of all, making sure that my kids get to school on time and they do their homework."[22]

Thus the Obama campaign sought at times to present the candidate and his wife as "conventionally" American, by emphasizing his Midwestern roots, patriotism, Christian faith, and "everydayness." This bundle of Americana was aimed squarely at moderate-to-conservative whites, and designed to invoke "tradition," the past, and comforting, gender-appropriate, white cultural normativity.

There's the United States of America

These images were not the dominant ones circulated by the campaign, however, as they did not suit Obama's candidacy particularly well. It was not that they were utterly implausible; after all, one could even buy the beer-guzzling populism of Hillary Clinton for a while.[23] But flattening out Obama's life history in this manner was fundamentally out of line with the core messaging of the campaign, as the imagery did not begin to tap into what was seen as the "revolutionary potential" of Obama's candidacy.

A much more powerful set of images was found in Obama's articulation of a multicultural, cosmopolitan vision of nation. It was here that he appeared to be the most vibrant, dynamic, and visionary. Whereas the conservative nation was unified and defined in part by boundaries and exclusions, the multicultural nation purported to be broadly inclusive (see chapter 7). Obama's nation would not rely on divisions, it would triumphantly overcome them. In a much-quoted passage from his keynote speech at the 2004 Democratic National Convention, Obama stated:

> Now even as we speak, there are those who are preparing to divide us. . . . Well, I say to them tonight, there's not a liberal America and a conservative America—there's the United States of America. There's not a black America and a white America and Latino America and Asian America—there's the United States of America. The pundits like to slice-and-dice our country into red states and blue states. . . . But I've got news for them, too. We worship an awesome God in the blue states, and we don't like federal agents poking around our libraries in the red states. We coach Little League in the blue states and have gay friends in the red states. . . . We are one people, all of us pledging allegiance to the stars and stripes, all of us defending the United States of America.[24]

The speech referenced bridging many sorts of divides, but the central organizing trope around which all others revolved was race. Why race? Because race was the nation's most enduring wound, standing in for all other social divides.[25] Because Barack Obama was a black man giving a major political address in a country that had been built on the backs of slaves. Because the blood of two "warring races" coursed through his veins. And because he spoke, victoriously, in terms of unity and ending divisions, and seemed to offer a way beyond the "racial stalemate" of the post–civil rights era.[26] Much of the excitement over Obama, from this moment, lay in his implicit promise to heal the nation through the vehicle of race, or specifically through his blackness. As Joe Klein wrote in *Time*, "He transcends the racial divide so effortlessly that it seems reasonable to expect that he can bridge all the other divisions— and answer all the impossible questions—plaguing American public life."[27]

In No Other Country on Earth

In elaborating the multicultural nation, Obama played up the diverse and unconventional dimensions of his biography. The idea was that the extraordinariness of his life history was evidence of the extraordinariness of the nation. In a 2007 *New York Times Magazine* story titled "Is (His) Biography (Our) Destiny?," for example, Obama said to a reporter, "I think . . . that if you can tell people, 'We have a president in the White House who still has a grandmother living in a hut on the shores of Lake Victoria and has a sister who's half-Indonesian, married to a Chinese-Canadian,' then they're going to think that he may have a better sense of what's going on in our lives and in our country. And they'd be right."[28] Here he was leaps and bounds away from any sort of small-town, apple-pie presentation of self, but he repackaged these elements into a safe and depoliticized narrative. Rather than being a confused, miscegenated, un-American mess, he said, I'm actually the essence of the new America, a citizen of the world. Consider also his repeated references to himself as "a skinny kid with a funny-sounding name"—as if Barack Hussein Obama registered the same way in post-9/11 America as "Pippi Longstocking" may have in years gone by. Overall, Obama sought not so much to over-turn or supplant the foundational myths of American nationalism as to expand them. Here and elsewhere, he carefully wove his story *into* the American dream narrative while claiming it as his own. He rewrote the Horatio Alger myth, placing himself not at the margins but squarely in the center. Consider again his 2004 keynote speech at the DNC, in which he stated:

> My father was a foreign student, born and raised in a small village in Kenya. He grew up herding goats, went to school in a tin-roof shack. His father, my grandfather, was a cook, a domestic servant to the British. But my grandfather had larger dreams for his son. Through hard work and perseverance my father got a scholarship to study in a magical place, America, that shone as a beacon of freedom and opportunity to so many who had come before him. . . . I stand here knowing that my story is part of the larger American story, that I owe a debt to all of those who came before me, and that in no other country on Earth is my story even possible.[29]

There are several interesting things to note about this passage. Like every immigrant of lore, Obama's father came to the United States "in pursuit of a dream." Obama thus offered a triumphal black American origins story, and one that was, crucially, vastly different from that of the overwhelming majority of African Americans. The nation itself was presented as magical, tolerant, and without original sin. The exploitation that his grandfather suffered had been under the British and was therefore *outside* the nation. The United States itself was allowed to stand as a model of democracy and progress.

Clearly, this was a triumphalist vision of nation, according to which the United States was figured as "overcoming all obstacles [in a] march towards the perfect fulfillment of its founding ideals."[30] Consider Obama's November 4, 2008, victory night speech, in which he stated, "If there is anyone out there who still doubts that America is a place where all things are possible; who still wonders if the dream of our founders is alive in our time; . . . tonight is your answer. . . . It's been a long time coming, but tonight, because of what we did on this day, in this election, at this defining moment, change has come to America."[31]

Note the crucial, though implicit, role of race in this formulation. Obama's allusion to the nation's racial history not only failed to blight or diminish the greatness of the United States, but was in fact key to the nation's ability to *manifest* its greatness. The implication was that Obama's campaign was the realization of both the original promise of the United States, as established by the founding fathers, and the fulfillment of the ideals of the civil rights movement. As "a simple band of colonists . . . left their homes and families in Lexington and Concord to take up arms against the tyranny of an Empire" in April 1775, so had "a young preacher from Georgia," generations later, "led a movement to help America confront our tragic history of racial injustice" (from Obama's 2008 "patriotism" speech).[32] Obama positioned himself as heir to each of those struggles. As he ascended, the loftiest and noblest ideals of the nation would be realized.

Throughout the election, Obama drew implicit but clear parallels between his campaign and the nation's triumphal struggle against racial injustice. In February 2007, he declared his intention to run for office in Springfield, Illinois, at the site where Abraham Lincoln had delivered a speech denouncing slavery and calling for national unity.[33] Before a crowd of 16,000, Obama invited Americans to join him in his quest: "It was here, in Springfield . . . that I was reminded of the essential decency of the American people. . . . And that is why, in the shadow of the Old State Capitol, where Lincoln once called on a divided house to stand together, where common hopes and common dreams still live, I stand before you today to announce my candidacy for President of the United States."[34] Though he was careful to distance himself from the controversial race men of today, Obama often invoked the leaders of the heroic civil rights past. As one journalist wrote of the speech Obama delivered after winning the January 3 Iowa primary, "[Obama's] voice and cadences suggested that he had studied Martin Luther King Jr.'s register and rhythms, the better to subtly evoke liberalism's great lost moment of revolutionary achievement and unfulfilled promise."[35] And while he made no explicit reference to the significance of the date, Obama accepted the Democratic nomination for president on August 28, 2008, 45 years to the day after King's historic "I Have a Dream" speech at the March on Washington. Here he said to black Americans, together we have reached the mountaintop; and whites could now claim the civil rights struggle as their own, being this time collectively on the right side of history.[36]

Sam Stein wrote in the *Huffington Post* that Obama aides had been particularly eager to get an endorsement from Senator Robert Byrd of West Virginia (which they did). Byrd, who had been a member of the Ku Klux Klan and an active opponent of equal rights, had "spent much of [the rest of] his life expressing contrition." Obama's strategists felt that an endorsement from Byrd "could help complete the moral arc of [Obama's] candidacy," Stein writes, "and they worked hard to ensure that voters understood its importance as well."[37]

In addition to its triumphalism, Obama's vision of nation derived its appeal from its articulation within the framework of the "new politics of race." As detailed in chapter 3, the new politics of race responds to the uncertainty and anxiety associated with race in the 21st century with "a strain of up-tempo, non-grievance, American-Dream-In-Color politics."[38] The new politics of race is not merely a "politics of deracialization" as some have argued, but rather it involves a specific orientation toward current and past issues of race.[39] In my view, it is a "racial pact" made between upwardly mobile blacks and the white mainstream. Public figures of color operating within the boundaries of the new race politics downplay the significance of racism and racial identity while emphasizing the greatness of the United States. Rather than presenting themselves as de-raced, they symbolically offer their (redemptive/diverse/"cool") blackness to whites, and by extension to the nation. Obama's unthreatening and bounded blackness could serve as a foundation for a revitalized, newly authentic American identity. Typical of other practitioners of the new racial etiquette, Obama was never angry and he displayed no "sense of grievance" for racial wrongs. Rather, he spoke often of the "core goodness of America" and of white Americans. He explained that he was "rooted in the black community" but "not limited to it."[40] Racism had a fairly minor role in Obama's worldview. Largely relegated to the past to begin with, the campaign implied that with Obama's ascent the remnants of racial injustice might be washed away once and for all.

Silences and Evasions of the Multicultural Nation

Obama's vision of a multiracial, globally oriented nation was in many ways remarkable. In the post-9/11 United States, he convinced a majority of voters that the nation would be stronger and better with him as its leader. Amid a culture war, he encouraged Americans to envision their core identity as much more than white, Christian, and heterosexual; not to retreat into nativism, but instead to see themselves as members of a global community. The "browning of America," he implied, was not to be feared, but celebrated; unity through diversity was the essence of who we are.

But there were downsides to this narrative as well. For one, the unity of the nation was achieved in part through obfuscations and silences concerning the racial past and present. Obama's portrayal of the African American struggle, for example, greatly diminished the role of whites in black oppression. Consider Obama's own biography, which was central to the racialized narrative of his campaign. As noted above, it was British, not American, tyranny that his grandfather sought to escape. His father came to the United States not as a slave but as a student who eventually achieved the American dream. In Obama's 2004 DNC keynote address, "slaves sitting around a fire singing freedom songs" were positioned as rhetorically equivalent to the founding fathers, who appeared as their fellow freedom fighters. This nearly unbelievable analogy was forwarded despite the fact that it was the founding fathers who provided the ideological rationale for the institution of slavery. And through Obama's emphasis on black "personal responsibility," and his tendency to deflect or avoid discussion of racism, he assured whites that he did not blame them for racial oppression, either today *or in the past*.[41]

Further, despite its pretense to be broadly multicultural, Obama's nation was largely organized around a binary notion of race. As Jonathan Tilove wrote, "[Obama's] candidacy at times seems less a campaign, than a crusade to transform the political culture and, implicitly, to bind the nation's racial wounds."[42] But the reconciliation that the campaign promised referred primarily to healing the divide between black and white. As for other racialized groups, their disparate paths to incorporation, their histories of exclusion, oppression, exploitation, and marginalization, were largely ignored. In Obama's United States of America, there was no mention of the Chinese Exclusion Act, the Bracero worker program, the Trail of Tears, or the Japanese internment. The triumphal nation was incompatible with mass deportations, predatory subprime lending, housing and employment discrimination, crumbling schools, racial profiling, and the prison-industrial complex. Not only were these realities overlooked, but the role of whites in either creating them, or passively benefitting from them, was erased. We were envisioned, all of us, as Americans, equally free to pursue our dreams in a nation that was tolerant, generous, and colorblind.

As the Chicana activist Cherrie Moraga has written, this was a "multiculturalism that is not multicultural" in that it was designed largely by, and for the benefit of, whites.[43] Obama's narrative of nation deployed a kind of racial "happy talk" that celebrated "diversity" but was entirely absent an agenda for racial justice.[44] The campaign was figured as a modern-day civil rights movement, in which support for Obama appeared as a form of anti-racist activism. As his victory was achieved, the implication was, whites would be absolved of the issue of race. They could leave behind the sins of the past and consider themselves exempt of responsibility to deal with race in the future. In accordance with the new politics of race, it was now up to blacks and other people of color to get on board, "get over race," and pull themselves up by their bootstraps. Obama—who generally avoided discussion of the issue of racism, backed away from support of policies designed specifically to remedy racial inequality, and repeatedly demonstrated that he would not be "the angry black man"—himself promised to lead the way.

But how did the narrative deal with the issue of slavery, the nation's original sin? Obama's blackness and his immigrant background allowed for slipperiness around this history. He could be the black Horatio Alger without irony, and tell a classic American origins story that demonstrated only the generosity and goodness of the nation. As he stood at the podium, addressing crowds of thousands, one could imagine the slave transformed into a voluntary migrant. Or at least one could see clearly how very far the nation had come. The painful historical comparisons could be sidestepped in favor of a triumphal vision of nation. As the law professor Patricia Williams wrote in a February 2007 article in *The Nation*, Obama was as "bright as a newly minted coin, 'cleansed' of baggage, of roots, of the unacknowledged rupture that is, paradoxically, our greatest national bond."[45]

Thus Obama's blackness was not simply made to seem unthreatening in the election; it also had a definite appeal. *Because of* his blackness, Obama was able to offer the nation symbolic absolution and make us feel good about being American again.[46] As one British journalist wrote during the week of Obama's victory:

> Those of us who have admired America since childhood . . . felt increasingly beleaguered after 2001. How to admire the land of "you're with us or against us," embodied by a president with a cowboy swagger, waging a fraudulent war and threatening to choke the planet by belching out a quarter of the world's CO_2 and damn the consequences? . . . But on Tuesday night I stood in Grant Park and watched a crowd of 200,000 erupt as they saw Barack Obama become America's next president. From now on, admiration for the US will no longer need to be whispered nor weighed down with a thousand qualifiers.[47]

There is no black America or white America, Obama claimed, no red states or blue states. In other words, there is no conflict over race, we're over it, let's move on. This is the ideology of racial colorblindness articulated through the language of multiculturalism. The nation would be united, and its wounds healed, through the tacit agreement to leave the unpleasantness of race alone.

6

Asian and Latino Voters in the 2008 Election

The Politics of Color in the Racial Middle

In an article published in the *Asian American Law Review*, the critical race scholar Robert Chang discussed his difficulty apprehending the relevance of the debate about Obama's race in 2007/2008 for Asian Americans. Despite wide claims that Obama's candidacy demonstrated that the United States had transcended race, Chang was not sure that scholars had even begun to fully grasp the place of Asian Americans in the country's racial hierarchy. He wrote, "Obama has been said to be running the first post-racial campaign, that his success somehow marks a post-racial moment or ushers in a new post-racial era. If that is so, where do Asian Americans fit within post-racial America?" Chang wrote that he was particularly "vexed" by this question "because I've spent much of my academic career talking about where Asian Americans fit within America's *racial* landscape, a landscape dominated by the black-white racial paradigm."

Though he felt that this work was far from complete, Chang stated, "Here I am, now having to think about it and to retool and say, 'Where do we fit in the post-racial landscape?'" It was therefore not clear to Chang at all that declaring the nation to have transcended race was a good thing. It was as if whites, and some blacks, were seeking to close inquiry into an area in which there were a good many questions still to be answered— especially with regard to Asian Americans. "What could 'post-racial' mean," Chang asked, "and how can we get to the post-racial without working through the racial?"[1]

These are the kind of questions I explore in the present chapter. Here I examine racial politics among "non-black non-whites" in the 2008 race—those the sociologist Eileen O'Brien has characterized as being in the "racial middle."[2] This chapter focuses on Latinos and Asian Americans, two groups whose demographic, cultural, and political impact has increased tremendously in the past several decades. As stated in a 2010 report by the U.S. Census Bureau, "Over the last 40 years, immigration from Latin America and Asia has been the major force changing the racial and ethnic composition of the American population."[3] Latinos are currently the largest non-white group in the United States at 15% of the overall population, followed by blacks at 12% and Asians at 4%.[4] It is projected that by 2050, the Latino and Asian share of the population will double, to nearly 30% and 9%, respectively.[5] As the aim of this book is to use Obama's presidential candidacy as a lens through which to understand emergent trends in U.S. race relations, it is clear that the politics of race in the racial middle merit consideration. Even if—as I argue throughout this book—the conversation about race in 2008 was overwhelmingly framed in terms of black and white, this fact itself begs for analysis.

On the one hand, I look at portrayals of Latino and Asian American communities in the mainstream media: how they were positioned in relationship to other racial groups; what their political concerns, interests, and motivations were understood to be; and how the wider racial narratives that circulated during the election were understood to pertain to them. I also consider Latino and Asian racial politics from within. I analyze an array of articles, editorials, and blog postings by non-black writers of color in both the mainstream and ethnic media. I look at debates about the 2008 election, race, and what an Obama victory might mean for the racial middle itself.

I also seek to understand the place and perspectives of Asian and Latino voters in comparison to those of whites and blacks. I ask, What was the relevance of race in the 2008 election for members of these groups? How did they respond to the themes of racial reconciliation, redemption, and new race politics? To what extent, if any, was Barack Obama's political success interpreted as evidence of the nation's definitive triumph over the problem of racism?

Other questions pertain to the issue of blackness and the black/white divide. How important, or relevant, was Obama's race to non-black communities of color? Was it appealing, unappealing, or largely irrelevant? Was Obama seen as black? As "brown?" Or as something other? What evidence, if any, was there of racial solidarity or a sense of shared fate as people of color? To what extent did Asian American and Latino writers look to black history as a point of reference for their own experiences in this country?

Lastly, I ask, What kinds of debates about Latinos, Asians, race, and politics emerged during the 2008 race? What do these debates tell us about the perceived place of the racial middle in American society, especially in relationship to blacks and to whites? What might a consideration of the broader ways that race played out in the 2008 election tell us about the contours of the U.S. racial hierarchy at present and in the near future? If the racial middle is neither simply a darker shade of white nor a lighter shade of black, then what exactly does it look like?

The Racial Middle and the Black/White Binary

As the discussion above suggests, this chapter is motivated in part by a series of broader theoretical questions pertaining to the racialization of the non-black non-whites in the 21st century. Observing the profound demographic and cultural shifts of the post–civil rights era—including the widening class gap among African Americans, rising rates of interracial marriage, and the dramatic growth of new populations of color since the 1965 immigration reform law—scholars have increasingly questioned the viability of a black/white, binary understanding of race relations.[6]

According to the black/white perspective, racial matters in the United States may be largely understood with reference to the history of relations between the nation's two most historically significant racial groups. As Eduardo Bonilla-Silva wrote in 2004, "For demographic . . . and historical reasons . . . the United States has [long] had a bi-racial order (white versus the rest) fundamentally anchored in the black-white experience."[7] While this was largely true in the past,[8] given the changes of the past several decades, we must ask whether it is true now. Have the broader workings of race in the United States significantly expanded past the limits of the binary?

A related question concerns the relevance of the black/white paradigm for non-black populations of color. The binary perspective posits that the core, or fundamental, pattern of racialization in the United States has been that experienced by black Americans in their relationship with whites.[9] The experiences of Latinos, Asians, and others are understood to take place somewhere along the black/white continuum—being either more like those of blacks, or more like those of whites. Those in the "racial middle" evidence more racial consciousness to the degree that their views and attitudes approximate those of blacks, and greater assimilation to the degree that their experiences and points of view mirror those of whites.

Recognizing the shortcomings of this perspective, some authors have argued that the single-axis approach should be abandoned for one that recognizes disparate trajectories of racialization for different racial groups.[10] In the second edition of their classic text *Racial Formation in the United States*, for example, the sociologists Michael Omi and Howard Winant "reject the project of dichotomizing race," arguing instead that the histories of the Chinese in California, Mexicans in Texas, Native Americans in the Midwest, and so forth should be understood as distinct from the experiences of African Americans in the U.S. South.[11]

Other scholars, however, have argued that this approach goes too far.[12] Race, after all, is a relational concept whose definitional subcategories (black, white, brown) acquire meaning only in relationship with one another. Race relations in different parts of the country, they remind us, evolved within a wider system of meaning, hierarchy, and oppression. Tiffany Davis argues that while "it is true that the histories of most non-black groups of color are absent from the race literature," it is also true "that the racialization of many of these groups in the U.S. was largely influenced by and structured around whites' treatment of and response to blacks." Davis cites the sociologist Joe Feagin, who argues that U.S. history is "not a multiplicity of disconnected racisms," but rather "emanates from a white supremacist core initially designed in the interests of exploiting African American labor and decimating indigenous societies."[13]

Similarly, in her study of the racialization of Asian Americans, the political scientist Claire Jean Kim notes: "The problem with the different trajectories approach is that it imputes mutual autonomy to respective racialization processes that are in fact mutually constitutive of one another. Asian Americans have not been racialized in a vacuum, isolated from other groups; to the contrary, Asian Americans have been racialized relative to and through interaction with Whites and Blacks. As such, the respective racialization trajectories of these groups are profoundly inter-related." Kim describes the conundrum facing scholars as how to discuss the experiences of "the other non-Whites" in a way that "appreciates both how racialization processes are mutually constitutive of one another and how they can unfold along more than one dimension or scale at a time."[14] She describes this approach as "racial triangulation."

In the single, black/white axis perspective, anti-black racism is seen as the core racism from which all other racisms are derived. Further, blacks are understood to be universally at the bottom of the U.S. racial hierarchy. But this last supposition is not actually always true. As the historian Evelyn Hu-DeHart argues, when it comes to the issue of national belonging and identity, African Americans in fact rank higher than many other groups. "Despite deep-seated and widely distributed hostility against them," Hu-DeHart writes, "only the most virulent and crudest white supremacist would deny that blacks are American, or that Americans can be black." "The same cannot be said about Latinos/as or Asians in America," she states, "regardless of how many generations they have been here."[15]

Similarly, Kim argues that there are at least two axes of racial domination in the United States (though she concedes that there may in fact be more)—superior/inferior and insider/foreigner. While blacks are seen as inferior to whites, they are nonetheless seen as integral members of the nation. Asian Americans, on the other hand, are viewed as fundamentally outside the nation, "immutably foreign and unassimilable with Whites on cultural and/or racial grounds." Thus, while Asian Americans may be considered culturally superior to blacks, they are also viewed as inherently un-American.[16]

Consider also the recent experiences of Arab Americans. While they have long been classified as white in the census, since 9/11 Arab Americans have been re-racialized as a distinct, suspicious, and newly threatening minority. Their racialization has elements akin to both those of lower-income blacks (intense antipathy) and to Asian Americans (being seen as inherently foreign). There are also important aspects of the Arab American experience that are unique. While Asian, Latino, and Native American writers have lamented the invisibility of their communities in discussions of U.S. racial politics, the sociologist Antonio A. Chiareli argues that Arab Americans and Muslims in the United States are experiencing the opposite—a crisis of hyper-visibility.[17] For these reasons, Eileen O'Brien argues that attempts to understand those in the racial middle as existing along a singular racial continuum (being either more like whites or more like blacks) are inherently limiting. There are crucial dimensions of the experiences of Latinos, Asians and others that neither the binary nor the continuum is able to capture.[18]

The immigration experience is by far the most important. Though Asians and Latinos have been present in the United States in smaller numbers for centuries (Chinese, Japanese, and Mexican Americans have particularly long histories in this country), these populations have greatly increased in size, visibility, and diversity in the last four and a half decades, due primarily to immigration. According to U.S. census estimates, at present, nearly 70% of the Asian population and 40% of the Hispanic population is made up of individuals who were born outside the United States. These facts have only reinforced the view that the racial middle is not, and can never be, truly American.[19]

The processes of globalization and transnationalism—greatly facilitating travel and communication back and forth across national borders—also mean that the kind of one-way assimilation into the American "melting pot" witnessed among white ethnics in the past is extremely unlikely to occur today. Rather, we may expect many members of immigrant communities to acquire "transnational identities," as citizens of the United States and also of wider diasporas stretching across the globe.[20]

We must consider the changing demographics that immigration is bringing about as well. Due both to an influx of new immigrants and higher birthrates among certain immigrant groups, whites' share of the population is shrinking. Non-Hispanic whites will decline to less than half the population by the year 2050, as racial minorities become the new majority. One possible response to these changes would be to embrace them and redefine the United States as a nation that is black, white, and brown. Often enough, however, the nation's changing demographics seem to be leading to widespread panic and alarm among certain whites, repressive new anti-immigration laws, and attempts to maintain the core of the culture as white and Christian.[21]

These factors cast doubt on the thesis put forth by George Yancey in his 2003 book *Who Is White?* Yancey argues that the United States is developing a new racial binary—a black/non-black divide. In order to preserve their majority group status, he argues, whites will assimilate Asians, Latinos, and others into a newly defined category of whiteness, in juxtaposition to African Americans. While blacks are "destined . . . to remain an outcast race," he claims, "other, non-black racial minorities will achieve dominant group status over time." In the remainder of his book, Yancey presents an array of survey data designed to support his conclusion that the members of the racial middle are in fact "becoming white."[22]

Another major perspective on the United States' racial future comes from Eduardo Bonilla-Silva, who predicts the emergence of a Latin America–like "tripartite" racial structure. In the next several decades, he argues, African Americans, black immigrants, and low-income Latinos and Asians will become part of the "collective black" category, relegated to the bottom of the racial hierarchy. Most Asians and Latinos, however, will become "honorary whites," meaning that they will receive some, but not all of, the benefits of whiteness (and their honorary white status can be revoked at any time). Bonilla-Silva also believes that a few light-skinned, highly assimilated non-whites (but no blacks) will be accepted into a slightly expanded category of whiteness.[23]

Bonilla-Silva's model, in my view, is a great improvement over Yancey's. It takes into account the importance of skin color, ethnicity, and the timing and conditions of entry into the United States. It also points toward potential areas of solidarity among non-whites who may confront similar types of marginalization. The key weakness of both models, however, is that they rely on a single axis of racialization. This perspective forces each author to oversimplify, ignore, or simply avoid inquiry into the dimensions of Latino and Asian racialization that do not correspond to the experiences of either blacks or whites.[24] As Claire Jean Kim suggests, a better model would acknowledge the differing but mutually constitutive trajectories of different racial groups, and the existence of more than one dimension of racialization. This framework guides the analysis found in this chapter.

The Workings of Race in the 2008 Election

The first finding of my research is that the national discussions about race that took place during the 2008 presidential campaign were overwhelmingly about blacks and whites, referring almost exclusively to the history of relations between these two groups. The overarching themes of the election—racial reconciliation, absolution, redemption, post-race triumphalism, and new race politics—were constructed around black and white racial archetypes. "Race" in discussions of the election generally meant blackness (as gender usually meant white women), and the members of the racial middle were for the most part invisible.

My second finding is that to the extent that Latino and Asian voters were discussed in the mainstream media at all, they were most often presented as the racial antagonists of African Americans. Their early, overwhelming support for Hillary Clinton was taken as a manifestation of deeply held anti-black prejudices, and as confirmation of the raging antipathies said to exist between blacks and other non-whites. Therefore, far from being seen as model minorities, those in the racial middle stood in implicit moral contrast to white Americans, who figured in the wider, mostly liberal narrative of the election as having overcome the pettiness of race, via the vehicle of Obama's candidacy. Thus Latino and Asian voters tended to be presented in reductive, racialized terms, and as different, in important respects, from both whites and blacks. The implicit comparisons drawn between Asians, Latinos, blacks, and whites in the election constituted a form of racial "triangulation," wherein different groups were racialized in relationship to one another.

As for views of the election from the perspectives the racial middle, I find first that the racialized imagery surrounding the Obama candidacy did not have tremendous resonance. Neither discussions of Obama as a "new type" of black man (new race politics), nor those of the nation's purported triumph over racism (post-race American triumphalism), were salient themes among Latino or Asian writers. And comparisons between Barack Obama and Martin Luther King—ubiquitous elsewhere—were generally not found in the non-black ethnic media.

But this is not to say that issues of race and culture were irrelevant to Latino and Asian voters. Toward the close of the primary season, Obama's heritage emerged as a clear point of pride, especially among Asian American and Pacific Islanders. Non-black writers of color identified with the senator as a fellow immigrant (via his Kenyan-born father), as an "honorary Asian American," or as a son of the third world—but not as a black man. In fact, among the communities of the racial middle, Obama's blackness did not appear to be an important source of appeal. Obama's self-presentation as a post-racial politician, however, seems to have been relevant to the members of the racial middle in that it allowed them to focus on the parts of his biography to which they could relate—none of which, again, were related directly to his blackness. Each of these issues is addressed, in turn, in the sections below.

Framing the Race in Black and White

After Obama won the first primary of the Democratic race (the January Iowa caucuses), one conservative pundit wrote that with the victory, "one of our great national sins is being obliterated." "I don't agree with Obama and I don't particularly like him," he continued, "but I am proud of this moment."[25] Even for some observers on the right, then, the racial symbolism of Obama's candidacy was a very meaningful aspect of the 2008 contest. When considered from the perspective of the racial middle, however, it is apparent that this symbolism was largely constructed in terms of black and white.

Imagery drawn from the African American struggle for equality was woven throughout the campaign. Obama declared his candidacy at the historic Illinois site where Abraham Lincoln had given a major address calling the nation to unite and end the practice of slavery. He and Clinton both delivered speeches in Selma, Alabama, on the anniversary of a famed civil rights march. And Obama accepted the Democratic nomination one day after the 45th anniversary of Martin Luther King's "I Have a Dream" speech. As an August 2008 article from MSNBC stated, "If King inspired Americans to confront their bigotry or at least dream of a more perfect union, a candidate with Obama's profile surely seems part of that dream's fulfillment." These actions, and this narrative, appealed most directly to white and to black voters.[26]

Even the discourses of racial progress and redemption were fundamentally rooted in the racial binary. The "new politics of race" that Obama was said to embody (discussed in chapter 3) were essentially a new *black* politics; a set of rules, or expectations, laid out for black Americans in the 21st century. The "post-race narrative of American triumphalism" (discussed in chapter 2) was at heart a story about whites overcoming the vestiges of racial prejudice by elevating Obama to the White House. Through the election of a black man, white Americans would be forgiven for the sins of the past, and black Americans would be drawn more fully into the national embrace. As the liberal critic Paul Waldman wrote in the *American Prospect*, "Obama offers his identity as the vehicle of our redemption, as individuals and as a nation. . . . He is both white and black, Kansas and Kenya, the racial synthesis through which the clash of thesis and antithesis is resolved."[27]

The members of the racial middle, while not entirely absent from the discourse about race, were mostly peripheral to it. In February 2008, Isaac Chotiner commented in the *New Republic* that while Obama had begun "peppering his speeches" with appeals to Latino and Asian voters, "he still faces the reality that his words are, too often, not 'post-racial' or 'colorblind' but actually dichotomous."[28] The precarious legal and economic status of millions of undocumented immigrants in the United States, the detention (without trial) of hundreds of Middle Eastern men in the Guantanamo Bay detention center, and the many other issues pertaining mostly to the racial middle were left unresolved, and unaddressed, in this story of black/white reconciliation.

Commenting on the discourse about the election, *Newsweek*'s Richard Rodriguez stated in May 2008, "I hear often enough that America is becoming a post-racial nation. This election season was supposed to prove it. Yet I am struck by the contrary—how mired our politics remain in the dialectic of black and white."[29] Similarly, in a 2009 article in the journal *Meridians*, the Chicana activist Cherrie Moraga argued that the campaign had "laid bare what most non-African-American people of color already know . . . that when this country thinks about 'race,' it thinks black." Why was this? "The bitter history of black slavery," Moraga argued, "still haunts the collective psyche of white America. For better or worse, black people represent white America's greatest fear and loathing as well as its greatest hope for moral redemption. Other people of color as a whole remain invisible or are perceived as of little political consequence, except as the scapegoats for economic and national security anxiety."[30]

Thus, in the larger national debate about race, those in the racial middle were, for the most part, simply not included in the conversation. Interestingly, perhaps, Asian Americans did not even appear here as shining examples for blacks to emulate, or as "model minorities."[31] In 2007/2008, it was "Obama-like" blacks who were juxtaposed against the irresponsible black lower classes and the problematic African American political old guard. In fact, to the extent that Asian and Latino voters were discussed in the media at all, they most often appeared as problematic racial actors themselves, as individuals unready for change, who stood in the way of Obama's revolutionary candidacy.

The Interracial Conflict Narrative

Hillary Clinton was extremely popular with Latino and Asian voters in the Democratic primary. In some areas, the racial middle favored Clinton by a margin of three to one. The polls projected that Clinton would handily defeat Obama in places such as California, Arizona, New York, and New Jersey, which had large non-black communities of color.[32] The story that emerged in the media to explain this phenomenon was one of interminority conflict: the notion that hostility toward blacks was driving the members of the racial middle toward Obama's democratic rival.

Several stories on the racial roots of Asian lack of interest in Obama appeared in 2007/2008. In a February 2008 article in *Time*, Lisa Takeuchi Cullen claimed that electoral results thus far had "raised a very sensitive, ugly question: could some Asian Americans not be voting for Obama simply because he's black?"[33] Cullen quoted a Taiwanese American scholar who argued that many Asian immigrants came to the United States with "a very uninformed bias" against blacks. Later in the article, a Chinese American financial analyst explained the preference for Clinton by stating, "Chinese people are really racist at times." Other stories offering at least partial credence to the Asian racism thesis appeared in *Time* (again), the *Seattle Times*, the *New Republic*, and on CNN's *Anderson Cooper 360*.[34]

With respect to Latinos, the purported conflict between black and brown was the biggest story of the election cycle by far. More than a dozen major stories on this issue appeared in the mainstream press.[35] In the *New York Times*, Adam Nagourney and Jennifer Steinhauer claimed that "Mr. Obama confronts a history of often uneasy and competitive relations between blacks and Hispanics, particularly as they have jockeyed for influence in cities like Chicago, Los Angeles, and New York." The authors quoted one local resident who opined, "I don't think many Latinos will vote for Obama. There's always been tension in the black and Latino communities." In another story from National Public Radio, Mandalit del Barco wrote, "How years of simmering tensions between California's Latinos and African Americans will play out in the presidential race" was "a hotly contested matter."[36] The conservative writer Robert Novak argued in the *Washington Post* that the Clinton campaign was "not only relying on a brown firewall built on an anti-black base" but also "reinforcing it." Others drew similar conclusions. A *New York* magazine article stated that Clinton was seeking "to play off, even exacerbate, historical tensions between black and brown voters."[37]

While several pointed the finger at the Clinton camp, many other writers blamed Obama's poor poll numbers on Latinos themselves. In the *New Republic*, John Judis stated that "over the last two decades, there has been evidence of growing hostility from Hispanics toward African Americans." He claimed that surveys had found that Latinos consistently "display more prejudice toward African Americans" than do whites.[38] A similar note was struck in *Newsweek*, where Earl Ofari Hutchinson stated that while whites had shown that they were "ready to vote for an African-American candidate," "the rules of political engagement" would "fall apart" when it came to Latinos. "I do not believe Latino voters will vote even for a candidate like Obama," Hutchinson claimed. "The tensions between blacks and Latinos and negative perceptions that have marred relations between these groups for so long unfortunately still resonate."[39] In the *New Yorker*, Ryan Lizza argued that though the primaries had been "refreshingly absent" of racial politics thus far, that was "about to change" due to the black and Latino populations of South Carolina and Nevada. Whereas whites in previous races had managed to transcend racialized thinking, Lizza claimed, black and Latino voters would inevitably introduce an unwelcome racial element into the contest.[40]

In the end, the racial middle did vote overwhelmingly for Hillary Clinton. Clinton won 86% of Asian American Democrats in New York, 73% in New Jersey, and 75% in California. She beat Obama among Latinos by a two-to-one margin overall, winning 73% in New York, 68% in New Jersey, and 66% in Texas.[41] The implication of most of the coverage of these races was that, motivated largely by their prejudices, Asians and Latinos had not so much voted for Clinton as they had voted against Obama.

Latino and Asian American Writers Respond

While the interracial conflict narrative was the most convenient explanation for Clinton's popularity with the racial middle, it was vigorously contested by bloggers and journalists of color.[42] In the *Huffington Post*, Roberto Lovato wrote that it was "tragicomic" "to watch the white, and some African American, political commentators on MSNBC, CNN and other networks tell us that the Latino vote for Clinton reflected 'Black-Latino tensions.'" Lovato found it particularly absurd that a story on the black/brown divide had appeared in the *New Yorker*, given that the publication "has no Latino editorial staff" to speak of. "Everybody," he wrote, "seems to have something to say about Latino politics. Everybody that is, except Latinos."[43]

The Puerto Rican blogger Liza Sabater characterized the conflict narrative as a tactic designed to foment tension among non-whites. She described Nagourney and Steinhauer's *New York Times* article as "one of the most poorly researched, poorly fact checked, backed by barely just one expert in Caribbean and Latin American history, anthropology, or public policy race-baiting piece of drivel about how Latinos will not vote for Obama because they can't relate to his blackness."[44] On her blog, the Cuban American writer Alisa Valdes-Rodriguez described the *New York Times* article as a "sloppy and inaccurate" story that "goes on for 32 agonizing paragraphs, using the terms 'black' and 'Latino' as though they were mutually exclusive—which they are not." She continues, "I suggest the reporters and editors of the *New York Times* . . . take the subway uptown for a spell. Walk around. Go to a bodega or two. Listen to people talk. All those 'black' people you see in Washington Heights? They're Latinos."[45]

The interracial conflict narrative provoked considerable frustration among Asian American writers as well. Jeff Chang referred to it as one of a number of "crackpot theories" about the non-white electorate. New America Media reported that CNN's February 12 story on the racial roots of Asian opposition to Obama had led to "outrage" among Asian American viewers.[46] The 80–20 Initiative circulated a petition stating that the story was misleading and insulting.[47] And the blogger Jennifer Fang wrote that while she was initially excited to learn that CNN had produced a story on the Asian American community, she was ultimately disappointed to find that the segment was "a half-assed fluff piece by a disinterested reporter." At the conclusion of her post she wrote, "So, I guess we exist. Sorta."[48]

Is He Black Enough?

There were many reasons to question the interracial conflict thesis. The first was its clear parallels to the "Is Obama black enough?" story, which dominated press coverage of the black electorate for months. Early polls had shown that Hillary Clinton's support among African Americans far exceeded Obama's. A national survey taken in January 2007, for example, gave Clinton a *40-point lead* over Obama among blacks.[49] The argument crafted by the press was that Hillary Clinton's stronger showing among blacks resulted from the fact that Obama was not culturally familiar, or "black," enough for most African Americans. He was too well educated, too articulate, too light-skinned, not angry enough, and so forth. That Bill Clinton had been extremely popular with African Americans in the 1990s—leading the novelist Toni Morrison to declare him the "first black president"—was entirely overlooked, along with the fact that among blacks, Obama was a relative unknown.[50]

In 2007, the "black enough" issue was furiously debated on MSNBC, *60 Minutes*, CNN, the *CBS Evening News*, the daytime talk show *The View*, and throughout the print media.[51] The British paper the *Guardian* declared that "with his mixed-race background, Ivy League education and Midwestern accent, one of [Obama's] greatest challenges has been convincing African-Americans that he is 'one of them.'" The host of National Public Radio's *Talk of the Nation*, Neal Conan, claimed that many blacks were openly questioning "whether in effect [Obama] is black enough, or whether he can be described as African American at all." The conservative pundit Juan Williams argued that most blacks were unable to relate to Obama because "the alienation, anger and pessimism that mark speeches from major black American leaders" were "missing" from his oratory. Williams characterized this as "the latest in self-defeating black politics."[52]

The "black enough" story caught on like wildfire. But the media's fascination with Obama's blackness revealed more about the media than it did about black politics. As the African American journalist Ta-Nehisi Coates wrote in *Time*, "What [the pundits] fail to understand is that African-Americans meet other intelligent, articulate African-Americans all the time." The claim that blacks did not accept Obama because he was not "black enough," Coates argued, "is a clever device, hatched by mainstream (primarily white) journalists who are shocked—shocked!—to discover that black people aren't as dumbstruck by Obama as they are."[53]

Brent Staples wrote in the *New York Times* that as the black community had "historically and eagerly embraced as black anyone and everyone with any African ancestry," the claim that Obama's mixed-race heritage made him "not black enough" simply did not "make sense in the black community itself." In the *Washington Post*, Amina Luqman wrote that many African Americans had scoffed at the media's questioning of Obama's blackness: "We know that the question has less to do with black America than with whether white America trusts that Obama is not too black for its [own] political taste." Middle-class blacks "live with a version of Obama's tightrope dance every day," she continued. "We do the same dance in our workplaces, with our supervisors, our neighbors and our college classmates. In that way we know Obama couldn't be more like us, he couldn't be more black."[54]

Thus the "black enough" meme painted a dramatically oversimplified portrait of black politics and black subjectivities. But it also manifested a perplexity and wonderment among members of the press about the nature of Obama's blackness. Having long understood African American politicians in monolithic, sometimes caricatured terms, the press greeted Obama with a kind of awe: what kind of black person *is* this? The ostensibly "color-blind" pundit class granted itself permission to explore the authenticity and dimensions of Obama's blackness by claiming to be merely reporting on a conversation that was taking place in the black community. It was not that the press was obsessed with Obama's blackness, it was that blacks were.

But the actual conversation in the black community was never framed in these terms. The questioning was less about Obama's cultural credentials than it was about his allegiances, policies, and positions. The senator was being hailed in the press as the greatest black person of all time, a man who would change the conversation about race forever, the "one" that the country had been waiting for. As MSNBC's Chris Matthews stated in 2007, "I don't think you can find a better opening gate, starting gate personality than Obama as a black candidate." Obama was also constantly praised for the ways in which he appeared to *differ* from most other blacks—who, in the words of one reporter, all too often evidenced the "crippling psychological legacy of slavery."[55]

The "black enough" argument began to disintegrate as soon as African Americans began to shift their allegiance to Obama en masse. As one reporter wrote in early 2008, "Remember all the commentator chatter last summer: Is Barack Obama black enough? Well, he's black enough now."[56] Obama garnered well over 80% of the black vote in most of the Democratic primaries and 95% in the general election.[57] By November 4, 2008, Obama had attained near messianic status in the black community, with blacks irrespective of age, gender, and class supporting him with an almost religious fervor, and criticism of the senator taken to be a kind of heresy.[58] Obama did not remain criticism-proof in the black community for long, however, as the "honeymoon" lasted less than two years.[59] But in 2007/2008 many blacks came to see Obama as a brilliant, visionary leader who represented the best of black America, admiring in him many of the characteristics that the press had claimed African Americans were constitutionally unable to relate to.

This Deserves Some Actual Reporting

Barack Obama did not achieve the same degree of adulation in the racial middle. But the interracial conflict narrative also revealed more about the wider white public than it did about voters of color. The clearest evidence of the falseness of the notion that deep-seated anti-black hostility would prevent Latinos and Asians from voting for Obama was found again in electoral results. In the general election, Obama won 67% of Latino voters and 62% of Asian Americans. In some contests, he was even more popular with the racial middle than Clinton had been in the primaries.[60] As a number of observers have pointed out, it was black and Latino voters who delivered Obama the presidency. Had it been up to whites alone, McCain would have won. Commenting on the decisive role of the non-white vote, Laura Carlsen wrote that the real lesson of the 2008 race "was that the white elite no longer have a stranglehold on U.S. politics."[61]

Further, while many of the early reports suggested that immigrants, being the most racist toward blacks, were the least likely to support Obama, several studies found that Latino immigrants actually voted for Obama in *higher* proportions than their native-born counterparts.[62] The original logic was that (1) immigrants detested blacks more because they brought to the United States deeply held prejudices learned in their home countries, or that (2) being especially preoccupied with getting ahead in the United States, immigrants were particularly desirous to distance themselves from the group most clearly at the bottom of the social hierarchy.[63]

I do not wish to imply that anti-black prejudices held by other non-whites are trivial or nonexistent. But the issue of interest here is why the interracial conflict narrative was so eagerly pursued by the media despite very thin evidence of its relevance to the 2008 race. Even the anecdotal evidence was spotty. As Lisa Cullen wrote in the follow-up to her February 18, 2008, *Time* story, "Does Obama Have an Asian Problem?" "Some of you wrote to say you too found [Anderson Cooper's] CNN report patently offensive. Others of you found my post's title patently offensive. . . . That got me to thinking. This deserved some actual reporting."[64]

Much of the frustration on the part of activists and bloggers of color stemmed from the fact that the conflict narrative supplanted substantive exploration of the experiences and interests of the racial middle. As Lovato argued in the *Huffington Post*, "Story after story tries to fit the Latino vote into the procrustean bed of old-school, black v. white politics" through the use of "awkward" and "simplistic" rhetoric. He wrote that the diversity and complexity of the Latino community was something that "news organizations, the political parties and the society as a whole" were "ill equipped to understand and to deal with."[65]

The interracial conflict thesis thus reflected a lack of attention to the diversity and complexity of political thought among non-whites. But it also had a functional role in the larger narrative of the election. This broader narrative portrayed Obama's campaign as a movement for racial justice and national redemption, one in which certain people were on the side of progress and others were against it. On the right side were educated, affluent white voters, liberals, youth, and some conservatives. In the wrong were blacks obsessed with racial authenticity, Asians and Latinos hampered by prejudice, and most of the political right. As racially motivated opponents of Obama's historic election, Latinos and Asians stood in contrast to liberal white Americans, who had themselves managed to transcend the issue of race. The implicit reprobation of non-white voters found throughout the press in 2007/2008 thus furthered the self-congratulatory narrative of whites' triumph over racism in the presidential race.[66]

But the focus on conflict between minorities was not new. The sociologist John Lie took aim at the black/Asian conflict thesis in an article published in 2004. Lie wrote that while social scientists generally assume that intergroup contact inevitably leads to tension and discord, this misunderstands "an effect for a cause." For example, scholars often blame desegregation for increases in ethnic conflict, rather than acknowledging the practice of segregation itself to have been the root cause. Lie also wrote that people often blame race for conflict that may be driven by differences in education, occupation, and politics. According to Lie, despite the fact that inter-minority conflict is actually quite rare, "contemporary Americans are wont to highlight ethnic tension and conflict." Blacks and Asians—"the ideologically antipodal minorities—the urban underclass against the model minority"—seem to be the perfect racial antagonists.[67]

But why? If conflict between racial minorities is relatively rare, why do we have the impression that it is quite prevalent? In a 2007 article titled "The Fantasy of L.A.'s 'Race War,'" the Los Angeles Times columnist Gregory Rodriguez offered a series of thought-provoking insights.[68] Rodriguez began with the observation that whites routinely estimate far higher levels of black-Latino conflict than do either blacks or Latinos. While 75% of whites in one national study said that relations between whites and blacks "were either very good or somewhat good," less than half viewed black-Hispanic relations in a positive light. Rodriguez found white pessimism concerning black/Latino relations to be "particularly interesting given that 68% of blacks and 59% of Latinos considered black-Latino relations generally good."[69] Rodriguez argued that the explanation for this phenomenon might lie in what he called "Anglo race fatigue": "Over the last generation, a growing number of white Americans have expressed their exasperation with the seeming intractability of racial issues in the U.S. . . . I imagine that plenty of them are eager to consign the issue of race to a new set of players and, indeed, may be relieved that the media's preoccupation with black versus brown has eclipsed that of white versus black. They want to say, 'Look at them. It's not just us.'"

Given that the narrative about race, Latinos, and Obama that emerged in the next several months so closely fit this pattern, Rodriguez's analysis was extremely prescient. Elements of his argument in fact echoed those made by Benjamin Wallace-Wells. In a *Washington Post* article from November 2006, Wallace-Wells observed that "whatever racism remains in this country. . . coexists with a galloping desire to put that old race stuff behind us, to have a national Goodbye to All That moment."[70] He predicted that whites' desire to prove themselves to be over the issue of race would make Obama a much more appealing candidate than Hillary Clinton, despite the historic nature of both their candidacies. The black/brown conflict narrative helped to satisfy that deep desire—which Obama's candidacy had ignited—by allowing whites to displace the society's remaining racial tensions onto racial minorities themselves.

But Rodriguez cautioned against equating black/white conflict with hostility between blacks and browns. In that same article, he wrote, "Contemporary black/Latino tensions don't somehow erase—or render routine—the historical divisions between white and black in America." "To pretend the two relationships are equivalent," he claimed, "is to downplay the official role and legacy of white supremacy in American history."

Ta-Nehisi Coates made a similar point in *The Atlantic* in 2009. Coates was objecting to a *Time* story that had characterized Sonia Sotomayor's nomination to the Supreme Court as "perhaps the most potent symbol yet of a 21st-century rapprochement between . . . Latino Americans and African Americans, who in the 20th century could be as violently distrustful of each other as blacks and whites were."[71] Coates wrote, "It is amazingly self-serving to suggest that the evil [of white supremacy] even approaches anything that's happened between blacks and Latinos in this country. It also conveniently allays American discomfort with an ugly, shameful past that we'd love to see go away."[72]

As the quotes above suggest, the inter-minority conflict narrative also played directly into the ideology of colorblind individualism—the core ideology undergirding the story of whites' triumph over racism in the 2008 election.[73] By drawing parallels between white/black and black/ brown conflict, the narrative naturalized the violent and repressive history of white supremacy as an inevitable outcome of intergroup contact. It located the source of contemporary U.S. racial problems in minority communities themselves, rather than in broader patterns of institutional discrimination that help to preserve white racial privilege. And by presenting non-whites as irrationally preoccupied with race, the narrative confirmed that race was a not a white problem, but rather a problem of people of color.

The conflict narrative also evidenced what Claire Jean Kim has called "racial triangulation." As discussed earlier in this chapter, this concept refers to the ways in which other non-whites are racialized not *along*, but *in relationship to*, the black/white binary. In the narrative forwarded during the election, Asians and Latinos were neither like whites nor like blacks, but rather stood in contrast to both groups. Obama represented the "good minorities" in this scenario; those who were working together with whites to help heal the country's racial divides. Asians, Latinos, and certain other blacks on the other hand, were figured as sources of racial tension, conflict, and confusion. In the 2008 race, they "injected racial politics" into an arena in which liberal whites themselves had remained colorblind.

The Fact of His Blackness

While the interracial conflict narrative was misleading and self-serving, Obama's race was not irrelevant to the racial middle. Though African Americans had not rejected Obama as "inauthentic," they needed to be clear who he was before they would support him. For Latinos and Asians, some of the same issues were at play. At first, Obama's outreach to non-black communities of color was not particularly good. As the columnist Mario Solis-Marich wrote in June 2008, "Obama himself has admitted time and time again that he has not matched Clinton's outreach efforts to Hispanics."[74] Ana Rivas wrote in the *Wall Street Journal* that Obama's use of the slogan "Sí, se puede" (the Spanish translation of "Yes, we can") fell into the category of "Mariachi Politics"—token gestures that would be insufficient to capture Latino interest.[75] Clinton had greater name recognition, and spent much more time and money pursuing Latino and Asian votes than did Obama in the early part of the race.

Nonetheless, racial factors did influence political sentiment among the racial middle. Given that the predominant narrative forwarded to explain the significance of Obama's candidacy was framed in terms of black and white, its relevance to Asian and Latino voters was not readily apparent. On the blog of the Asian American Action Fund, Maytak Chin discussed her difficulty figuring out where she and other Asians "fit" in the discussions of identity politics taking place during the election.[76] And in May 2008, Richard Rodriguez urged Obama to "talk to Hispanics as a brown man who has made his way through a black and white America." "We would understand you better," he wrote in *Newsweek*, "if you understood your story in ours."[77]

Part of the reason that Obama was not at first embraced by the racial middle, then, was the emphasis placed on his blackness. The early fascination in the press with Obama's blackness seems to have been more a source of estrangement and alienation than of inter-minority identification. As a black man, Obama was expected to be far more concerned with African Americans than with other voters. According to an article in the *Latino Times*, Obama's focus on gaining black votes "has created the perception amongst Hispanic people that he doesn't care about their situation."[78] And as Professor Chang wrote in the article cited at the beginning of this chapter, "In the beginning perhaps I was not listening closely enough, because clearly he is someone who thinks beyond and cares for more than the black community."[79] A major shift in the perception of Obama occurred toward the end of the primary season, when the racial middle swung its support his way. The idea that Obama was a "post-racial" politician—"rooted in the black community but not limited to it"—seems to have been part of the equation.

Post-Racial Politics

This notion, it should be noted, played differently to different audiences. Many African Americans viewed Obama's "new race politics" as a welcome change in black political leadership. As one blogger wrote, "I'm personally tired of the old, permed out, sweatin', jive-preacher representation."[80] Obama was widely admired for his savvy, cool temperament, and ease in both black and non-black worlds. But there was an undercurrent of wariness about Obama's next-generation blackness as well. Many African Americans understood the importance of his not appearing to be a traditional "civil rights–style" leader. (Even Al Sharpton stated that Obama was running to be the president of America, not the president of black America.) Some took on faith that his silences on racial issues and his overtly conciliatory nature were tactical concessions necessary for success in his endeavor. But if elected, some wondered, would Obama look out for the interests of black Americans at all? Were his speeches on black personal responsibility truly designed to promote racial uplift, or were they primarily meant to score points with whites?[81]

Among whites, Obama's new politics of race were met with much less ambivalence and more outright celebration. Conservatives in particular praised the candidate for giving up the "protest politics" and "divisiveness" of the past, and for seeming to be the one who would put the Sharptons and the Jacksons out of business forever. One of the many other positive functions of Obama's post-racial blackness was that it allowed whites to move beyond the issue of race themselves. As a former chairman of the Tennessee Democratic Party was quoted in the *Wall Street Journal* as saying, "Obama is running an emancipating campaign. . . . He is emancipating white voters to vote for a black candidate."[82]

For the racial middle, the new politics of race meant something else entirely. First, as such—as "new race politics"—the issue received virtually no discussion among Latino and Asian writers.[83] Obama's "post-racial" presentation of self, however, seems to have allowed non-black voters of color to identify with those aspects of his heritage most relevant to them. According to Thomas Chen in Harvard's *Perspective Magazine*, Asian Americans switched their allegiance to Obama "once they learned about his diverse background" and realized that he was a "different kind of African American."[84]

Pareng Barack

In speeches before predominantly Asian American audiences, Obama often mentioned his familial ties to Asian American and Pacific Islander communities—his childhood in Hawaii and Jakarta, his Indonesian stepfather, half-Indonesian sister, and his Chinese American brother-in-law.[85] These connections were clear points of pride for Asian American and Pacific Islander writers and activists. In a piece titled "Our Man Obama," the Vietnamese immigrant Andrew Lam wrote, "I see the rise of Barack Obama as the beginning [of] the end of a 500 year-old colonial curse."[86] In

January 2008, the blogger Jennifer Fang wrote that having been raised in Hawaii and "surrounded by a majority of Asian American people," Barack Obama was "the candidate who most closely understands what it is like to be an Asian American."[87] Similarly, in *Time* magazine a native Hawaiian politician was quoted as saying, "From the first time I heard that he referred to his grandmother as 'Toot' [derived from the Hawaiian word for grandmother], I felt a profound linkage to this man."[88]

The Filipino American journalist Benjamin Pimentel referred to Obama as Pareng Barack, or "Brother Barack," in his book of the same name. Interestingly, Pimentel was one of the only writers to draw parallels between the histories of blacks and Asians in the United States. In the *Philippine Star*, Pimentel wrote that an Obama victory would honor the memories of the "young blacks and whites who gave their lives for civil rights in the American south," as well as those "of Vera Cruz, Itliong and other [Filipino] farmworkers whose sacrifices now also are part of the [American] story."[89]

Some argued that Obama's life experiences uniquely positioned him to understand the kinds of racism faced by Asian Americans. As Jeff Yang wrote in the *San Francisco Chronicle*, "Beneath the charges that [Obama is] 'anti-American,' is the lingering insinuation that the 'exotic' candidate with the 'funny name' is, in fact, not an American at all." "For Asian Americans," Yang continued, "that's an implication with a familiar and frightening ring." Elsewhere Yang wrote that Obama's memoir "reads like it was written to an Asian template." Upon reading *Dreams from My Father*, he argued, "the Asian American reader's feelings of déjà vu will slip from amusing to uncanny." Yang suggested that given these realities, Obama could in fact become "the first Asian American president."[90] Pimentel made a similar assertion in a story from January 2008. He wrote that if Toni Morrison "can claim that Bill Clinton was the first African American president, well, I should be able to make a similarly wild claim about Barack Obama." "I mean he looks Pinoy, doesn't he?," he asked. "He could very well be Pareng Barack."[91]

Latinos, Immigration, and Barack

Latino writers and political commentators expressed some degree of identification with Obama as well. The Fox News commentator Geraldo Rivera, for example, claimed in early 2009 that Obama was "the first Hispanic president," echoing the sentiments of Yang and Pimentel discussed above. Among Latinos, however, much more important than personal identification with Obama was optimism about his stance on immigration.[92]

The Republican candidate, John McCain, was hindered in his efforts to capture the Latino vote by his party's overt nativism. As Ben Smith wrote, "McCain seems to have wound up with the worst of both worlds: He appears to be getting no credit from Latino voters for his past support for immigration reform, while carrying the baggage of other Republicans' hostility to illegal immigration."[93] But Obama benefitted from both the comparatively positive reputation of the Democrats on immigration and from his January 2008 expression of support for granting driver's licenses to the undocumented. By the time of the general election, there was tremendous hope that if elected, Obama would introduce comprehensive immigration reform legislation during his first year in office.[94]

In the three years since the election, Latino commentators have had quite a lot to say about President Obama. There is a general acknowledgement that he has appointed an unprecedented number of Latinos to positions of power in the federal government. The nomination of Sonia Sotomayor to the Supreme Court was seen as particularly important act in this regard.[95] Consistent with a broader souring toward Obama on the part of the liberal wing of the electorate, however, Latino commentators have also registered profound disappointment with the president. That he has failed to make comprehensive immigration reform a top legislative priority has been seen as a form of betrayal.[96] Some have expressed anger that the Obama administration has stepped up arrests and deportations of undocumented workers, pointing out that more detentions have taken place under Obama than during the Bush years.[97] In general, there is a feeling that many of the promises Obama made during the campaign may have been little more than lip service.[98] As the Univision television anchor Jorge Ramos, described as "the most influential Latino in America," said of the president in August 2010, "He has a credibility problem right now with Latinos."[99]

By early 2011, however, this credibility problem had only persisted. While Obama's approval rating among Latinos stood at nearly 75% in January 2009, the Gallup Organization reported in March 2011 that it had fallen to somewhat over half.[100] In a recent post titled "Some Latinos Wondering Why Vote for Obama in 2012," one blogger wrote, "People can only be strung along for so long and then something has to be shown as a sign of good faith that things will be different a second term around."[101] Given the openly anti-immigrant rhetoric and legislation forwarded by Republican politicians over the last several years, few believe that Latinos would defect to the GOP en masse. The chief threat facing Obama at this time, however, is that many members of this crucial voting block will simply sit out the 2012 presidential election altogether.[102]

Conclusions

Looking back at the 2008 race from the perspective of the racial middle, a number of conclusions may be drawn. First, it is clear that the black/white binary was the central axis around which the national conversation on race revolved. The dominant racial themes of the election, as well as most of the public discourse about race, were overwhelmingly phrased in terms of black and white.

The racial middle was not entirely invisible in 2007/2008, however. The story of interracial conflict put forth to explain the early strong support for Clinton's candidacy reflected a lack of attention to the depth and diversity of thought among Latino and Asian voters. But it also helped to solidify the larger story of the election—one of white triumph over racism—by drawing contrasts between the race consciousness of the racial middle and the colorblindness of liberal whites. In equating contemporary manifestations of conflict between minorities with the history of white supremacy in the United States, the narrative also downsized white culpability for racial injustice in the past.

A central argument of this book is that many white and black Americans were drawn to Obama's candidacy not despite his blackness, but because of it. But this was not so straightforwardly the case for the racial middle.[103] The Latino journalists and bloggers I read did not overtly identify with Obama as a fellow person of color, nor did they draw parallels between the historical experiences of blacks and Latinos in the United States. Though Asian American and Pacific Islander writers did identify with Obama far more personally, they did not identify him as a black man, focusing rather on the Asian dimensions of his biography.

Latino and Asian writers did not describe Obama, or the significance of his candidacy, in black or in white terms. References to the new politics of race, to transcending race, and to the concept of post-racialism were largely absent. Much more common were discussions of frustration about being overlooked and ignored in broader conversations about the election—except to the degree that they were figured as obstacles to racial progress. Race did matter to the racial middle, but not in the same way that it did to others, and perhaps not even to the same degree. This makes sense given that many Latino and Asian communities include large numbers of immigrants not raised under the regimes of U.S. racial logic. And it also makes sense given that the members of the racial middle were not viewed in the same way as were whites or blacks.

A review of the 2008 race, therefore, provides considerable evidence that black/white models of race relations are inadequate to capture the experiences and subjectivities of those racialized as neither white nor black. The racial middle is a "triangulated" space, existing not along the constructed axis of black and white, but in dialogue, and in contestation, with it.

7

In Defense of
the White Nation

The Modern Conservative Movement and

the Discourse of Exclusionary Nationalism

A t an October 2008 rally in Greensboro, North Carolina, the Republican vice presidential nominee, Sarah Palin, then governor of Alaska, made the following statement:

> We believe that the best of America is in these small towns that we get to visit, and in these wonderful little pockets of what I call the real America, being here with all of you hard working very patriotic . . . pro-America areas of this great nation. This is where we find the kindness and the goodness and the courage of everyday Americans. Those who are running our factories and teaching our kids and growing our food and are fighting our wars for us. Those who are protecting us in uniform. Those who are protecting the virtues of freedom.[1]

The "real America" also might have been called "Middle America," the "heartland," or "red state USA." In fact, the conservative commentator Glenn Beck had published a book titled *The Real America* in 2003. But Palin revived the real America in the 2008 presidential race, bringing along all its ideological trappings.

The real America was a conservative, exclusivist vision of nation. If there was a real America, then there was also a not real, not authentic, not worthy America. There were "others" who were not so hardworking, not so patriotic, not so good. And following the logic of the narrative, we knew, more or less, who the real Americans were and who they weren't. We knew in part because throughout the 2008 campaign, McCain and Palin utilized a dizzying array of terms to outline the boundaries of the real America and to differentiate between "us" and "them."

In this chapter I unearth the racial roots of the real America narrative, as I critically examine the political discourse of the American right. For the Democrats, the trope of race was used to create an expansive, broadly inclusive nation. As Obama's nation would triumphantly overcome the divide of race, so would it overcome all other divides (religion, gender, sexuality, class, disability, etc.). For the Republicans, however, race was a key element in constructing a delimited, bounded nation in which defining who was out was as important as defining who was in. For the McCain/Palin campaign in the 2008 election, this vision of nation was the real America.[2]

The real America was populated by hockey moms, NASCAR dads, Joe Six-Pack, and Joe the Plumber.[3] Real Americans, we were told, were small-town voters, regular folks, hardworking people, your neighbors, and Middle Americans. As simple, God-fearing people, they cared more about kitchen table issues than any libel that might be written in the *New York Times*.[4] In 2007/2008, Clinton and Obama occasionally referred to segments of the electorate in similar terms. The labels did not have the same resonance when coming from the Democrats, however, because the terrain they were treading on was fundamentally conservative. Though repackaged in 2008 by the major-party candidates, these terms derived from the racially coded populist discourse that the right had been aggressively forwarding since the late 1970s.[5]

The real America narrative articulated a vision of a good, white America, one that could be identified by country music, guns, small towns, flags, and pickup trucks.[6] The idyllic heartland that the architects of the red state nation invoked was far from the gritty urban cores where black and brown people were imagined to reside in large numbers. The nation was understood to be Christian, heterosexual, and conservative as well. Thus "realness" (authenticity, legitimacy, righteousness, morality) and "American-ness" were defined using whiteness as one of several key criteria.[7]

The real America narrative was also embedded with a series of moral binaries. According to the broader discourse, there were "two Americas"—one righteous, humble, observant, and hardworking, and the other alternately arrogant and elitist, foreign, criminal, and profane.[8] Real Americans were simple men or women who'd take a cup of black coffee over a latte any day. They knew right from wrong (they were not cultural relativists) and would pledge allegiance only to the red, white, and blue (they were not citizens of the world). Real Americans believed in family (not feminism) and marriage (but not for gays). And while there might be a few brown faces at the PTA or the neighborhood barbecue, the real America was decidedly not multicultural. In God's country, Christmas would never be supplanted by Hanukah, Kwanza, or "winter break." As the cultural critic Rich Benjamin observed in 2009, "Obama's [ascendance] raises the stakes in a battle royal between two versions of America: one that is segregated yet slap-happy with its diversity . . . and an America that 'does not mind a little ethnic food, some Asian math whizzes, or a few Mariachi dancers—as long as these trends do not overwhelm the white dominant culture.'"[9]

As the race progressed, the McCain/Palin campaign increasingly relied on polarizing cultural cues distinguishing "our side" from "theirs." Whereas Obama was at first largely criticized as inexperienced and naive, by the closing months of the election he had become an enemy of the nation and a foreign other.[10] At a series of highly publicized rallies in the closing months of the race, the McCain-Palin camp attempted to tap into the existing well of white national and racial anxiety and channel it into activism. As I discuss below, the ideological groundwork for the campaign had been laid by a generation of conservative discourse on immigration, race, nation, and culture.

Roots of the Real America Narrative: Paradigms of Exclusion and Inclusion

The discourse of the real America derives from a strain of conservative nationalism that seeks to delimit and unify the nation in part through boundaries and exclusions. There is a fixation in this paradigm with defining who is an authentic, legitimate, and loyal member of the nation, and who is a usurper, an outsider, a traitor, or an enemy. Obama's campaign narrative, on the other hand, deployed the inclusive discourse of multicultural liberalism. Obama spoke of a big-tent nation that would comprise many different kinds of Americans (gay and straight, able-bodied and disabled, black, brown, and white, Muslim, Jewish, and Christian).

While the basic tendencies toward inclusion or exclusion have existed in this country, in some form or another, since the nation's founding, they have not remained static. These competing paradigms—which scholars refer to variously as pluralism, ethno-culturalism, cosmopolitan liberalism, essentialism, incorporationism, and nativism—have been rearticulated time and again in response to changing political and economic conditions.[11] The earliest expressions of exclusionary nationalism were characterized by strong anti-Catholic sentiment, inherited from the Protestant colonists.[12] By the late 1880s, in response to mass immigration from southern and eastern Europe, those who advocated a delimited model of nation became obsessed with the problems of ethnicity. Many expressed fears that the "Anglo-Saxon race" would become extinct as Europeans of inferior stock overran the United States. By the end of World War II, however, the predominant nationalist sentiment in the United States had shifted markedly.[13] As their socioeconomic position improved, Poles, Italians, and Jews were upgraded from members of the lesser races to "meltable" ethnics eligible for assimilation into the mainstream. As James Barrett and David Roediger point out, for these immigrant groups, "the process of becoming white and becoming American were connected at every turn."[14]

In the last half-century, debates about exclusion and inclusion have centered around Latinos and Asians—the new sources of immigration anxiety—as well as blacks, women, gays, and lesbians. Further, inclusivism has attained primacy as the dominant paradigm of national identity, as reflected in the widespread (though vague) valorization of "diversity" and "multiculturalism."[15]

Exclusivist tendencies, however, have remained an important part of the culture, and in recent years they have gained steam. Among the most important factors in the growth of contemporary conservative nationalism were the social justice movements of the 1960s and 1970s and the widespread immigration of non-whites following the abolition of national origins quotas in 1965. These developments have profoundly shifted the country's cultural, political, and demographic balance, leading to accelerated fears of a brown takeover.[16]

The most immediate point of reference for conservative nationalist discourse today is 9/11. The attacks that took place that day have heightened perceptions that the white nation is endangered, and they have revived doubts about the viability and wisdom of the inclusivist paradigm. As the conservative Mark Steyn wrote in 2006, "Liberals will still tell you that 'diversity is our strength'—while Talibanic enforcers cruise Greenwich Village burning books and barber shops."[17]

Threats to the White Nation

Martin Spencer points out that each of the major historic waves of exclusionary nationalism in the United States were characterized by "a profound identity-anxiety," or "the fear that the 'American identity'—however this might be conceptualized—was in jeopardy."[18] Deep anxiety about the nation is a particularly salient feature of conservative nationalism today. According to the chorus on the right, the United States is under siege, its values, freedom, and traditions imperiled. The white, Judeo-Christian foundation on which the nation was built is said to be in "eminent danger" of erosion. Unless there is a major course correction on the part of our national leaders, we are told, the country that so many "knew and loved" will vanish from the earth.

Such sentiments have been reflected in the words of numerous right-wing political commentators. Among the best known are the anti-immigration activist Peter Brimelow, the polemical writer Ann Coulter, the Hoover Institution fellow Victor Davis Hanson, the political scientist Samuel Huntington, the radio commentator Rush Limbaugh, and former Colorado representative and Tea Party leader Tom Tancredo, as well as Glenn Beck, Bill O'Reilly, and many others from the Fox News cable television network.[19]

Patrick Buchanan is one of the most prolific and high-profile members of this cohort. He has railed against non-white immigration, abortion, secularism, liberalism, feminism, homosexuality, and "reverse racism" for decades. Buchanan is a former Republican presidential candidate and a regular commentator on the (generally left-leaning) MSNBC cable news network. In his 2002 book *The Death of the West*, Buchanan painted the picture of a civilization in its final days:

> "Pat, we're losing the country we grew up in." Again and again in the endless campaign of 2000 I heard that lament from men and women across America. . . . In half a lifetime, many Americans have seen their God dethroned, their heroes defiled, their culture polluted, their values assaulted, their country invaded, and themselves demonized as extremists and bigots for holding on to beliefs Americans have held for generations. . . . Our world has been turned upside down. What was right and true yesterday is wrong and false today. What was immoral and shameful—promiscuity, abortion, euthanasia, suicide—has become progressive and praiseworthy.[20]

Buchanan believes that much of the blame for the decline of the United States may be placed on the shoulders of white women. As he stated in a July 2007 broadcast of the *McLaughlin Group*, "The rise of women to power in a civilization is very often the mark of its decline."[21] But even more concerning to Buchanan is the fact that so many women have become "hostile" to the ideas of birth and motherhood. "Why," he asks, "have Europe's nations and peoples stopped having babies and begun to accept their disappearance from this earth with such seeming indifference?"[22]

It is non-white immigration, however, that many conservatives believe to pose the greatest threat to the nation. In 2007's *State of Emergency*, Buchanan wrote that millions of the immigrants in the United States today "are strangers in our midst." They are culturally inferior others who come to the United States with "malevolent motives" and an assembly line of diseases.[23] In the opening pages of the book, he described the new immigration in terms that implied that the nation was being taken over and defiled:

> The African, Asian, Islamic, and Hispanic peoples that the West once ruled are coming to repopulate the mother countries. What can be said for a man who would allow his home to be invaded by strangers who demanded that they be fed, clothed, housed, and granted the rights of the firstborn? What can be said for a ruling elite that permits this to be done to the nation, and that celebrates it as a milestone of moral progress? . . . We are witnessing how nations perish. We are entered upon the final act of our civilization. The penultimate scene, now well underway, is the invasion unresisted.[24]

Peter Brimelow sounded a similar alarm in his 1996 book *Alien Nation*. The current wave of immigration, he wrote, is "so huge and so systematically different" from anything past "as to transform—and ultimately, perhaps, even to destroy" the United States. "The racial and ethnic balance of America is being radically altered," he continued. "*Is that what Americans want?*"[25] Note that these authors are even more concerned with immigrants than they are with blacks. "Completely different" from previous (i.e., white) immigrants, these "visible minorities" have entered the United States in such numbers as to fundamentally alter its character.[26] With its culture every day more debased, corrupted, and polluted, the nation is said to be faced with extinction.

This is not say that African Americans escape the scrutiny of the architects of the right-wing nation. Blacks most often figure in the narrative as ungrateful racial bullies who benefit at the expense of whites. They are held back not by economic or racial barriers, but by their own crippling sense of victimhood and culture of failure. In March 2008, at the height of the controversy over Senator Obama's relationship with Jeremiah Wright, Pat Buchanan argued that Obama's former pastor "ought to go down on his knees and thank God he is an American." "America has been the best country on earth for black folks," Buchanan argued. "It was here that 600,000 black people, brought from Africa in slave ships, grew into a community of 40 million, were introduced to Christian salvation, and reached the greatest levels of freedom and prosperity blacks have ever known."[27] Thus, Buchanan claimed, blacks had been saved, civilized, and liberated by the slave experience. Therefore they should be thankful to the nation and to whites, *even for slavery.* "We hear the grievances," he groused. "Where is the gratitude?"

The conservative paradigm of nation expresses concern not only for the nation at large, but for the welfare of whites in particular. The fear is that whites will be displaced or oppressed in a nation in which non-whites hold the reins of power. The scholar Aimee Carrillo Rowe writes that "the discourse of white victimization" is a key element of contemporary conservatism. This discourse has been used "to rearticulate the terrain of the national space," following "advancements made by white women and people of color." In this context, she writes, "the discourse of whiteness has adapted by constructing white men as the new minority."[28]

Rush Limbaugh has been an especially prolific architect of this discourse. In September 2009, he argued that a vicious interracial beating on a St. Louis school bus was an example of the kind of treatment that whites could expect under a black president: "You put your kids on a school bus you expect safety, but in Obama's America the white kids now get beat up with the black kids cheering 'yeah, right on, right on, right on.'" On his July 2, 2010, radio show, Limbaugh further claimed that President Obama had *created* the recession "as payback" for 230 years of racial oppression.[29]

Similarly, in the 2008 essay referred to above, Patrick Buchanan claimed that anti-white discrimination on the part of universities, businesses, and government was an extremely common occurrence. While the public had heard "ad nauseam" about the Jena Six and the Duke lacrosse rape case, "about the epidemic of black assaults on whites that are real," he railed, "we hear nothing." This sense of victimization was also clearly articulated by Fox News's Glenn Beck in July 2009. Despite Obama's strongly accomodationist posture on most matters pertaining to race, Beck claimed that the new president had demonstrated over and over again that he was a "racist" with a "deep-seated hatred for white people." Thus, far from considering themselves to be chauvinists or bigots, conservative ideologues identify themselves as freedom fighters, defending their rights and those of the nation. As Bill O'Reilly said in a May 30, 2007, interview with John McCain, "Do you understand what the *New York Times* wants, and the far-left want? They want to break down the white, Christian male power structure, of which you're a part and so am I. They want to bring in millions of foreign nationals to basically break down the structure that we have."[30]

Exclusionary nationalisms define the nation in large part by whom it stands against, and who stands against it. Thus America (the real America) has many enemies. In countless conservative tracts from the last several decades, America's enemies have been identified, variously, as multiculturalism, political correctness, black racism, the liberal media, coastal elites, third-world immigration, radical Islam, feminism, abortion, gay marriage, and secularism.[31] Where some see progress in attempts to extend full rights and recognition to members of historically oppressed groups, others see a liberal plot to disparage and destroy the real America.

Many conservatives have answered the threats they perceive with the language of war. As Bill O'Reilly wrote in his 2006 manifesto *Culture Warrior*, "I have chosen to jump into the fray and become a warrior in the vicious culture war that is currently under way in the United States of America. War is exactly the right term. On one side of the battlefield are the armies of the traditionalists like me, who believe the United States was well founded and has done enormous good for the world. On the other side are the committed forces of the secular-progressive movement that want to change America dramatically."[32] Many of the threats the conservative nation references today (multiculturalism, gay marriage, terrorism, etc.) are products of the recent era. Thus, while the nation is "traditionalist," in that it is characterized by nostalgia for an uncomplicated white past, it is also distinctly modern. With ideological roots extending back to the early days of the republic, the exclusionary nationalism of today is articulated around 21st-century sociopolitical and demographic concerns.

Combating the Enemy Other

These were precisely the sentiments—white resentment, fear, and anger—that were exploited by John McCain and Sarah Palin. By the time the 2008 presidential race came along, voters had been primed by years of conservative rhetoric.[33] The election was presented as part of the epic battle between the defenders of freedom and those who wished to tear the white Christian nation apart. Thus the real America would go to war.

In the early months of the campaign, John McCain mostly avoided sharply attacking Obama, maintaining what one reporter called an "easygoing," "endearing" "campaign presence."[34] From the outset of her emergence on the scene, however, Sarah Palin was a different story. The Alaska governor had an appetite for confrontation and polarization. As the conservative journalist David Brooks observed in October 2008, "No American politician plays the class-warfare card as constantly as Palin. Nobody so relentlessly divides the world between the 'normal Joe Sixpack American' and the coastal elite."[35] And as I argue above, the war that Palin and other conservatives sought to incite was racialized as well.

Like Bill O'Reilly and others, Palin often made use of the language of battle and confrontation. In her September 3, 2008, speech at the Republican National Convention, she began by mentioning John McCain's 22 years in uniform and her own son's recent deployment to Iraq. "You know they say the difference between a hockey mom and a pit bull?," she famously quipped, "Lipstick." Similarly, a month later, Palin opened a speech in Carson, Colorado, by saying, "OK, the heels are on, the gloves are off."[36] In both instances, she positioned herself as a patriot-soldier while emphasizing her fealty to aspects of the conservative gender code.[37] She might be a fighter, but she was no emasculating, unattractive, liberal feminist.

Anti-American Obama

Patriotism was a major issue in the 2008 campaign, a basic litmus test of belonging to the real America. As the historian John Higham writes, "Seeing or suspecting a failure of assimilation, [the nativist] hears disloyalty. Occasionally the charge of disloyalty may stand forth naked and unadorned, but usually it is colored and focused by a persistent conception about what is un-American."[38] In the 2008 race, Barack Obama's patriotism was questioned at every turn. He was assailed for a purported unwillingness to wear the flag pin, for failing to put his hand over his heart during the national anthem, and for cancelling a visit with troops in Iraq. During an appearance on MSNBC's *Hardball with Chris Matthews*, the Minnesota congresswoman Michele Bachmann claimed that she was "very concerned" that Obama and other liberal members of Congress "may have anti-American views."[39]

Senator Obama was especially likely to be accused of being anti-American by association. In March 2008, a series of taped sermons by his former pastor, the Reverend Jeremiah Wright, came to light. In these sermons, which were broadcast again and again throughout the 24-hour news cycle, Wright denounced America's histories of institutional racism and imperialism. Outraged conservatives claimed that the tapes proved that both Wright and Obama were anti-American and anti-white.[40] A firestorm of controversy also surrounded statements made by Obama's wife, Michelle, in February 2008, when she declared that she was "really proud of my country" for "the first time in my adult life." Conservatives denounced this statement as arrogant, anti-American, and racist.[41]

As in the Wright case, a perceived attack on the United States was taken as an attack on white Americans as well. Charges of "reverse racism" are a basic feature of the discourse of white racial victimization, and an increasingly common feature of contemporary American racial politics.[42] As if to defend the candidate's wife, Bill O'Reilly declared on Fox News, "I don't want to go on a lynching party against Michelle Obama *unless there's evidence, hard facts*, that say this is how the woman really feels." "If that's how she really feels, that America is a bad country or a flawed nation, whatever—*then that's legit*," he continued. "We'll track it down."[43]

But Barack Obama was said to be un-American in more than sentiment. The deeper implication was that patriotism was not truly possible for him because he was simply not American.[44] For the right, Obama's core was not just too exotic to be recognizably American, it was fundamentally inimical to the nation. Throughout the campaign, the conservative media and McCain/Palin used innuendo and direct accusation to associate Obama with terrorism and Islam. In the summer of 2008, Fox News ran several segments about Osama Bin Laden in which the Saudi 9/11 mastermind was "mistakenly" identified as "Obama" Bin Laden.[45] Right-wing commentators regularly referred to the Democratic candidate as Barack *Hussein* Obama, in order to draw parallels between Obama and the executed Iraqi dictator.[46] When Fox News's Alan Colmes suggested that his guest Bill Cunningham's repeated references to Obama (and not to McCain) by his full name constituted a double standard, Cunningham replied, "My standard, Alan Colmes, is for the American people and the American way of life."[47]

From early 2007 onward, the Internet was flooded with websites and e-mails claiming that Obama was a Muslim with jihadist leanings.[48] In January of that year, the Fox News anchors Steve Doocy and John Gibson alleged that Obama had been educated at a radical Islamist school during his boyhood in Indonesia, in one instance of the network's ongoing rumoring about the candidate's likely Muslim roots.[49] And even the Clinton campaign appears to have attempted to raise fears by linking Obama to Islam: the pictures of Obama dressed in "Muslim garb" that appeared on the *Drudge Report* website in February 2007 were widely believed to have been submitted by a Clinton staffer.[50]

In an attempt to parody the anti-American and anti-white rumors that had dogged Senator Obama for months, the *New Yorker* published a drawing on the cover of its July 21, 2008, edition that proved to be terrifically controversial. The drawing featured Michelle Obama as a fist-bumping black radical with an Angela Davis–style afro and a machine gun, and Barack Obama dressed as an "Arab" or as a "Muslim." The two stood in the Oval Office of the White House, where an American flag burned in the fireplace and a portrait of Bin Laden hung on the wall. While some saw the image as satire, others believed it to be offensive and incendiary.

Who Is the Real Barack Obama?

McCain and Palin only fanned the flames. Faced with dropping poll numbers, John McCain's strategists decided to adopt a "very aggressive" strategy in last month of the race.[51] Obama would be presented not merely as under-qualified and overhyped, but also as a dangerous unknown. At an October 6 rally in Albuquerque, McCain asked ominously, "Who is the *real* Barack Obama? . . . What is his plan for America?"[52] Sarah Palin ratcheted the rhetoric up considerably higher. In a series of speeches in early October, she repeatedly and forcefully raised the issue of Obama's association with the former radical William Ayers.[53] "This is not a man who sees America as you see it and how I see America," she claimed. "Our opponent . . . is someone who sees America it seems as being so imperfect that he's palling around with terrorists who would target their own country." When accused of greatly exaggerating the extent of Obama's relationship with Ayers, Palin refused to back down, saying that Obama had in fact "kicked off his political career in the guy's living room."[54]

In the final days of the race, McCain staffers publically accused Palin of going off message and taking things too far. By then, however, the explosive rhetoric of the campaign had caught fire. As Eleanor Clift wrote in *Newsweek*, "The cultural arsenal is about all McCain has left against Obama. . . . Whatever else Palin does in this race, she has ignited the culture war." As Andrew Sullivan wrote in *The Atlantic*, "There was always going to be a point of revolt and panic for a core group of Americans who believe that Obama simply *cannot* be president. . . . This is that point. As the polls suggest a strong victory, the Hannity-Limbaugh-Steyn-O'Reilly base are going into shock and extreme rage."[55]

As November 4 approached, the alarm and anger among conservative voters reached palpable proportions. McCain/Palin rallies increasingly appeared to be populated by volatile crowds of fearful, angry white voters. One Clearwater, Florida, man yelled "Kill him!" in response to Palin's claim that Obama consorted with terrorists. In Jacksonville, an audience member cried "Treason!" after Palin stated that he did not support the troops. Agitated throngs at Republican events were reported to jeer and to hiss at the mention of Obama's name. At a town hall meeting in Wisconsin, the *Washington Post* reported, "there were boos, middle fingers turned up and thumbs turned down as a media caravan moved through the crowd." As McCain raised the issue of Obama's tax plan at an event Pennsylvania, one supporter yelled "Off with his head!" and another screamed "Traitor!" The hostility spread into other electoral contests as well. At an October 9 Senate debate in Perry, Georgia, a woman was heard to shout "Bomb Obama!" at the mention of the candidate's name.[56]

It soon became clear that the emotions the campaign had incited had gotten beyond the control of the Republican presidential nominee. At a mid-October event in Lakeville, Minnesota, McCain was unable to rein in the hostility of his supporters. When McCain told fearful crowd members, "I have to tell you [Obama] is a decent person and a person that you do not have to be scared [of] as president of the United States," he was booed and hissed by the crowd. Later, a woman told McCain, "I don't trust Obama. I have read about him. He's an Arab." As an apparently startled McCain responded, "No, ma'am, he's a decent family man, [a] citizen that I just happen to have disagreements with," he was again met with a chorus of boos.[57]

While many observers to the center and left of the political spectrum found the developments of the last weeks of the campaign to be alarming, most conservative commentators dismissed their concerns as vastly overblown.[58] For me, however, there are two important things to note about the turn the race took. First, it is evident that neither Palin nor McCain could have stirred up that degree of antipathy by means of several weeks of speech making alone. Clearly, the GOP candidates had tapped into an existing well of deeply held fears and resentments. In the context of the election, the allegations of McCain and Palin ignited these sentiments like a powder keg. For some, it must have seemed that their worst nightmare was coming to life. Obama's ascendance was the culmination of the immigrant takeover, the beginning of a new era of white racial oppression, the end of the real America.

I believe that it is also important to consider the content of the attacks on Obama during the race. Many commentators have argued these attacks were fundamentally grounded in anti-black racism. I think this was part of the story, but not all of it. Also crucial in understanding the conservative opposition to Obama is the extent to which he was portrayed as a foreign, dangerous, alien other. It should be noted that this is a different form of racialization, and a different positioning in relationship to the construct of nation. Being seen as a lesser member of the nation is not the same as being seen as inherently foreign to the nation.[59] In the 2008 election, Obama was subjected to two kinds of exclusionary racialization—as black (inferior, lazy, ungrateful, racist against whites, incompetent) and, separately, as an enemy alien (foreign, dangerous, inimical to the nation). And during the 2007/2008 electoral season, in the mainstream conservative discourse that this chapter has focused on, the second set of accusations seemed to have more ideological currency than the first. The fundamental danger that Obama was believed to pose to the nation came less from his blackness than from his third-world, terrorist roots.

This point has some interesting implications for scholarly analyses of the election. A number of progressive observers have complained that in 2007/2008, the press and the major-party candidates discussed race in almost exclusively black-and-white terms, basically ignoring other populations of color.[60] As I have argued in previous chapters of this book, it is evident that the Obama camp, the Clinton campaign, and the Obama-adoring segments of the media were chiefly fixated on the black/white divide—either overcoming it or exploiting it. For the right-wing attack machine, however, it was Obama's other racial otherness that was key. Both the real America narrative and the broader conservative nationalist discourse from which it was derived displayed a deeper preoccupation with the browning of America writ large.

One might argue that the fear-mongering and hostility of the last months of the campaign tell us little about the views of most white conservatives, as these extreme attitudes were representative of only a minority of voters and a handful of vocal conservative talking heads. But it is important to remember that John McCain won the majority of white voters, beating Obama among this cohort by a 12-point margin.[61] Thus, while the attempts to stir up anti-Muslim sentiment and the specter of jeering crowds likely turned off some white voters, a sizeable majority were either drawn to these developments or not bothered enough by them to abandon the ticket. This reality, along with the even more virulent displays of rage, xenophobia, and racism by members of the "Tea Party" movement in 2009/2010, suggests that the ride from here to a majority-minority America is likely to be a bumpy one. It seems that the transition to a nation envisioned as red, white, blue, and brown is far from complete.

8

Racial Politics under the
First Black President

To conclude the book, I briefly discuss racial politics since Barak Obama's electoral victory, and ponder the larger meaning of his political ascent for racial dynamics in the future. In the previous chapter, I examined the racial and national politics of members of the conservative mainstream (i.e., the Republican Party presidential nominees, other elected officials, well-known authors, and commentators from the major conservative news outlets). Here, however, I begin by looking at two political movements that are further to the right of the political spectrum—the "birthers" and the Tea Party. Each gained substantial notoriety in the first two years after the election, in part because of the racially tinged nature of their intense opposition to the president.

The Birthers

The seemingly irrational belief that Obama could not be truly American has found its clearest expression in the "birther" movement. Despite all evidence to the contrary, birthers insist that Barack Obama is not a natural-born citizen, and thus he is ineligible to hold the office of president. The birther movement includes conservative activists, attorneys, bloggers, and others who have claimed, since the Democratic primary, that Obama's Hawaiian birth certificate (released by the campaign in 2007) is a forgery.[1] Birthers cloak themselves in the language of patriotism and constitutionalism. They maintain that the president's alien status means that the country has no legally appointed head of state and therefore is in a state of constitutional crisis. The language of the movement is also decidedly conspiratorial. As one website claims, "No doctor has [ever] come forward to state that he or she was the doctor that brought Barrack Hussein Obama, II, into the world on August 4, 1961."[2]

The birther myth has proved extraordinarily tenacious. Almost three years (at this writing) after the election, activists on the far right persist in disputing the validity of Obama's citizenship. By mid-2011, the website *WorldNetDaily* had published more than 600 articles on the topic.[3] Since Obama's January 2009 inauguration, numerous challengers (including the former Republican presidential candidate Alan Keyes) have brought lawsuits before the lower and higher courts demanding that Obama provide "valid" proof that he was born in the United States. As Ben Smith writes, "The suits share a vague, underlying notion that Obama must be some sort of foreigner, probably Kenyan, Indonesian or British, though none have any evidence or a coherent narrative to support the claim."[4] Similarly, in July 2009, the army reservist Stefan Cook grabbed headlines when he refused to deploy to Afghanistan on the grounds that Obama did not have the authority to send him there.[5]

Though it is tempting to assume that the birther myth is confined to a minority of individuals on the fringe, a poll conducted by CNN in August 2010 suggested that more than one in four Americans had doubts about Obama's citizenship.[6] Further, support for the theory that Obama was not born in the United States appears to provide traction for conservative politicians seeking to appeal to constituents on the far right. In fact, the movement has gained the open or tacit endorsement of a number of Republican elected officials. In March 2009, Representative Bill Posey of Florida introduced a House bill to require that all candidates for president present a birth certificate before running for office. In February 2010, the Tennessee state senator Ron Ramsey, who was then running for governor, went on record to question Obama's citizenship. In July 2010, then Republican congressman (and now U.S. senator) David Vitter of Louisiana stated that he would "support conservative legal organizations and others who would bring [the issue of Obama's citizenship] to court." And in April 2011, the billionaire real estate developer and reality T.V. show star Donald Trump, said to be considering a run for the White House, grabbed the headlines by repeatedly declaring that Obama's citizenship "may be a scam." Soon after, the *Washington Times* reported that "since Mr. Trump embraced the issue of Mr. Obama's birth . . . he has gone from nowhere to the top tier of possible 2012 Republican candidates."[7]

Though the former Republican presidential nominee John McCain was born in the Panama Canal, this fact has been entirely ignored.[8] The facts, after all, are beside the point. The birther myth refuses to die because it seems to provide evidence for a belief—deeply held among some Americans—that Obama's presidency is illegitimate. Barack Hussein Obama—black, Muslim, Arab, foreign—is simply incompatible with the nation.

The Tea Party

The festering rage of the last months of the GOP campaign spilled over into what would become, in 2009, the "Tea Party" movement. While a detailed examination of the Tea Party is beyond the scope of this book, I do want to highlight some of its dimensions here. The Tea Party began as a loose coalition of groups (the Tea Party Express, the Tea Party Patriots, Tea Party Nation, the National Tea Party Federation, etc.) lying generally to the right of the GOP. Among the most distinguishing features of the movement in the first two years of its existence were its virulent opposition to the president and the defiant, angry tone of the protests that were staged in cities across the United States. Armed with the rhetoric of revolution, patriotism, and liberty, Tea Party members expressed outrage over "out-of-control spending," "government bailouts," "government-run health care," and President Obama's "socialist agenda."

Tea Party groups repeatedly declared their independence from the Republican Party, and many in the GOP in turn expressed considerable wariness about being openly associated with the movement. Yet there were clear linkages between the Tea Party and the Republicans. A July 2010 poll conducted by the Gallup Organization found that eight in ten Tea Party members considered themselves to be conservative Republicans.[9] On July 16, 2010, Congresswoman Michele Bachmann of Minnesota filed paperwork to establish a "Tea Party Caucus" in the House of Representatives. By the 21st of the month, 50 other members of Congress had joined Bachmann's group.[10] Later that year, the Tea Party transitioned from a fringe protest movement to one with real political power. In the November 2010 midterm elections, more than three dozen Tea Party–backed candidates were elected to Congress, helping the Republican Party regain control of the House and make major gains in the Senate.[11]

The Tea Party has also developed particularly close ties to the former Republican vice presidential nominee Sarah Palin. During her February 2010 keynote speech at the party's first national convention, Palin delivered a "blistering criticism" of President Obama that "was greeted with

wild enthusiasm." "This is about the people," she stated, "and it's a lot big-
ger than any charismatic guy with a teleprompter." Declaring that "America is ready for a revolution!," she brought audience members to their feet.
The former Alaska governor continued to use militaristic rhetoric following her February appearance. In March 2010, after the Obama administration managed to secure passage of a major health care reform bill that
had been reviled by conservatives, Palin urged "Commonsense Conservatives & lovers of America" not to "retreat," but instead to "reload."[12]

Far more strident rhetoric came from other members of the Tea
Party. The most controversial aspect of the movement in 2009/2010 was
the way its supporters positioned themselves with regard to race. Echoing the "two Americas" discourse of the McCain/Palin campaign (see
chapter 7), the former Colorado representative Tom Tancredo declared
at the February convention, "People who could not spell the word 'vote'
or say it in English put a committed socialist ideologue in the White
House—name is Barack Hussein Obama. . . . The revolution has come.
It was led by the cult of multiculturalism aided by leftist liberals all over
who don't have the same ideas about America as we do."[13] In September
2009, Mark Williams, then leader of the Tea Party Express, told CNN's
Anderson Cooper that he believed Obama to be an "Indonesian Muslim," a "welfare thug," and the "racist-in-chief."[14] In May 2010, in protest
of the planned building of an Islamic cultural center near the site of the
9/11 attacks in New York, Williams stated that Muslims were "savages"
who worshipped a "monkey god."[15]

In July 2010, the NAACP passed a resolution condemning the racism
of the Tea Party. As if to prove their point, Williams countered that the
NAACP was itself a "vile racist group" that had "made more money off
of race than any slave trader ever." A few days later, he published on his
blog an "open letter" to Abraham Lincoln from the "the coloreds" of the
United States, which stated:

> We Coloreds have taken a vote and decided that we don't cotton
> to that whole emancipation thing. Freedom means having to work
> for real, think for ourselves, and take consequences along with the
> rewards. That is just far too much to ask of us Colored People and
> we demand that it stop! . . . Mr. Lincoln, you were the greatest rac-
> ist ever. We had a great gig. Three squares, room and board, all our
> decisions made by the massa in the house. Please repeal the 13th and
> 14th Amendments and let us get back to where we belong.[16]

Williams was expelled as leader of the Tea Party Express shortly thereafter.[17]

Similarly extreme sentiments, however, were reflected in the signage found at Tea Party rallies. Like the GOP rallies of the final month of the election, the protests at times appeared to be cauldrons of resentment and rage. Some people came with shotguns.[18] Crowd members carried posters depicting as Obama as a terrorist, as an African witch doctor with a bone through his nose, or as Hitler. A protester in Chicago carried a sign reading "The American Taxpayers Are the Jews for Obama's Oven." A poster from a Wisconsin rally read, "Obama's Plan: White Slavery." And one Florida man carried a sign featuring Obama slitting Uncle Sam's throat with a knife.[19]

One particularly common image featured Obama in whiteface, channeling the homicidal Joker of the 2008 Batman movie. Obama wore a crazed, maniacal expression, his eyes circled in black, and the red paint on his lips extending to his cheeks and chin, as if they had been sliced open. The color symbolism of this image—particularly the whiteface—was both striking and disturbing. It seemed to suggest that Obama was a sinister black villain who had usurped a white man's role. Most often the word "socialism" ran across the bottom of the image.[20]

In addition to the hundreds of race crimes reported to have been perpetrated in the wake of Obama's victory, this imagery reminds us that while "old style" racism may be marginalized in the United States, it is far from dead.[21] Further, when one considers the content of the various charges leveled against Obama—that he is a Muslim, a socialist, an Arab, a madman, a terrorist, a racist, the Antichrist, or Hitler—and their simultaneous irrationality, illogic, and tenacity, it seems particularly clear that for many of his accusers, panic about race in general has been inextricably tied to anxiety about the nation, and about the place that whites "like them" will be relegated to in the post-9/11, majority-minority United States.

Conclusions

One of the goals of this book was to uncover the subtle and blatant ways that race was used against Obama by his liberal and conservative opponents alike. But an even more important goal of the work has been to demonstrate the ways in which Obama's race contributed to his electoral appeal. Obama brought to the forefront a new kind of black public persona—"mainstream," "articulate," less angry, and less confrontational.

Far from transcending race, Obama was still clearly marked as black. The antidote to the Jacksons and the Sharptons, he offered a way through the "stagnant" and "stilted" racial politics of recent decades. In some ways, Obama seemed the answer to many of the anxious questions that had been posed about race in the 21st century. While campaigning on a message of unity, hope, and change, Obama was clear, nonetheless, that he would make no race-based demands of white Americans, nor attempt to significantly modify the existing racial order.

Though conservatives did express concerns about terrorism and non-white immigration in 2007/2008, what we saw in the election was that the national debate about race was primarily framed as a conversation between black and white. The focal point of racial anxiety and conflict was understood to be the fraught and contested relationship between white Americans and the descendants of slaves. Obama was a chance for reconciliation and redemption, notions that were particularly important in a deeply polarized nation mired in an unpopular war. If Obama could redeem the United States and heal the wound of race, it seemed, he might heal all other national wounds and make it feel good to be American again.

Throughout this book, I have critiqued the colorblind perspectives on race found in the rhetoric of the Obama campaign and in mainstream press. But I have also distanced myself somewhat from the deeply pessimistic points of view found in the work of several scholars on this issue.[22] I have attempted to move beyond both the simplistic, binary assumptions inherent in the colorblind individualist perspective, and, to a certain extent, in the predominant critique of this paradigm. Issues are not simply about race, and therefore racist, or not at all about race, and therefore anti-racist. As I have demonstrated in this book, there is lots of middle ground. That many whites voted for Obama in 2008 in no way proves that they were indifferent to his color. But the prevailing counterargument, that whites were drawn to Obama largely because he validated their hidden racist sentiments, is also, in my view, far too simplistic.[23] Further, by claiming either that Obama's win was largely meaningless (or even, as some have, that it was primarily a victory for white supremacy), scholars of race and other progressives risk becoming dismissed as ideologues blindly committed to a belief in the unchanging and intractable nature of racial oppression.[24]

To be clear, I believe that the election of Barack Obama represented a definitive, positive step forward for the nation overall. Black, biracial, middle-class, and born to an immigrant father, Obama was in many ways the face of the new America. He put forth a vision of a vibrant, multicultural nation that would embrace the full range of its diversity. There was something undeniably powerful about seeing Obama give his victory night speech in Chicago on November 4. It was almost unbelievable that a black man, and his black American family, would soon move into the White House and represent the United States to the world.

On that November day, Obama triumphantly declared that "at this defining moment . . . change has come to America." But three years out, many are asking what this really means. As president, Obama has faced strong criticism from both right and left. Throughout his term, many progressives have expressed disappointment about his timid or centrist stances on major political issues such as health care, the Afghan war, the environment, gay rights, financial reform, and race. As Eric Alterman wrote in *The Nation* on July 7, 2010, "If one examines the gamut of legislation passed and executive orders issued that relate to the promises made by candidate Obama, one can only wince at the slightly hyperbolic joke made by late night comedian Jimmy Fallon, who quipped that the president's goal appeared to be to 'finally deliver on the campaign promises made by John McCain.'" And in mid-2011, the Nobel Prize–winning economist and *New York Times* columnist Paul Krugman asked, "What have they done with President Obama? What happened to the inspirational figure his supporters thought they elected? Who is this bland, timid guy who doesn't seem to stand for anything in particular?"[25]

President Obama has generally not shown the kind of leadership in dealing with racial matters either. He has tended to shy away from discussions of race, and to declare accusations of racism made by his political allies (such as Jimmy Carter and Eric Holder) to be invalid. His infamous July 2009 "beer summit" read largely as an apology to white Americans for having raised the issue of institutional racism in a forceful manner.[26] In a late July 2010 address before the National Urban League, Obama urged Americans to discuss racial matters "around kitchen tables and water coolers and church basements." But he dismissed the idea of taking the discussions to a higher level, arguing that there was no need to have "a bunch of academic symposia or fancy commissions or panels."[27]

In chapter 3, I suggested that the new politics of race had the potential to evolve into a genuine racial dialogue. Such a dialogue would allow for an open exchange of ideas without demanding silence on issues of racial injustice. Currently, the "new racial calculus" seems instead to be functioning as a kind of straightjacket for the president. During his almost three years in office, Obama has failed to forward policies that would directly address the persistent problems of racial inequality, leading prominent black critics to charge that he has no agenda for black America. In April 2011, the black intellectual Cornel West, who had come to express *qualified* support for candidate Obama, declared that the president had become a "puppet" of powerful interests, a "black mascot" of Wall Street oligarchs, and "the friendly face of the American empire abroad."[28] Latino writers have been particularly vocal in their criticism of Obama's failure to comply with his promise to pursue comprehensive immigration reform. Some have argued that he has stepped up rates of arrest and detention—currently *higher* than rates during the Bush administration—in order to appease conservatives.[29] Obama has seemed at times to be more willing to let the reactionary right control the national dialogue on race than to take a firm stand himself.[30]

Barack Obama found a way of dealing with the issue of race in the United States that enabled him to ascend to the White House. This was a major accomplishment. But Obama's brand of racial politics becomes deeply problematic to the extent that it justifies heaping further scorn on the most economically and politically marginalized people of color; or that it requires upwardly mobile non-whites to join in the chorus of condemnation in exchange for integration and acceptance; or that it invalidates the pursuit of racial equality in fact rather than merely in principle. While Obama's successful campaign for the presidency was an important historical breakthrough, it certainly did not represent the nation's definitive triumph over the problems of race—not only because we are still profoundly unequal in many non-electoral domains (housing, education, criminal justice, wealth, etc.), but also because the way that race factored into Obama's own ascent was complicated and problematic. Barack Obama helped to create a space for new conceptions of national identity and a new kind of racial politics. But we must continue to push that space open much further.

Notes

NOTES TO CHAPTER 1

1. Schorn, "Transcript Excerpt," 2007.

2. Hu-DeHart, "21st-Century America," 2001; Omi, "Changing Meaning of Race," 2001; Winant, *New Politics of Race*, 2004.

3. Bobo, "Inequalities That Endure?," 2004; Essed, *Understanding Everyday Racism*, 1991; Trepagnier, *Silent Racism*, 2010; Picca & Feagin, *Two-Faced Racism*, 2007; Blauner, "Talking Past One Another," 1992; Bonilla-Silva, *White Supremacy and Racism*, 2001; Steinhorn & Diggs-Brown, *By the Color of Our Skin*, 2000.

4. Collins, *Black Feminist Thought*, 1990; Bhavnani, *Feminism and "Race,"* 2001; Breines, "Struggling to Connect," 2007.

5. Yancey, *Who Is White?*, 2003; Bonilla-Silva, "We Are All Americans!," 2002; O'Brien, *Racial Middle*, 2008; Perea, "Black/White Binary Paradigm of Race," 1997; Kim, "Racial Triangulation of Asian Americans," 1999; Davis, "American Dream Deferred," 2007; Gans, "Possibility of a New Racial Hierarchy in the 21st-Century United States," 1999.

6. Gillespie, *Whose Black Politics?* 2010; Pew Research Center, *Blacks See Growing Values Gap*, 2007; Cose, *Rage of a Privileged Class*, 1995; Lacy, *Blue-Chip Black*, 2007.

7. Chideya, "Nation of Minorities," 1999; Mills, *Arguing Immigration*, 1994; Stein, "Palin Explains What Parts of Country Not 'Pro-America,'" 2008.

8. Given the resurgence of strong anti-immigrant sentiment, Islamophobia, and the highly racialized imagery of the Tea Party movement in 2009/2010, we might also ask if racism is likely to become more blatant and overt. See Bonilla-Silva, *Racism without Racists*, 2010; Feagin, *Racist America*, 2000; Sniderman & Piazza, *Scar of Race*, 1993; Thernstrom & Thernstrom, *Beyond the Color Line*, 2002; and others for discussion of this last set of questions.

9. Crouch, "What Obama Isn't," 2006; Wallace-Wells, "Is America Too Racist for Barack?," 2006.

10. See Collins, "Toward a New Vision," 1993; Collins, *Black Feminist Thought*, 1990; Lourde, *Sister Outsider*, 1984; Bhavnani, *Feminism and "Race,"* 2001, Breines, "Struggling to Connect," 2007; for discussions of intersectionality.

11. Gallagher, "Introduction," 2008, p. ix; Bonilla-Silva, *Racism without Racists*, 2010, chapter 1.

12. Winant, *Racial Conditions*, 1994, p. 22.

13. Boger & Orfield, *School Resegregation*, 2005; Bonilla-Silva, *Racism without Racists*, 2010; Conley, *Being Black*, 2009; Dickerson & Jacobs, "Race Differentials in College Selectivity," 2006; Guinier & Torres, *Miner's Canary*, 2003; Herring, "Is Job

Discrimination Dead?," 2002; Johnson, *The American Dream and the Power of Wealth*, 2006; Roberts, *Shattered Bonds*, 2002; Krysan & Bader, "Perceiving the Metropolis," 2008; Massey, "Residential Segregation," 2000; Pager, "Mark of a Criminal Record," 2003; Powell, "Post-racialism or Targeted Universalism?," 2009.

14. Ngai, *Impossible Subjects*, 2004, p. 267; see also Davis, "American Dream Deferred," 2007; Lee, "American Gatekeeping," 2004; O'Brien, *Racial Middle*, 2008; Omi, "Changing Meaning of Race," 2001; Winant, *Racial Conditions*, 1994.

15. Brunsma, *Mixed Messages*, 2006; Butterfield, "We're Just Black," 2004; Daniel, *More Than Black?*, 2002; Waters, *Black Identities*, 1999; Winant, *Racial Conditions*, 1994.

16. Younger whites may feel especially anxious about racial identity in our current times. According to the Temple University sociologist Matt Wray, many white students believe that "to be white is to be culturally broke." "They might be privileged, they might be loaded socioeconomically," he continues, "but they feel bankrupt when it comes to culture" (quoted in Hsu, "End of White America?," 2009). As Jason Rodriguez states, for many white youth, "whiteness seems to provide very little substance on which to base an identity" ("Color-Blind Ideology," 2006, p. 646). According to Barbara Trepagnier (*Silent Racism*, 2010), even liberal whites, afraid to appear racist and yet unable to challenge the anti-black stereotypes that they and others hold, often end up "perpetuating the racial divide" through their passivity. On white racialization, see Hartmann, Gerteis, & Croll, "Empirical Assessment of Whiteness Theory," 2009; Twine & Gallagher, "Future of Whiteness," 2008; Winant, *Racial Conditions*, 1994; and dozens of other relevant cites.

17. Carrillo Rowe, "Whose 'America?,'" 2004; Frankenberg, "Mirage of Unmarked Whiteness," 2001; Gallagher, "Color-Blind Privilege," 2003.

18. Benjamin, *Searching for Whitopia*, 2009; Carrillo Rowe, "Whose 'America?,'" 2004; Hechtkopf, "Tom Tancredo Tea Party Speech," 2010; Hsu, "End of White America?," 2009; Rodriguez, "Color-Blind Ideology," 2006; Stein, "Palin Explains What Parts of Country Not 'Pro-America,'" 2008; Waters, *Ethnic Options*, 1990.

19. Ansell, "Casting a Blind Eye," 2006; Bonilla-Silva, *Racism without Racists*, 2010, Brown et al., *Whitewashing Race*, 2003; Frankenberg, "Mirage of Unmarked Whiteness," 2001; Gallagher, "Color-Blind Privilege," 2003; Powell, "Post-racialism or Targeted Universalism?," 2009.

20. Winant, *New Politics of Race*, 2004; *Racial Conditions*, 1994; and *The World Is a Ghetto*, 2001; Gallagher, "Color-Blind Privilege," 2003; Omi, "Changing Meaning of Race," 2001; Omi & Winant, *Racial Formation in the United States*, 1994, Feagin, *Racist America*, 2000; and *Systemic Racism*, 2006; Wingfield and Feagin, *Yes We Can?*, 2010; Bonilla-Silva, *Racism without Racists*, 2010; "Rethinking Racism," 1997; "We Are All Americans!," 2002; *White Supremacy and Racism*, 2001; and "From Bi-racial to Tri-racial," 2004; Bonilla-Silva and Ray, "When Whites Love a Black Leader," 2009; O'Brien, *Racial Middle*, 2008; Kim, "Imagining Race and Nation in Multiculturalist America," 2004; and "Racial Triangulation," 1999; Yancey, *Who Is White*, 2003; Gillespie, *Whose Black Politics?*, 2010.

21. For discussion of these controversies, see Robinson, "Pique and the Professor," 2009; Loury, "Obama, Gates, and the American Black Man," 2009; Washington, "Obama Takes a Stand on Race," 2009; Berger, "Tea Party Launches 'Counter-Revolution,'" 2010; Tubman, "Rotting Racist Underbelly of the Tea Party Protests," 2009;

Corley, "NAACP, Tea Party Volley over Racism Claims," 2010; Steele, "Sotomayor and the Politics of Race," 2009; Giroux, "Judge Sonia Sotomayor and the New Racism," 2009; Harshaw, "Sotomayor, Race, and the Right," 2009; Rich, "Rage Is Not about Health Care," 2010; and later chapters of this book.

22. More than 125 students between the ages of 18 and 29 were asked to discuss the roles of race and gender in the 2008 election and in the wider society. The questions asked pertained to reverse racism, colorblindness, patriotism, meanings of "blackness," and feminism. Though I quote from some of these interviews in the present book, the bulk of the analysis will be found in a separate study.

23. Bonilla-Silva, *Racism without Racists*, 2010; Carrillo Rowe, "Whose 'America?,'" 2004; Frankenberg, "Mirage of Unmarked Whiteness," 2001.

24. Bell & Hartmann, "Diversity in Everyday Discourse," 2007.

25. Kim, "Racial Triangulation of Asian Americans," 1999. The term "racial middle" comes from Eileen O'Brien's 2008 book of the same name.

NOTES TO CHAPTER 2

1. Ansell, "Casting a Blind Eye," 2006; Bonilla-Silva, *Racism without Racists*, 2010; and *White Supremacy and Racism*, 2001; Gallagher, "Colorblind Privilege," 2003; Guinier & Torres, *Miner's Canary*, 2003; Powell, "Post-racialism or Targeted Universalism?," 2009.

2. The most frequently referenced sources are listed in the introduction to this book. It is important to note that while many of these sources are considered to be more "liberal" in orientation, the narrative framing that predominated in media coverage of the election regarding racial matters was fundamentally neoconservative in orientation.

3. Coates, "Deeper Black," 2008; DiMaggio, "Transcending Race," 2008.

4. Kim, "Imagining Race and Nation in Multiculturalist America," 2004, p. 989.

5. Ansell, *New Right, New Racism*, 1997; Bonilla-Silva, *Racism without Racists*, 2010; Brown et al., *Whitewashing Race*, 2003; Carr, *"Color-Blind" Racism*, 1997; Gallagher, "Color-Blind Privilege," 2003; and "Introduction," 2008; Guinier & Torres, *Miner's Canary*, 2003; Winant, *World Is a Ghetto*, 2001.

6. Carr, *"Color-Blind" Racism*, 1997; Cochran, *Color of Freedom*, 1999. In July 2010, in fact, Senator James Webb (D-VA) published an op-ed piece in the *Wall Street Journal* calling for an end to race-based affirmative action; see "Diversity and the Myth of White Privilege," 2010.

7. Guinier & Torres, *Miner's Canary*, 2003. As Amy Ansell wrote in *New Right, New Racism*, 1997, p. 6, "The New Right has succeeded in setting the ideological agenda and influencing the development of government policy formation in a conservative direction. . . . Many counter-trends can be noted . . . but the manner in which the opposition expresses its voice is very much informed by the rightward lurch; people from all parts of the political spectrum are being forced to adapt or fail." Evidence of the continuing move to the right in the last decade alone includes the Supreme Court's severe restrictions on affirmative action policies in 2003, its 2007 ruling against school desegregation plans, and its 2009 narrowing of the provisions of the Voting Rights Act. Stephen

Steinberg writes that liberals began to retreat from a commitment to full racial equality as early as the late 1960s; see *Turning Back*, 1995.

    8.   Gallagher, "Color-Blind Privilege," 2003; Bonilla-Silva, *White Supremacy and Racism*, 2001; Winant, *The World Is a Ghetto*, 2001.

    9.   Ansell, "Casting a Blind Eye," 2006; Bonilla-Silva, *Racism without Racists*, 2010; and *White Supremacy and Racism*, 2001; Bobo, "The Color Line, the Dilemma, and the Dream," 1999; Frankenberg, "Mirage of Unmarked Whiteness," 2001; Frederickson, "Beyond Race?," 2001; Gallagher, "Color-Blind Privilege,"2003; Herring, "Is Job Discrimination Dead?," 2002; Lewis, "There Is No 'Race' in the Schoolyard," 2001; Lui, "Doubly Divided," 2004; Pager, "Mark of a Criminal Record," 2003; Picca & Feagin, *Two-Faced Racism*, 2007; Powell, "Post-racialism or Targeted Universalism?," 2009; Sweeney & González, "Affirmative Action Never Helped Me," 2008; Wingfield & Feagin, *Yes We Can?*, 2010.

    10.   Gallagher, "Colorblind Privilege," 2003, p. 22; see also Ansell, *New Right, New Racism*, 1997; Omi and Winant, *Racial Formation in the United States*, 1994, Steinberg, *Turning Back*, 1995. Winant's arguments can be found in *Racial Conditions*, 1994; *New Politics of Race*, 2001; and *The World Is a Ghetto*, 2004.

    11.   Ansell, "Casting a Blind Eye," 2006, p. 333.

    12.   I thank David Pellow for drawing these analogies.

    13.   Steele quoted in Weisman & Meckler, "Obama Sweeps to Historic Victory," 2008; Redenbaugh, "Barack Obama," 2008.

    14.   Carlson quoted in Kurtz, "When Journalism Turns Personal," 2008; Simon quoted in Hart, "Obamamania," 2007.

    15.   Keillor, "Wow! America Is Cool," 2008; Cain, "How Long Will the GOP Be in the Cold?," 2008.

    16.   Dyson, "Race, Post Race," 2008; Bacon, "Election Underscores New Hope for a Colorblind Society," 2008.

    17.   Connerly quoted in Williams & Negrin, "Affirmative Action Foes Point to Obama," 2008; Page, "Jackson's Eloquent Tears," 2008.

    18.   Morris, "America Begins Its Journey into a Post-racial Era," 2008.

    19.   Bykofsky, "My First Post-racial Column," 2008. In a particularly perverse celebration of Obama's win, Bykofsky continued, "America is like a big college fraternity. When new 'pledges' come along, whether from Senegal or South America, they get hazed. I don't like it, I wish it weren't so, but it is. 'Outsiders' *everywhere* get the short end of the stick until they 'prove' themselves. In many countries they never can. In America, they can. Barack Obama just did." Thus slavery, lynching, Jim Crow, and other dimensions of black oppression were rendered natural if unpleasant rites of passage, things that all "newcomers" should reasonably expect to go through.

    20.   "President Elect Obama," 2008.

    21.   George Will cited in Younge, "An Obama Victory Would Symbolise a Great Deal and Change Very Little," 2008; *New Republic* quote found in Peretz, "Barack Obama," 2008. For other repudiations of the black political "old guard," see also "O'Reilly to 'Race Hustlers' and 'Race-Baiters,'" 2008; Huston, "AP Finds Race Hustler to Say Obama Isn't the Cure," 2008; McWhorter, "ObamaKids," 2008; Taylor, "Great Black-White Hope," 2007.

    22.   Elder, "Obama or Not, America Still a 'Racist Nation,'" 2008; Williams, "What Obama's Victory Means for Racial Politics," 2008.

23. Steyn, "Post 'Post-Racial Candidate,'" 2008.
24. Obama, "A More Perfect Union," 2008; Tapper, "Wright Assails Media, Cheney, Obama," 2008.
25. "Mr. Obama and Rev. Wright," 2008.
26. For positive and negative assessment of the personal responsibility rhetoric, see Tilove, "'Pookie' Keeps Popping Up in Obama's Speeches," 2008; Bosman, "Obama Sharply Assails Absent Black Fathers," 2008; Page, "Obama to NAACP," 2008; Coates, "This is How We Lost to the White Man," 2008; Schaeffer, "Jesse Jackson Just Handed the White House to Obama," 2008; Olopade, "Father 'Hood," 2008; Walsh, "Obama on Father's Day," 2008; Gray, "Why Does Barack Obama Hate My Family?," 2008; Ford, "Obama Insults Half A Race," 2008.
27. Raspberry, "Path beyond Grievance," 2008; Taylor, "Great Black-White Hope," 2007; Williams, "What Obama's Victory Means for Racial Politics," 2008.
28. Barras, "He Leapt the Tallest Barrier," 2008; Graves, "No More Excuses," 2008; Neiwert, "Bill Bennett," 2008; Blow, "No More Excuses?," 2009; Branch-Brioso & Roach, "With Nation's New President, Promise and 'No Excuses' for Black Students," 2009; Holcomb, "Smith: Obama Sets Bar High," 2009; Williams, "After Obama, No Excuses," 2009.
29. Kaufman & Fields, "Election of Obama Recasts National Conversation on Race," 2008; Merida, "America's History Gives Way to Its Future," 2008; Vennochi, "Closing the Door on Victimhood," 2008.
30. Winant, *The World Is a Ghetto*, 2001, p. 175.
31. Coates, "This Is How We Lost to the White Man," 2008; Lacy, *Blue-Chip Black*, 2007; Feagin & Sikes, *Living with Racism*, 1994; Cose, *Rage of a Privileged Class*, 1995.
32. The importance of redemption and renewal as themes of Obama's campaign narrative is explored further in chapter 5, "The Trope of Race in Obama's America." I argue that the campaign consistently relied on civil rights imagery to present Obama's race for the White House as a 21st-century movement for racial justice and national unity, and as the definitive fulfillment of Martin Luther King's dream.
33. See further discussion of race-based attacks in chapters 4 and 7 of the present book. In focusing on the appeal of Obama's race, my approach is quite different from that taken by Wingfield and Feagin in *Yes We Can?*, 2010. These authors highlight instances of racist opposition to Obama's candidacy to explain how race mattered to white voters.
34. Wallace-Wells, "Is America Too Racist for Barack?," 2006.
35. Steele, "Obama's Post-racial Promise," 2008; Steele, "Obama Bargain," 2008.
36. Hsu, "End of White America?," 2009; Walker, "Whassup, Barbie?," 2003; Steele, "Obama's Post-racial Promise," 2008; Kamiya, "It's OK to Vote for Obama Because He's Black," 2008.
37. Hart, "Obamamania," 2007.
38. See Mabry, "Color Test," 2008; Lilpop, "Is Black Racism Obama's Greatest Advantage?," 2008.
39. Kim, "Imagining Race and Nation in Multiculturalist America," 2004.
40. Snell, *Capital Punishment*, 2009; Pager, "Mark of a Criminal Record," 2003; Massey, "Residential Segregation and Neighborhood Conditions in U.S. Metropolitan Areas," 2000; Bond & Williams, "Residential Segregation and the Transformation of Home Mortgage Lending," 2007.

41. Boger & Orfield, *School Resegregation*, 2005; Kozol, *The Shame of the Nation*, 2005; Schott Foundation, *Yes We Can*, 2010; Edelman, Holzer, & Offner, *Reconnecting Disadvantaged Young Men*, 2006. For other cites on the educational outcomes of students of color, see Harris, Trujillo, and Jamison, "Academic Outcomes among Latino/a and Asian Americans," 2008; Hausmann et al., "Sense of Belonging and Persistence," 2009; Lee, "From Du Bois to Obama," 2009.

42. Income refers primarily to wages or salary. Wealth is defined as homes, commercial real estate, other land, stocks, bonds, savings—that is, one's net worth. Whites are estimated to take in twice the income of blacks on average. See Barsky et al., "Accounting for the Black-White Wealth Gap," 2002; Lui, "Doubly Divided," 2004; Oliver & Shapiro, *Black Wealth/White Wealth*, 2006.

43. Conley, *Being Black, Living in the Red*, 2009; Johnson, *The American Dream and the Power of Wealth*, 2006; Lui, "Doubly Divided," 2004; Lui et al., *Color of Wealth*, 2006; Oliver & Shapiro, *Black Wealth/White Wealth*, 2006.

44. Tate, "Political Representation of Blacks in Congress," 2001; Herring, "Is Job Discrimination Dead?," 2002.

45. See Carroll, "Behind the Scenes," 2008; Chude-Sokei, "Redefining 'Black,'" 2007; Coates, "Is Obama Black Enough?," 2007; Crouch, "What Obama Isn't," 2006; Dickerson, "Colorblind," 2007; Sarmah, "Is Obama Black Enough?," 2007; Younge, "Is Obama Black Enough?," 2007. Also see my discussion of the "black enough" debate, and other questionings of Obama's racial authenticity, in chapter 6 of this book.

46. Kozol, *The Shame of the Nation*, 2005.

47. Waters, "Intersection of Gender, Race, and Ethnicity," 1996; and *Black Identities*, 1999; Herring, "Is Job Discrimination Dead?," 2002; Vickerman, "Jamaicans," 2001.

48. Waters, *Black Identities*, 1999; Scheiber, "Race against History," 2004; Bonilla-Silva & Ray, "When Whites Love a Black Leader," 2009.

49. Keith & Herring, "Skin Tone and Stratification in the Black Community," 1991; Hochschild & Weaver, "The Skin Color Paradox and the American Racial Order," 2007, pp. 9–10.

50. See, for example, D. G., "Does 'Postracial' Just Mean Light-Skinned?," 2008.

51. Matthews quoted in Williams, "Obama's Color Line," 2007.

52. Grossman quoted in Dedman, "Historians' Write 1st Draft on Obama Victory," 2008.

53. Of the Democratic presidential candidates since 1972, Obama was eclipsed only by Jimmy Carter, who gained 47% of whites in 1976. See "National Exit Polls Table," 2008. Obama won 53% of the popular vote overall, compared to Johnson's 61% against Barry Goldwater. He also won 95% of blacks (who made up 12% of the electorate) and 67% of Latinos (7.5% of all voters). See also Lopez & Taylor, "Dissecting the 2008 Electorate," 2009. For further discussion of the importance of voters of color in the 2008 race, see chapter 6.

54. Omi, "Changing Meaning of Race," 2001.

NOTES TO CHAPTER 3

1. He has also said that he is "not limited *by*," or "not *defined by*," the black community (emphasis mine). See Obama's 2004 interview with the *Washington Post*

reporter Mark Leibovich ("The Other Man of the Hour") and his 2007 *60 Minutes* interview with Steve Kroft (Schorn, "Transcript Excerpt," 2007).

2. Extended discussion of the "next generation" of African American political leaders is found in Bai, "Is Obama the End of Black Politics?," 2008; Barras, "He Leapt the Tallest Barrier," 2008; Boyer, "Color of Politics," 2008; Cohen, "Obama's Path to Power Typical of New Generation of Black Political Leaders," 2007; Freedman, "After Obama Victory, Test for the Black Clergy," 2008; Harris, "Young, Gifted, Black," 2008; MacGillis & Bacon, "Obama Rises in New Era of Black Politicians," 2007; Moynihan, "Transformation on Race," 2008; Remnick, "Joshua Generation," 2008; Samuel, "Young, Black, and Post–Civil Rights," 2007; Smith, "New Generation of Black Leaders Emerging," 2008; Younge, "Obama Effect," 2007; and the collection of essays found in *Whose Black Politics?*, 2010, edited by Andra Gillespie. See especially the important article "The 'Steele Problem' and the New Republican Battle for Black Votes" by Tyson King-Meadows, which appears in the Gillespie volume.

3. Will, "Misreading Obama's Identity," 2007; Steele, "Identity Card," 2007; Sullivan, "Jackson vs. Obama," 2007.

4. Lochhead, "Obama's Candidacy Shakes Up Racial Politics," 2008.

5. Simply consider the title of Matt Bai's 2008 *New York Times Magazine* article, "Is Obama the End of Black Politics?"

6. Obama, "Election Night," 2008.

7. Dawson, *Behind the Mule*, 1994; and *Black Visions*, 2001; Walters, *African American Leadership*, 1999; and *Freedom Is Not Enough*, 2005; Persons, *Dilemmas of Black Politics*, 1993; Perry, *Blacks and the American Political System*, 1995; and *Race, Governance, and Politics in the United States*, 1996; Gillespie, *Whose Black Politics?*, 2010.

8. McCormick & Jones, "Conceptualization of Deracialization," 1993, p. 76.

9. Orey, "Deracialization or Racialization," 2006, p. 816.

10. See, for example, the collection of essays in Gillespie, *Whose Black Politics?*, 2010.

11. "President-Elect Obama," 2008.

12. See Steele, *A Bound Man*, 2007; "Identity Card," 2007; "Obama Bargain," 2008; "Obama's Post-racial Promise," 2008; and "Sotomayor and the Politics of Race," 2009.

13. Steele, "Identity Card," 2007.

14. Steele, "Sotomayor and the Politics of Race," 2009.

15. Bonilla-Silva, *White Supremacy and Racism*, 2001; and *Racism without Racists*, 2010; Guinier & Torres, *Miner's Canary*, 2003; Gallagher, "Color-Blind Privilege," 2003, Carr, *"Color-Blind" Racism*, 1997; Winant, *The World Is a Ghetto*, 2001.

16. Powell, "Post-racialism or Targeted Universalism?," 2009.

17. D'Souza, *End of Racism*, 1995; Gallagher, "Color-Blind Privilege," 2003.

18. Bonilla-Silva, *White Supremacy and Racism*, 2001.

19. Elder, *Ten Things You Can't Say in America*, 2000; Prelutsky, "Black Racism," 2007; McWhorter, *Losing the Race*, 2000; Will, "Misreading Obama's Identity," 2007; Kamiya, "Is Race Dying?," 2007; Raspberry, "Path beyond Grievance," 2008.

20. It is *not*, therefore, a pact between the white mainstream and the black poor, who appear as objects, rather than subjects, of the new race politics.

21. This typology is not set in stone and is likely to evolve as new political developments emerge, perhaps during the 2012 presidential race.

22. Patrick quoted in MacGillis & Bacon, "Obama Rises in New Era of Black Politicians," 2007.

23. Mabry, "Color Test," 2008.

24. Thernstrom, "Subtle, Serious, Patriotic," 2008.

25. Moynihan, "Transformation on Race," 2008; Williams, "What Obama's Victory Means for Racial Politics," 2008; Barras, "He Leapt the Tallest Barrier," 2008; Raspberry, "Path beyond Grievance," 2008; Narcisse, "New Agenda for Black America?," 2008; Kessler, "Obama Encourages Black Victimhood," 2008.

26. McWhorter, *Losing the Race*, 2000; Will, "Misreading Obama's Identity," 2007; Kamiya, "Is Race Dying?," 2007; Raspberry, "Path beyond Grievance," 2008.

27. Moynihan, "Transformation on Race," 2008; Williams, "What Obama's Victory Means for Racial Politics," 2008; Kirsanow, "Obama and the Aspirations of Black Kids," 2009.

28. Coates, "More Dumb Questions about Barack Obama and Black Folks," 2008. See also Adam Serwer's very insightful article "He's Black, Get over It," 2008.

29. Obama, "Selma Voting Rights March Commemoration," 2007.

30. Obama, "A More Perfect Union," 2008; Obama, "Election Night," 2008.

31. Orr, "Jimmy Carter Racism Charge," 2009.

32. Cooper, "Attorney General Chided for Language on Race," 2009.

33. Elder, *Ten Things You Can't Say in America*, 2000; D'Souza, *End of Racism*, 1995; Taylor, "Racism Marginalized," 2008; Gallagher, "Color-Blind Privilege," 2003; Mac Donald, "Promoting Racial Paranoia," 2009; Prelutsky, "Black Racism," 2007.

34. Bonilla-Silva, *Racism without Racists*, 2010; Carr, *"Color-Blind" Racism*, 1997.

35. Such condemnations were an important aspect of the *Tyra Banks Show*, for example. Banks frequently featured white and non-white guests who opposed interracial dating (ostensibly for equivalent reasons) while audience members shook their heads in disgust. Other aspects of Banks as a "post-racial" figure are discussed in Joseph, "Tyra Banks Is Fat," 2009.

36. Rasmussen, "Only 22% Say McCain Ad Racist," 2008.

37. Gandelman, "Rasmussen Poll," 2008.

38. Pew Research Center, *Obama's Ratings Slide across the Board*, 2009.

39. Erbe, "Obama's Henry Louis Gates Arrest Comment," 2009; Calderone, "Fox's Beck," 2009; Caddell and Schoen, "Our Divisive President," 2010.

40. Powell, "Post-racialism or Targeted Universalism?," 2009; Frankenburg, "Mirage of an Unmarked Whiteness," 2001.

41. See Bill O'Reilly, Larry Elder, Stuart Taylor, and others for such statements during the 2008 election. Specific cites found in Malkin, "Michelle Obama's America," 2008; and D'Souza, *End of Racism*, 1995.

42. Beinart, "Black Like Me," 2007. Andrews and Hartmann have made similar points about "good" and "bad" blacks in sports; see Andrews, "Fact(s) of Michael Jordan's Blackness," 1996; Hartmann, "Bound by Blackness or Above It?," 2006.

43. Salant, "Jackson's 'Crude' Remarks May Give Boost to Obama," 2008; Obama, "Selma Voting Rights March Commemoration," 2007.

44. Sullivan, "Jackson vs. Obama," 2007.

45. Samuel, "Young, Black, and Post–Civil Rights," 2007.

46. Barras, "He Leapt the Tallest Barrier," 2008. Typifying the "anti-grievance" rhetoric that was heard throughout the campaign, Barras continued, "Some African Americans don't get it. Despite measurable advances over the past 30 years, they still perceive themselves as beleaguered, as the once and present victims of discrimination, struggling to keep pace with their white counterparts. This portrait of a currently besieged people is mostly fiction."

47. Younge, "Obama Effect," 2007.

48. Bonilla-Silva, *Racism without Racists*, 2010.

49. As the columnist Burt Prelutsky wrote on the conservative website Townhall.com ("Black Racism," 2007), "When we finally stop patronizing loafers, louts and criminals, stop encouraging people who were born 120 years after the Emancipation Proclamation, 20 years after the passage of the Civil Rights Act, to pretend that their sloth and ignorance are the fault of whites, only then will blacks come one step closer to having that colorblind society they claim they want."

50. Tilove, "'Pookie' Keeps Popping up in Obama's Speeches," 2008.

51. Obama, "Text of Obama's Fatherhood Speech," 2008.

52. Amira, "Obama's Tough Talk on African-American Fathers," 2008; Olopade, "Father 'Hood," 2008.

53. Gray, "Why Does Barack Obama Hate My Family?," 2008; Reed, "Obama No," 2008. See also Ford, "Obama Insults Half a Race," 2008.

54. As one journalist wrote of the next generation, "They are just as likely to see themselves as ambassadors *to* the black community as they are to see themselves as spokesmen for it." Bai, "Is Obama the End of Black Politics?," 2008.

55. McCormick & Jones, "Conceptualization of Deracialization," 1993.

56. Powell, "Post-racialism or Targeted Universalism?," 2009; Guinier & Torres, *Miner's Canary*, 2003.

57. Carr, *"Color-Blind" Racism*, 1997.

58. Quotes from Byrne, "Time to Give Race a Respite," 2008; and Williams & Negrin, "Affirmative Action Foes Point to Obama," 2008. See also Babington, "Might Obama's Success Undercut Affirmative Action?," 2008; Eubanks, "Affirmative Action and After," 2009; Connerly, "Triumph of Principle over Color," 2008; Kahlenberg, "Barack Obama and Affirmative Action," 2008; and "What's Next for Affirmative Action?," 2008; Kuhn, "Obama Shifts Affirmative Action Rhetoric," 2008; Price, "Obama Victory," 2008; Lithwick, "Shades of Gray," 2008; Melber, "Obama, Race, and the Presidency," 2008; Robinson, "Obama Opens Debate on Affirmative Action," 2007; Swarns, "Delicate Obama Path on Class and Race Preferences," 2008; Wooten, "Obama and Race Preferences," 2008.

59. Robinson, "Obama Opens Debate on Affirmative Action," 2007; Lithwick, "Shades of Gray," 2008.

60. Ansell, *New Right, New Racism*, 1997; Bonilla-Silva, *Racism without Racists*, 2010; Carr, *"Color-Blind" Racism*, 1997; Cochran, *Color of Freedom*, 1999; Gallagher, "Color-Blind Privilege," 2003; Omi, "Changing Meaning of Race," 2001; Webb, "Diversity and the Myth of White Privilege," 2010.

61. Klein & Williams, "Obama's Silence on Imus Alarms Some Blacks," 2007; Liss, "Report: Jesse Jackson Says Barack Obama 'Acting White,'" 2007; Zeleny, "Obama and Clinton Statements on Police Trial," 2008.

62. West stated, "I want to know, how deep is your love for the people? What kind of courage have you manifested in the stances that you have? . . . You can't take black people for granted just because you're black. . . . We've got a lot of these candidates running, and they are characterized by unadulterated mediocrity. . . . He's got to be accountable." See "Cornell West on Barack Obama" video at on YouTube at http:// www.youtube.com/watch?v=HXj3_pjTTwg (accessed January 12, 2011). Though Obama was again absent from the State of the Black Union in 2008, his democratic rival Hillary Clinton did attend the event that year.

63. Will, "Misreading Obama's Identity," 2007; Koppelman, "Bill Bennett Knows Black People," 2008.

64. Luqman, "Obama's Tightrope," 2007.

65. It has also been a key component of Oprah Winfrey and Michael Jordan's presentations of self. For discussion of Jordan's Americanism, see Kellner, "Sports Spectacle, Michael Jordan, and Nike," 2004.

66. Buchanan, "Brief for Whitey," 2008; Limbaugh, "Michelle Obama Slams America," 2008; Parker, Sawyer, & Towler, "A Black Man in the White House?," 2009.

67. Newton-Small, "Obama's Flag Pin Flip-Flop?," 2008; Oinounou & Kapp, "Michelle Obama Takes Heat," 2008; Martin, "The Full Story behind Wright's 'God Damn America' Sermon," 2008; Ross and Rehag, "Obama's Pastor," 2008. Michelle Obama was widely criticized for her February 2008 claim to be "really proud of my country" for "the first time in my adult life." See Oinounou & Kapp, "Michelle Obama Takes Heat," 2008; Prelutsky, "Obama," 2008. As one commentator bitterly opined, "Compared to the eloquent grace of Jackie Kennedy, Nancy Reagan, Barbara Bush and yes, even Rosalind Carter, she portrays herself as just another angry black harridan who spits in the face of the nation that made her rich, famous and prestigious. The dichotomy and depth of loathing is stunning." Massie, "Michelle Obama," 2008.

68. Huntington, "The Insider," 2003.

69. I discuss McCain/Palin's "real America" narrative and the defense of the white nation in chapter 7.

70. Martin & Smith, "Obama's Apple Pie Campaign," 2008.

71. Traub, "Is (His) Biography (Our) Destiny?," 2007.

72. Obama, "Keynote Address," 2004.

73. Gallagher, "Color-Blind Privilege," 2003; Rodriguez, "Color-Blind Ideology," 2006.

74. As one young black writer (Coates, "Deeper Black," 2008) stated admiringly in *The Nation*:

> When Obama greets his political allies . . . he offers the sort of dap—a little English in the wrist and a one-armed hug—that black males spend much of their adolescence perfecting. If elected, surely Obama will be the first President to greet foreign dignitaries with a pound. Obama warms up on election morning not by running a three-miler or swimming laps but by shooting hoops. The Illinois senator sports a flawless and ever-fresh Caesar demonstrative of the razorwork native to only one side of the tracks. Think Jay-Z—"I'm not looking at you dudes/I'm looking past you"—not Jay Rockefeller.

75. Obama, "A More Perfect Union," 2008. Wright, Obama's pastor for over 20 years, had sharply criticized the racism and imperialism of the United States in a series of taped sermons that surfaced during the campaign. His most controversial statement was that God (should or would) "damn America" "for killing innocent people . . . for treating our citizens as less than human . . . for as long as she acts like she is God and she is supreme." Martin, "The Full Story behind Wright's 'God Damn America' Sermon," 2008.

76. See Bonilla-Silva & Ray, "When Whites Love a Black Leader," 2009; Street, *Barack Obama and the Future of American Politics*, 2009; Wise, *Colorblind*, 2010. Wingfield and Feagin, however, offer an analysis similar to mine. The authors believe that Obama speaks courageously about race in certain parts of the speech but in others "retreats" into what they call "the white racial frame"; see *Yes We Can?*, 2010.

77. Obama, "A More Perfect Union," 2008.

78. Conniff, "Jeremiah Wright's Bombshell," 2008; Tapper, "Wright Assails Media," 2008.

79. See, for example, Bevan, "Ballentine's Racist Attack on Juan Williams," 2009.

80. Bonilla-Silva & Ray, "When Whites Love a Black Leader," 2009.

81. Walker, "Whassup, Barbie?," 2003; Hsu, "End of White America?," 2009; Rodriguez, "Color-Blind Ideology," 2006; Ehrenstein, "Obama the 'Magic Negro,'" 2007; Steele, "Obama Bargain," 2008; Hart, "Obamamania," 2007.

82. As discussed by Winant, *Racial Conditions*, 1994; and *The World Is a Ghetto*, 2001; Hsu, "End of White America?," 2009; and others, such anxieties include a perceived loss of power, influence, and relevance, being outnumbered demographically, feeling materially disadvantaged, victimized, culturally bereft, and without a clear sense of identity.

83. Kamiya, "'It's OK to Vote for Obama Because He's Black,'" 2008.

84. Omi & Winant, *Racial Formation in the United States*, 1994; Steinberg, *Turning Back*, 1995; Ansell, *New Right, New Racism*, 1997. In this perspective, equality is defined as abstract or formal equality, rather than as equality of results or outcome. See Ansell, "Casting a Blind Eye," 2006; Lewis, "There Is No 'Race' in the Schoolyard," 2001; Powell, "Post-racialism or Targeted Universalism?," 2009. The proper role of the state is (or was) to remove overt or explicit references to race from the law and public policy. However—especially in the neoconservative paradigm—doing anything more (to address inequalities created by past discrimination or by the covert mechanisms of discrimination that persist today) is viewed as illegitimate and unfair to whites.

85. Ansell, *New Right, New Racism*, 1997; Steinberg, *Turning Back*, 1995, p. 107.

86. Omi, "Changing Meaning of Race," 2001; Winant, *New Politics of Race*, 2004.

87. Ansell, "Casting a Blind Eye," 2006, p. 352; see also Winant, *The World Is a Ghetto*, 2001; Frederickson, "Beyond Race?," 2001; Logan, "El apóstol y el comandante en jefe," 1999; Bonilla-Silva, "Rethinking Racism," 1997.

88. "Yet," the article continued, "it was precisely the American longing for post-racialism—relief from this sort of racial calculating—that lifted Mr. Obama into office." Steele, "Sotomayor and the Politics of Race," 2009.

89. Bell & Hartmann, "Diversity in Everyday Discourse," 2007; Gallagher, "Color-Blind Privilege," 2003; Rodriguez, "Color-Blind Ideology," 2006; Lewis, "There Is No 'Race' in the Schoolyard," 2001.

90. Erbe, "Obama's Henry Louis Gates Arrest Comment," 2009; Pew Research Center, *Obama's Ratings Slide across the Board*, 2009; Rasmussen Reports, "Only 22% Say McCain Ad Racist," 2008; Steele, "Sotomayor and the Politics of Race," 2009.

91. Cesa, "Fooled Again by Breitbart and the Wingnut Right," 2010; Blow, "No More Excuses?," 2009; Edney, "Obama Needs Race Staff in the White House," 2010.

92. Consider the controversies involving Professor Henry Louis Gates Jr. (which prompted Obama to call a conciliatory "beer summit"), Attorney General Eric Holder, and former president Jimmy Carter, as discussed above. For a more recent example, consider the reaction to the NAACP's July 2010 call for the "Tea Party" movement to renounce racism in its ranks, which led some conservatives to counter that the NAACP was itself a racist organization. See Orr, "Jimmy Carter Racism Charge," 2009; Cooper, "Attorney General Chided for Language on Race," 2009; Blow, "No More Excuses?," 2009; Corley, "NAACP, Tea Party Volley over Racism Claims," 2010.

93. Serwer, "Obama's Racial Catch-22," 2008; Blow, "Obama's Race War," 2010.

94. See Thompson, "Activist Al Sharpton Takes on New Role as Administration Ally," 2010; Wallsten, "Obama's New Partner," 2010; Washington, "Obama Carefully Courts Black Votes With Sharpton," 2011.

95. Here I refer to the manifestations of overt anti-black racism by members of the Tea Party, Republican attempts to revise the 14th Amendment to deny citizenship rights to children born in the United States to noncitizen parents, Arizona's repressive anti-immigration law, and widespread protests against the building of an Islamic cultural center near the site of the 9/11 attacks in New York.

NOTES TO CHAPTER 4

1. Bonilla-Silva, *Racism without Racists*, 2010; Frankenberg, "Mirage of an Unmarked Whiteness," 2001.

2. English, "Diversity Bloc Is Divided," 2008.

3. Steinem, "Women Are Never Front-Runners," 2008; Morgan, "Goodbye to All That (#2)," 2008; Feldt, "Why Women Need to Learn History's Election Power Lesson," 2008.

4. Stan, "The Feminist Case for Obama," 2008; Darko, "Race Trumps Gender Theme," 2008; Martin, "More Than a Mother-Daughter Debate," 2008.

5. Bravo, "Why So Many Feminists Are Deciding to Vote for Barack Obama," 2008; O'Rourke, "Death of a Saleswoman," 2008; Kissling, "Why I'm Still Not for Hillary Clinton," 2008; Douglass, "Why Women Hate Hillary," 2008.

6. Traister, "Hey, Obama Boys," 2008.

7. Martin, "Dear Hillary," 2008.

8. See, for example, Breines, "Struggling to Connect," 2007; Collins, *Black Feminist Thought*, 1990; Lourde, *Sister Outsider*, 1984; Bhavnani, *Feminism and "Race*," 2001; Hull, Scott, & Smith, *All the Women Are White*, 1982; Baca Zinn & Dill, "Theorizing Difference," 1996; hooks, *Ain't I A Woman?*, 1981.

9. See Saslow, "To Women, So Much More Than Just a Candidate," 2008.

10. McLarin, "Family Fight," 2008.

11. Hirshman, "Looking Forward, Feminism Needs to Focus," 2008.

12. Jill, "Has Feminism Lost Its Focus?," 2008; Brownfemipower, "OOOh, Look a Thoughtful Intelligent Analysis of Intersectionality!," 2008. See also Ashley, "This Just In!," 2008; and Donna, "White Women Feminism," 2008, responding to Saslow's article, cited above.

13. Reed, "Race to the Bottom," 2008.

14. Rikyrah, "When It Comes to Michelle Obama," 2008; see also Curtis, "Loud Silence of Feminists," 2008. For an exception, see "Michelle Obama, Radically Awesome," 2008, in which Alexa Stanard elegizes the candidate's wife as "girl-crush inducing," "razor-sharp brilliant," and an icon "of badass womanhood."

15. Mitchell, "Full Transcript of Hillary Claiming Sexism Worse Than Racism," 2008; Long, "Painful Lessons," 2008; Steinem, "Women Are Never Front-Runners," 2008. Long was no Obama fan—in a July 25, 2008, blog post ("Obama Is a Megalomaniac"), she described Obama as a "megalomaniac," not unlike "serial killers," "dictators," "fundamentalists," and "genocidal maniacs" such as Adolf Hitler.

16. Fang, "Pitting Race against Gender in Election '08," 2008.

17. "Morning in America," 2008.

18. See, for example, comments by the blogger Donna Darko: "There was sexism in the campaign but also racism. yeah but there was a helluva lot more sexism in the campaign than racism. . . . Sexism gave Obama the nomination and race was only used to his advantage" ("Race Trumps Gender Theme," 2008).

19. Wise, "Your Whiteness Is Showing," 2008.

20. From mid-September 2008 through the morning of the general election, my research team and I conducted more than 125 in-depth interviews with undergraduates about the roles of race and gender in the 2008 presidential election. This study generated tremendous interest on the part of the students we spoke to. We achieved remarkable depth with regard to the racial diversity of those interviewed (more than half of whom were non-white), which was a key goal of the sampling strategy. This chapter draws on responses to a small subset of the questions that were asked. Detailed discussion of sample design and data collection, as well as a more extensive analysis of the interviews, will be found in future publications.

21. Winant, *Racial Conditions*, 1994, p. 23.

22. Wallace-Wells, "Is America Too Racist for Barack?," 2006.

23. Consider, for example, the degree of offense taken by someone who is accused of being "racist" compared to being called "sexist." Scholars have argued, however, that there is a critical distinction between being non-racist (i.e., having a commitment to the abstract ideals of equality, tolerance, and colorblindness) and being truly anti-racist (i.e., actively working against racial injustice). In fact, sociologists of race have found that adherence to the "non-racist" ideal of "colorblindness"—in the context in which this term is understood today—ironically prevents many whites from acknowledging the privileges they receive and how they themselves may be helping to reproduce racial inequality. On the ideology of racial colorblindness, see Bonilla-Silva, *White Supremacy and Racism*, 2001; and "'New Racism,' Color-Blind Racism, and the Future of Whiteness in America," 2003; Gallagher, "Color-Blind Privilege," 2003; Carr, *"Color-Blind" Racism*, 1997; Guinier & Torres, *Miner's Canary*, 2003; and chapter 2 of this book. On the distinction between non-racism and anti-racism, see O'Brien, "The Personal Is Political," 2003; Trepagnier, *Silent Racism*, 2010.

24. These ideas are explored further in chapter 3 of this book, which focuses on post-racialism and the "new politics of race."

25. Kamiya, "It's OK to Vote for Obama Because He's Black," 2008.

26. Limbaugh, "Does Our Looks-Obsessed Culture Want to Stare at an Aging Woman?," 2007; "Limbaugh: '[A] Lot of These Feminists and Women,'" 2008.

27. Givhan, "Hillary Clinton's Tentative Dip into New Neckline Territory," 2007.

28. Vennochi, "That Clinton Cackle," 2007; Achenbach, "End of the Clinton Era?," 2008; Fox News quoted in Wakeman, "Misogyny's Greatest Hits," 2008.

29. Venezia, "Nut Buster," 2007; Carlson quoted in Wakeman, "Misogyny's Greatest Hits," 2008; Linkins, "MSNBC Hosts Founder of Anti-Hillary Group 'C.U.N.T.,'" 2008.

30. See Breslau, "Hillary Tears Up," 2008, for a report of Clinton's display of emotion. Others responded quite differently to "Hillary's misty moment." Some were moved by her display of emotion. Others rallied to Clinton's defense not because of her tears, but because of the way she was subsequently ridiculed in the conservative and liberal media. See Traister, *Big Girls Don't Cry*, 2010, pp. 93–97. I thank the anonymous NYU Press reviewer for urging me to clarify this point.

31. Traister, *Big Girls Don't Cry*, 2010, p. 91.

32. See references to "dog whistle" racism during the Democratic primary in Cohn, "Why Obama Should Ignore Ferraro," 2008; Neiwert, "Blowing the Dog Whistle," 2008; Calabresi, "Obama's 'Electability' Code for Race?," 2008; Spaulding, "White Dog Whistles No More," 2008; Conason, "Was Hillary Channeling George Wallace?," 2008.

33. See discussion of the use of racial code words in post–civil rights politics in Sears et al., "Is It Really Racism?," 1997; Bonilla-Silva, *Racism without Racists*, 2010; Yetman, *Majority and Minority*, 1998.

34. The remark paraphrased above did lead Keith Olbermann to deliver a very angry "Special Comment" on May 23. The transcript, posted to the MSNBC website, is titled "Clinton, You Invoked a Political Nightmare: Referencing RFK's Assassination as a Reason for Staying in the Race Is Unforgiveable," 2008.

35. Morris, "How Clinton Will Win the Nomination by Losing S.C.," 2008.

36. Morrison, "Comment," 1998.

37. Samuel, "Young, Black, and Post-Civil Rights," 2007.

38. See Huddy & Terkildsen, "Consequences of Gender Stereotypes," 1993; Kelly & Duerst-Lahti, "Study of Gender Power," 1995; Johnson, *Gender Knot*, 1997; Witt, Paget, & Matthews, *Running as a Woman*, 1994.

39. Forrest & Foster, "25 Beautiful People," 2006.

40. Shiver, "Women Voters and the Obama Crush," 2008; Allen, "We Scream, We Swoon, How Dumb Can We Get?," 2008.

41. Woods, "Bringing Sexy Back," 2008; "Chris Matthews: 'I Felt This Thrill Going Up My Leg' as Obama Spoke," 2008.

42. "Rove: Obama Is the Type of Guy Who Hangs Out at Country Clubs," 2008.

43. See Huddy & Terkildsen, "Consequences of Gender Stereotypes," 1993.

44. For feminist disdain of Palin, see Goldberg, "Flirting Her Way to Victory," 2008; Muskal, "Steinem Criticizes Palin for Using Feminist Brand," 2010; Steinem, "Wrong Woman, Wrong Message," 2008; Traister, "Zombie Feminists of the RNC,"

2008; Valenti, "Sarah Palin's 'Feminism' Is Irrelevant to Her Irresponsible Record," 2008; Young, "Why Feminists Hate Sarah Palin," 2008.

45. For views of Clinton as a feminist hero, see, for example, Fortini, "Feminist Reawakening," 2008; Goldberg, "3 A.M. for Feminism," 2008; Milligan, "Clinton's Struggle Vexes Feminists," 2008; Robinson, "Standing at the Nexus of Change," 2008; Wilson, "Commentary: Clinton Started a New Political Movement," 2008. Robinson describes her as "quite possibly the last great feminist heroine we'll see from a passing generation." For opposing perspectives, see Douglass, "Why Women Hate Hillary," 2008; Kissling, "Why I'm Still Not for Hillary Clinton," 2008; O'Rourke, "Death of a Saleswoman," 2008.

46. See Liddle, "Hillary, They Just Don't Like You," 2008.

47. See interesting insights in Zeitlin, "Barack Obama Is My Imaginary Hip Black Friend," 2008.

NOTES TO CHAPTER 5

1. Balibar, "Racism and Nationalism," 1991, p. 37.

2. Anderson, *Imagined Communities*, 1991, p. 224.

3. Collins, "Like One of the Family," 1991; Skurski, "Ambiguities of Identity," 1994; Stoler, *Race and the Education of Desire*, 1995; Marx, *Making Race and Nation*, 1998.

4. See Appelbaum, Macpherson, & Rosenblatt, *Race and Nation in Modern Latin America*, 2003; Marx, *Making Race and Nation*, 1998; Roediger, *How Race Survived U.S. History*, 2008; Kutzinski, *Sugar's Secrets*, 1993; Twine, *Racism in a Racial Democracy*, 1998; Seigel, *Uneven Encounters*, 2009; Glenn, *Unequal Freedom*, 2002; Gerstle, *American Crucible*, 2001.

5. Omi & Winant, *Racial Formation*, 1994.

6. Collins, "Like One of the Family," 2001. These ideas did not arise because of any "natural" or "inevitable" feelings of difference or prejudice. Rather, they served to justify the socioeconomic structure on which the nation was being erected. The exclusion of Native Americans was necessary to justify the expropriation of lands, and the inferior status Africans legitimized their perpetual enslavement in the land of the free. See Bonilla-Silva, "Rethinking Racism," 1997; and *White Supremacy and Racism*, 2001; Nash, "Race and the Ideology of Race," 1962.

7. Layton, "International Pressure and the U.S. Government's Response to Little Rock," 1997, p. 258. This is a quote from the amicus brief filed by the State Department in the *Brown v. Board of Education* case, which led to the Supreme Court's 1954 school desegregation order.

8. Winant, *Racial Conditions*, 1994; Wallace-Wells, "Is America Too Racist for Barack?," 2006; Jacobs & Tope, "Politics of Resentment in the Post–Civil Rights Era," 2007; Moraga, "What's Race Gotta Do with It?," 2009.

9. See, for example, Wang, "Now Hip-Hop, Too, Is Made in China," 2009; Cornyetz, "Fetishized Blackness," 1994; Maira, "We Ain't Missing," 2008; Umlauf, "Cuban Hip-Hop," 2002; Fernandes, "Fear of a Black Nation," 2003. See also Rodriguez's discussion of hip-hop and colorblindness among white American suburban youth, "Color-Blind Ideology and the Cultural Appropriation of Hip-Hop," 2006.

10. Glod, "U.S. Teens Trail Peers around World on Math-Science Test," 2007; Caldwell, *American Narcissism*, 2006.

11. Huntington, *Clash of Civilizations*, 1996.

12. Orr, "Palin: Obama 'Palling around with Terrorists,'" 2008; Cooper, "McCain: 'Who Is the Real Barack Obama?,'" 2008; Tope, "Othering Obama," 2008.

13. Eilperin, "Palin's 'Pro-America Areas' Remark," 2008. The ideas that I have summarized here are the subject of chapter 7.

14. Martin & Smith, "Obama's Apple Pie Campaign," 2008.

15. Bell & Hartmann, "Diversity in Everyday Discourse," 2007.

16. For much stronger critiques of Obama's policy positions and ties to corporate interests, see Street, *Barack Obama and the Future of American Politics*, 2009; Bonilla-Silva & Ray, "When Whites Love a Black Leader," 2009; Lamont-Hill, "Not My Brand of Hope," 2008; Gonzalez, "Obama Craze," 2008; Reed, "Obama No," 2008.

17. Nicholas, "Meet the Guy Next Door," 2008.

18. Martin & Smith, "Obama's Apple Pie Campaign," 2008.

19. Frederick, "Put Michelle Obama in the Bacon Camp," 2008. Also see discussion of the "latte libel" as key element of contemporary conservative populist discourse in chapter 2 of Thomas Frank's 2004 book *What's the Matter with Kansas?*

20. First quote from Prelutsky, "Obama," 2008. See also Massie, "Michelle Obama," 2008; Oinounou & Kapp, "Michelle Obama Takes Heat," 2008; Berry, "If Michelle Obama Isn't Racist, What *Is* She?," 2008.

21. Fram, "Poll: Public Cool to Michelle, Doesn't Know Cindy," 2008.

22. Quote from Silva, "Michelle Obama's Popularity Soars," 2009; see also St. Clair, "Michelle Obama Image Makeover," 2009; Powell & Cantor, "Michelle Obama Looks for a New Introduction," 2008.

23. But not for too long. In a May 1, 2008, post, the blogger Daniel Koffler referred to Clinton as the "beer-swillin'est gun-shootin'est valedictorian of Wellesley *ever!*" See "And Now Hillary Clinton Wants to Sue OPEC"; see also McAuliff, "Hillary Clinton Tries to Bag Votes with Duck Tale," 2008; Suarez, "Bottoms Up," 2008.

24. Obama, "Keynote Address," 2004.

25. Winant, *Racial Conditions*, 1994; Jacobs & Tope, "Politics of Resentment in the Post–Civil Rights Era," 2007. As Winant writes, "Racial conflict is the very archetype of discord in North America, the primordial conflict that has in many ways structured all others" p. 22.

26. Obama referred to this stalemate in his March 18, 2008, speech "A More Perfect Union" (i.e., the "race speech").

27. Klein, "Fresh Face," 2006.

28. Traub, "Is (His) Biography (Our) Destiny?," 2007.

29. Obama, "Keynote Address," 2004.

30. Kim, "Imagining Race and Nation in Multiculturalist America," 2004, p. 989.

31. Obama, "Election Night," 2008.

32. Obama, "America We Love," 2008.

33. Tapper and Hinman, "Obama Declares His Candidacy," 2007.

34. Obama, "Full Text of Senator Barack Obama's Announcement for President," 2007.

35. Greenberg, "Why Obamamania?," 2008.

36. For other comparisons between Obama and King, see "MLK to Obama," 2008; Grieve, "We Are Ready to Believe Again," 2008; Gitell, "Is Obama Like King?," 2008;

Powell, "Embracing His Moment," 2008; Gane-McCalla, "Is Obama's Inauguration MLK's Dream?," 2009; McKinney and Pallasch, "Obama Draws Parallels to Martin Luther King Jr.," 2008.

37. Stein, "Robert Byrd," 2010.

38. Samuel, "Young, Black, and Post–Civil Rights," 2007.

39. McCormick & Jones, "Conceptualization of Deracialization," 1993.

40. Leibovich, "The Other Man of the Hour," 2004.

41. Page, "Obama to NAACP," 2008; Obama, "Selma Voting Rights March Commemoration," 2007.

42. Tilove, "Third Labor of Obama," 2008.

43. Moraga, "What's Race Gotta Do with It?," 2009.

44. Bell & Hartmann, "Diversity in Everyday Discourse," 2007; Lewis, "There Is No 'Race' in the Schoolyard," 2001; Bonilla-Silva & Ray, "When Whites Love a Black Leader," 2009.

45. Williams, "L'Étranger," 2007.

46. Bonilla-Silva & Ray, "When Whites Love a Black Leader," 2009; Kaufman, "Whites' Great Hope?," 2007.

47. Freedland, "America Has Not Lost Its Talent for Renewal," 2008.

NOTES TO CHAPTER 6

1. Chang, "Asian Americans and the Road to the White House," 2009/2010, p. 210.

2. O'Brien, *Racial Middle*, 2008; O'Brien's work is discussed in more detail below.

3. Grieco, *Race and Hispanic Origin of the Foreign-Born Population*, 2010.

4. Pew Hispanic Center, "Table 1: Population, by Race and Ethnicity," 2009; non-Hispanic whites currently make up 66% of the U.S. population.

5. Passel and Cohn, "Immigration to Play Lead Role in Future U.S. Growth," 2008.

6. The 1965 law, known as the Hart-Cellar Act, abolished national origins quotas restricting non-white immigration to the United States. The law has led to a mass influx of newcomers from Latin America, Asia, and Africa. For a discussion of the experiences of black immigrants in the United States, see Waters, *Black Identities*, 1999; Foner, *Islands in the City*, 2001; Kasinitz, *Caribbean New York*, 1992. For discussion of the importance of class in the black community, see Cose, *Rage of a Privileged Class*, 1995; Lacy, *Blue-Chip Black*, 2007; Pew Research Center, *Blacks See Growing Values Gap*, 2007. The increased visibility of the multiracial population is discussed in Dalmage, *Tripping on the Color Line*, 2000; Rockquemore and Brunsma, *Beyond Black*, 2002; Root, *Racially Mixed People in America*, 1992.

7. Bonilla-Silva, "From Bi-racial to Tri-racial," 2004, p. 931.

8. In 1960, 93% of the non-white population was African American. By 1990, that share had fallen to 61%. See Gibson and Jung, "Table 1: United States—Race and Hispanic Origin," 2002. I note, however, that some scholars disagree with my assessment, arguing that the black/white paradigm has never adequately captured U.S. racial dynamics. Claire Jean Kim, for example, writes, "The multiracial composition of the American populace has always given the lie to a bipolar racial framework" ("Racial Triangulation," 1999, p. 105).

9. See Feagin, *Racist America*, 2000; and *Systemic Racism*, 2006.

10. Kim identifies the "different trajectories approach" in "Racial Triangulation," 1999. For examples, see Omi and Winant, *Racial Formation in the United States*, 1994; Okihiro, *Margins and Mainstreams*, 1994; Perea, "Black/White Binary Paradigm of Race," 1997.

11. Omi and Winant, *Racial Formation in the United States*, 1994; quote from Kim, "Are Asians Black?," 1999, p. 2388.

12. As the legal scholar Janine Young Kim writes, "The black/white paradigm retains contemporary significance despite demographic changes in American society. It is, therefore, imperative that race scholars understand the paradigm's enduring resonance and potential before concluding that it nevertheless ought to be abandoned" ("Are Asians Black?," 1999, p. 2387).

13. Davis, "American Dream Deferred," 2007, pp. 47, 50.

14. Kim, "Racial Triangulation of Asian Americans," 1999, p. 106.

15. Hu-DeHart, "21st-Century America," 2001, p. 94.

16. Kim, "Racial Triangulation of Asian Americans," 1999, pp. 106–107, 130n9.

17. Manneh, "Census to Count Arabs as White," 2010; Chiareli, "Muslims and Arab Americans," n.d. Discussion of the invisibility of the racial middle in the 2008 election is found in Chang, "Asians Americans and the Road to the White House," 2009/2010; Chotiner, "Asian Alienation," 2008; Fang, "Anderson Cooper 360," 2008; Martin, "Election 2008," 2008; Moraga, "What's Race Gotta Do with It?," 2009; Rodriguez, "Obama Is More Brown Than Black," 2008; and later in this chapter.

18. O'Brien, *Racial Middle*, 2008, p. 18.

19. On the foreign-born population, see Grieco, *Race and Hispanic Origin of the Foreign-Born Population*, 2010. Claire Jean Kim points out that the view of Asian Americans as inherently foreign is very long-standing, dating at least from the mid-19th century. "Racial Triangulation," 1999, p. 107.

20. As Silvia Pedraza writes, "The concept of transnationalism arose when social scientists noticed that under the impact of changes in the nature of modern communications at this century's end, many immigrants fail to shed their old identities and totally assimilate. Instead, they develop new bicultural identities and live their lives and are quite involved in more than one nation, more than one world—in effect making the home and adopted countries both one lived social world." "Assimilation or Transnationalism?" 2005, pp. 422–423.

21. See further discussion of these issues in chapter 7 and the conclusion of this book.

22. Yancey, *Who Is White?*, 2003, pp. 3, 13, 14.

23. See Bonilla-Silva, "From Bi-racial to Tri-racial," 2004; "We Are All Americans!," 2002; and "Are the Americas 'Sick with Racism,'" 2009.

24. It is also my contention that both authors (and nearly the entirety of race scholarship at present) greatly underestimate the increasing importance of class in shaping the ways that African Americans experience and understand race. As the class gap widens, the cultural, geographic, economic, and familial affiliations that created a sense of shared fate and identity among blacks will weaken. In the next several decades, I believe, it will be increasingly difficult to speak of "the" black experience or "a" black community. Differential black racialization by class is thus a vital dimension of future research on African Americans. See Dawson, *Behind the Mule*,

1994; Pew Research Center, *Blacks See Growing Values Gap between Poor and Middle Class*, 2007; and Winant, *Racial Conditions*, 1994; for consideration of the issues raised in this note.

25. Brookhiser, "Let Us Not Forget," 2008; originally cited in Waldman, "Why Conservatives' Crush on Obama Is Doomed," 2008.

26. Quote from "MLK to Obama," 2008. For discussion of the announcement of Obama's candidacy, see Tapper and Hinman, "Obama Declares His Candidacy," 2007. For text of the Selma speech, see Obama, "Selma Voting Rights March Commemoration," 2007.

27. Waldman, "Why Conservatives' Crush on Obama Is Doomed," 2008.

28. Chotiner, "Asian Alienation," 2008. Obama did mention Asians and Latinos several times in his March 2008 "race speech," for example, yet most of the speech was organized around a discussion of points of conflict and disagreement between blacks and whites; Obama, "A More Perfect Union," 2008.

29. Rodriguez, "Obama Is More Brown Than Black," 2008.

30. Moraga, "What's Race Gotta Do with It?," 2009, p. 168.

31. For discussion of the Asian "model minority myth," see Takaki, *Strangers from a Different Shore*, 1990; Tatum, *Why Are All the Black Kids Sitting Together?*, 2003; Lee, *Unraveling the "Model Minority" Stereotype*, 2009. Tim Wise discusses "Obama-like blacks" on p. 93 of his 2009 book *Between Barack and a Hard Place*.

32. Roth, "Latino Vote Is the Winning Ticket for Super Tuesday," 2008.

33. Cullen, "Does Obama Have an Asian Problem?," 2008.

34. See Chuang, "Racial Rifts," 2008; Tuchman, "Anderson Cooper 360," 2008; Cullen, "Does Obama Have an Asian Problem? We're Still Debating," 2008; Chotiner, "Asian Alienation," 2008. See also chapters 1–2 of the 2008 book *Pareng Barack* by the Filipino American author Benjamin Pimentel.

35. See Arrillaga, "Hispanics' Reluctance on Obama Highlights Black-Brown Divide," 2008; del Barco, "Uneasy Black-Latino Ties a Factor in Calif. Primary," 2008; Contreras, "Bradley Effect Is Still in Effect," 2008; Heileman, "Evita Factor," 2008; Judis, "Hillary Clinton's Firewall," 2007; Lizza, "Minority Reports," 2008; Nagourney and Steinhauer, "In Obama's Pursuit of Latinos, Race Plays Role," 2008; Novak, "Clinton's Risky Gamble," 2008; Reno, "Black-Brown Divide," 2008; Roth, "Latino Vote Is the Winning Ticket for Super Tuesday," 2008; Shapiro, "Latino Vote," 2008; Smith, "Courting the Latino Vote," 2008; Traub, "Emerging Minority," 2008; Vick and MacGillis, "Obama Confronts Ethnic Tensions in Bid for Votes," 2008.

36. Nagourney and Steinhauer, "In Obama's Pursuit of Latinos, Race Plays Role," 2008; del Barco, "Uneasy Black-Latino Ties a Factor in Calif. Primary," 2008.

37. Novak, "Clinton's Risky Gamble," 2008; Heileman, "Evita Factor," 2008.

38. Judis, "Hillary Clinton's Firewall," 2007.

39. Hutchinson quoted in Reno, "Black-Brown Divide," 2008.

40. Lizza, "Minority Reports," 2008.

41. See Asian American Legal Defense and Education Fund, "Asian American Voters Favor Clinton and McCain in Northeast," 2008; Kim, "Did Asian Americans Swing California for Clinton?," 2008; Minushkin and Lopez, *Hispanic Vote in the 2008 Democratic Presidential Primaries*, 2008. Of the Asian American voters polled in the Northeast, 95% identified as Democrats.

42. See Barreto and Ramírez, "The Latino Vote Is Pro-Clinton, Not Anti-Obama," 2008; Chang, "Why Latinos and Asians Went for Hillary," 2008; Coates, "Especially the Blacks and the Latinos," 2009; Lovato, "Clinton's Latino Advantage Decreases," 2008; Lovato, "Everyone's an Expert on the Latino Vote, Except Latinos," 2008; Mitchell, "Facts Don't Back Black-Brown Divide in Texas," 2008; Navarrette, "Commentary: Latinos Will Vote for Obama," 2008; Reagan, "Fried Chicken Tacos," 2008; Rodriguez, "Black-Brown Divide," 2008; Sabater, "Divide and Conquer," 2008; Solis-Marich, "McAuliffe: Obama Has a Hispanic Problem," 2008; Valdes-Rodriguez, "Obama and the Latino Vote," 2008; Wang, "Asian Americans Outraged by CNN Election Report," 2008.

43. Lovato, "Everyone's an Expert on the Latino Vote, Except Latinos," 2008. Commenting in 2009 on coverage of the Sotomayor nomination, Lovato similarly argued, "What's fascinating is how [so many] liberal publications, media where Latinos, Latino issues, Latinos writers *brillan por su ausencia* (shine for their absence), are suddenly demonstrating expertise on Latino issues, Latino pols, judges, etc." See "New Republic Attacks Judge Sotomayor," 2009.

44. Sabater, "Divide and Conquer," 2008.

45. Valdes-Rodriguez, "Obama and the Latino Vote," 2008. For a few examples of the vast literature on populations of African descent in Latin America, see Logan, "Each Sheep with Its Mate," 2010; de la Fuente, *A Nation for All*, 2001; Twine, *Racism in a Racial Democracy*, 1998; Wade, *Blackness and Race Mixture*, 1993.

46. Chang, "Why Latinos and Asians Went for Hillary," 2008; Wang, "Asian Americans Outraged by CNN Election Report," 2008.

47. The 80–20 Initiative is an Asian American political action committee founded by former Delaware lieutenant governor S. B. Woo. In early January 2008, the initiative made waves by attacking Obama for his refusal to endorse its pledge to the Asian American community. (Obama signed a modified version of the pledge on January 31.) For more on the conflict between the 80–20 Initiative, the Obama campaign, and other Asian American activists (many of whom opposed Woo's position), see Chen, Kalayil, & Toy, "Response to 80–20 from Obama AAPI Leaders," 2008; Guillermo, "Why Is Obama Snubbing Asian Americans?," 2008; Dutta, "Divide and Dishonor," 2008; Asians Vote, "Fang, Obama, and Expanding the Definition of 'Asian American,'" 2008. The petition circulated in response to the CNN report is discussed in Wang, "Asian Americans Outraged by CNN Election Report," 2008.

48. Fang, "Anderson Cooper 360," 2008.

49. Burns, "Black Vote Support Not Sure Thing for Obama," 2007.

50. Morrison, "Comment," 1998.

51. Bacon, "Can Obama Count on the Black Vote," 2007; Coates, "Is Obama Black Enough?," 2007; Conan, "Can Barack Obama Win the Black Vote?," 2007; Coyne, "Blackness of Barack Obama," 2007; Chude-Sokei, "Redefining 'Black,'" 2007; Crowley and Johnson, "Is Black America Ready to Embrace Obama?," 2007; Dickerson, "Colorblind," 2007; Luqman, "Obama's Tightrope," 2007; "Obama Card," 2007; "Is Barack Obama Black Enough?," 2007; Pickler, "Democrats Face Off in 'YouTube' Debate," 2007; Reynolds, "Obama's Racial Identity Still an Issue," 2007; Sarmah, "Is Obama Black Enough?," 2007; Schorn, "Transcript Excerpt," 2007; Staples, "Decoding the Debate over the Blackness of Barack Obama," 2007; Valbrun, "Black Like Me?,"

2007; Williams, "Black Voters Aren't Fully Sold on Obama," 2007; Younge, "Is Obama Black Enough?," 2007. During one CNN debate, the journalist Suzanne Malveaux even asked Hillary Clinton if *she* was "black enough." See Martin, "Sen. Clinton, Are You Black Enough to Be President?," 2007.

52. See Younge, "Is Obama Black Enough?," 2007; Conan, "Can Barack Obama Win the Black Vote?," 2007; Williams, "Obama's Color Line," 2007. For an analysis of conservative infatuation with the way that Obama spoke, and did not speak, about race, see Waldman, "Why Conservatives' Crush on Obama Is Doomed," 2008.

53. Coates, "Is Obama Black Enough?," 2007.

54. Staples, "Decoding the Debate over the Blackness of Barack Obama," 2007; Luqman, "Obama's Tightrope," 2008.

55. Matthews from a January 2007 broadcast, quoted in Hart, "Obamamania," 2007; second quote from Klein, "Fresh Face," 2006.

56. Merida, "Obama Wave Stuns Clinton's Black Supporters," 2008.

57. Ibid.; Minushkin and Lopez, *Hispanic Vote in the 2008 Democratic Presidential Primaries*, 2008; Schaller, "How Hillary Clinton Botched the Black Vote," 2008. In addition to voting for Obama, blacks did begin to vote specifically against Clinton. There was a strong perception by mid-primary that the Clintons were attempting to mobilize white racism in their favor—by drawing constant attention to Obama's blackness, for example. In April 2008, Terence Samuel argued in the *American Prospect* that black anger toward the Clintons had "gotten so visceral it forces the question not just of whether blacks would support Clinton in a fall campaign, but whether a Clinton win would lose Democrats the support of the next generation of black voters altogether." See "On the 2008 Primary and Black Anger," 2008. I discuss these issues in chapter 4 as well.

58. These points discussed in Sanneh, "What He Knows for Sure," 2008; Bonilla-Silva, "2008 Elections and the Future of Anti-racism in 21st-Century Amerika," 2008. As Earl Ofari Hutchinson wrote in 2010, "It's no overstatement to say that Barack Obama would not be president if Latino and especially black voters had not turned the 2008 election into a holy crusade—not an election, in the traditional sense, but a holy crusade." See "Defecting Black Vote Spells Big Trouble for Democrats," 2010.

59. As Margaret Kimberly wrote in April 2011, "The novelty [of a black president] is now over and some of the bloom is off the rose." See also Grove, "Are Blacks Abandoning Obama?," 2009; Herbert, "Neglecting the Base," 2010; Hutchinson, "Defecting Black Vote Spells Big Trouble for Democrats," 2010; Kimberly, "Freedom Rider," 2011; Harris, "Sharpton and West's MSNBC Shouting Match," 2011.

60. "CNN Election Center," 2008; Hornick, "Poll: 'Sharp Reversal' for Obama with Latino Voters," 2008.

61. Carlsen, "Obama and the Minority Majority," 2008. Obama lost among whites 43% to 57%. He lost among older voters and men as well, but won blacks, Asians, Latinos, women, and youth. See "CNN Election Center," 2008. For discussions of the crucial role played by black and Latino voters in the 2008 race, see Carlsen, "Obama and the Minority Majority," 2008; Bialik, "Did Race Win the Election for Obama?," 2009; Feagin, "Which Voters Had the Most Impact?," 2010; Jordan and Eaton, "Big Turnout of Latino Voters Boosted Obama," 2008; Lopez and Taylor, "Dissecting the 2008 Electorate," 2009; Noah, "What We Didn't Overcome," 2008; Wing, "Obama,

Race, and the Future of US Politics," 2009; Yglesias, "The Rise of the Non-whites," 2008. Latinos constituted 7.5% of all voters in 2008, and blacks 12%. Lopez and Taylor point out that at 76%, the white share of the electorate was the lowest ever, but still quite a bit higher than whites' overall proportion of the population, which was 66%. The Asian American vote was not as decisive overall because Asians constituted just 2.5% of all voters.

62. According to one poll, Obama won 78% of foreign-born Latinos, compared to 67% of Latinos overall. See "AALDEF Exit Poll," 2009.

63. Such arguments are found in Cullen, "Does Obama Have an Asian Problem?," 2008; Pimentel, "Barack Obama through Filipino-American Eyes," 2008; and *Pareng Barack*, 2008; Roebuck, "Hispanics, Racism, and Obama," 2008; and the blog post "Hispanics and Barack Obama" by el Profe, 2008.

64. Cullen, "Does Obama Have an Asian Problem? We're Still Debating," 2008.

65. Lovato, "Everyone's an Expert on the Latino Vote, Except Latinos," 2008.

66. See Hart, "Obamamania," 2007; Swift, "Iowa Caucus Results Explained," 2008; and chapter 2 of this book for discussion of White self-congratulation in narratives of the election.

67. Lie, "Black-Asian Conflict?," 2004, pp. 306, 310.

68. Rodriguez, "Fantasy of L.A.'s 'Race War,'" 2007.

69. The study was conducted by the Gallup Organization. Gallup has reported similar findings from polls conducted every year since 2001. Commenting on the 2008 election, the Gallup Organization states, "While black-Hispanic animosity may exist and could even have been a factor in some state caucuses or primaries, the Gallup data indicates it is not overwhelmingly obvious to members of either group. Whites are much more likely to believe the two are in conflict." See Saad, "Whites May Exaggerate Black-Hispanic Tensions," 2008.

70. Wallace-Wells, "Is America Too Racist for Barack?," 2006.

71. Padgett, "Picking Sotomayor," 2009.

72. Coates, "Especially the Blacks and the Latinos," 2009.

73. Sociologists have identified colorblind individualism as the predominant ideological framework through which most Americans understand U.S. racial matters today. For a deeper discussion of this ideology and how it played out in the 2008 election, see chapters 2 and 3.

74. Solis-Marich, "McAuliffe: Obama Has a Hispanic Problem," 2008.

75. Rivas, "Latino Bloggers React to Candidates' Outreach Efforts," 2008.

76. Chin, "Identity Politics," 2008.

77. Similarly, in an August interview on National Public Radio, Rodriguez stated, "If Obama would have to come to Hispanics and [said], like you, I have lived my life between white and black America, I think Hispanics would more easily understand that as a narrative." See Corley, "Writer: Whites See Obama as a Black Exception," 2008. Quote in text from Rodriguez, "Obama Is More Brown Than Black," 2008.

78. Ballave, "Where Do Latinos Go Now?," 2008.

79. Chang, "Asian Americans and the Road to the White House," 2009/2010, p. 212.

80. The writer continued, "Contrary to how we are portrayed in the mainstream media and BET, there are plenty of black folks that are educated, articulate, and not turning everything into a damn race issue when it doesn't need to be. Barack Obama

just happens to be one of them—he is by no means a freak of nature." See "Is Barack Obama Black Enough?" on the blog *Walk Taken*, 2007.

81. The debate about these issues is discussed further in chapter 3.

82. Kaufman, "Whites' Great Hope?," 2007.

83. For one of the very rare references to the "new politics of race" by a writer from the racial middle, see Guillermo, "Obama's Colorblind Ambition," 2008. Also see the critical race scholar Robert Chang's discussion of Obama and post-racialism, quoted throughout this chapter.

84. Chen, "Why Asian Americans Voted for Obama," 2009.

85. For statements emphasizing Obama's ties to Asian American and Pacific Islander communities by Obama and his family members, see Kang, "Obama Announces Asian Americans and Pacific Islanders National Leadership Council," 2007; Weisman, "Obama, at Fundraiser, Pronounces Himself an 'Honorary AAPI,'" 2008; "A Conversation about Asian Pacific America," 2009/2010; Solomon, "All in the Family," 2008. Obama's half sister, Maya Soetoro-Ng, is married to Konrad Ng, a professor of critical studies at the University of Hawaii.

86. Lam, "Our Man Obama," 2009.

87. Fang, "One Asian Passionate about Obama," 2008. See similar sentiment in Asian Week Staff, "Endorsements," 2008.

88. Nakoso, "Obama's Hawaii Trip," 2008.

89. Pimentel, *Pareng Barack*, 2008; Pimentel, "Barack Obama through Filipino-American Eyes," 2008.

90. Yang, "American More Than a Birthright," 2008; and "Could Obama be the First Asian American President?," 2008.

91. Pimentel, "Obama, First Pinoy President?," 2008.

92. Starr, "Obama Is 'First Hispanic President,'" 2009. For pre – and immediate post-election discussion of the importance of immigration to Latino voters, see Cubias, "What Does an Obama Administration Mean for Latinos?," 2008; Munoz, "McCain-Palin Attacks Fall Flat with Latinos," 2008; Nezua, "Latinos [and Allies] Want Specifics," 2008; Ramirez, "McCain's Immigration Dilemma," 2008; Rivas, "Latino Bloggers React to Candidates' Outreach Efforts," 2008; Smith, "Hispanics Turn Cold Shoulder to McCain," 2008.

93. See Smith, "Hispanics Turn Cold Shoulder to McCain," 2008. Smith writes, "McCain seems to have wound up with the worst of both worlds: He appears to be getting no credit from Latino voters for his past support for immigration reform, while carrying the baggage of other Republicans' hostility to illegal immigration."

94. Lochhead, "Obama Takes Big Risk on Driver's License Issue," 2008; Cubias, "What Does an Obama Administration Mean for Latinos?," 2008.

95. See Gonzalez, "Day of Pride for Latinos," 2009.

96. The December 2010 Senate filibuster of the DREAM Act was described as having shut the door "on what perhaps was the last chance for pro-immigration legislation until at least the 2012 election." First introduced in 2001, the DREAM Act would offer permanent residency to undocumented minors seeking higher education or planning to enter the military. Obama claimed later in December that not having passed the DREAM Act was "maybe my biggest disappointment." See Wong and Toeplitz, "Dream Act Dies in Senate," 2010; Condon, "Obama," 2010.

97. Obama has continued the increase in yearly deportations begun under George W. Bush. There were 184,000 noncriminal deportations in fiscal year 2006, 220,000 in 2007, 262,000 in 2008, and 272,000 in 2009. While the proportion of noncriminal deportations decreased somewhat in 2010 (to just over half), the number of deportations overall last year reached an all-time high of 392,862. For fiscal year 2011, Immigration and Customs Enforcement set a goal of 404,000 deportations. See Slevin, "Deportation of Illegal Immigrants Increases under Obama Administration," 2010; "Deportations by Fiscal Year," 2010; Preston, "Deportations from U.S. Hit a Record High," 2010; "U.S. Deports Record Number of Migrants in 2010," 2010. For Latino criticism of the administration's policy, see Khimm, "Why Have Hispanics Soured on Obama?," 2010; Lovato, "Act Now to Stop to Obama's Administration's Racist 287G Immigration Policy," 2009; Gamboa, "Obama Woos Hispanic Vote on Education," 2011.

98. Latino writers have also criticized Obama's use of the term "illegal immigrant" during his 2009 address to Congress on health care, and his failure to substantively discuss immigration reform during the 2010 State of the Union. See "Hispanics Left out of the State of the Union Speech!," 2010; Falcón, "Latinos Left out of Obama's State of the Union Speech," 2010; Treviño, "Are Latinos Really Wanted by Either Party?," 2010. On the general liberal/left disappointment with Obama, see Beinart, "Why Obama Disappoints the Left," 2010. For criticism of his failure to advance immigration reform, and discussion of his broken promises to Latinos, see also "Enough with Empty Words," 2010; Lovato, "Act Now to Stop to Obama's Administration's Racist 287G Immigration Policy," 2009; Navarrette, "Dear Mr. President," 2010; and "Did Obama Break Promise to Latinos?," 2010; Schumacher-Matos, "Democrats Must Seize the Immigration Issue," 2010; Rodriguez, "Obama and Immigration Reform," 2009; Treviño, "Obama Explains Why He Used the Term 'Illegal Immigrant,'" 2009.

99. Description of Ramos found in Schumacher-Matos, "Democrats Must Seize the Immigration Issue," 2010. Quote from Brown, "Hispanic Media Turn on Obama," 2010. Ramos's statement parallels charges by some African American critics, who have recently argued that Obama has failed to do enough for black America. See Grove, "Are Blacks Abandoning Obama?," 2009; Washington, "What Has Barack Obama Done for Black America?," 2010; Kimberly, "Freedom Rider," 2011; Harris, "Sharpton and West's MSNBC Shouting Match," 2011.

100. Obama still polls considerably better among Latinos than whites, among whom only 39% approve of the president. Obama continues to receive highest marks among African Americans. In March 2011, his black approval rating registered at 85%, following a high of 93% at his January 2009 inauguration. See Jones, "Obama Approval Slips among Blacks, Hispanics in March," 2011.

101. Treviño, "Some Latinos Wondering Why Vote for Obama in 2012," 2011.

102. Wessler, "Hostile State Battles Now Define Immigration Debate," 2011; Dee, "Advice to President Obama on Winning the Hispanic Vote in 2012," 2011; Condon, "Obama's Challenge," 2011.

103. While I do not wish to discount the possibility that a sense of racial kinship with Obama was important to Latino voters in 2007/2008, there was little evidence of this in the more than two hundred articles and blog posts I reviewed.

NOTES TO CHAPTER 7

1. Eilperin, "Palin's 'Pro-America Areas' Remark," 2008.

2. Throughout this chapter, I refer to the Republican ticket as the McCain/Palin campaign because of the tremendous influence of the Alaska governor in shaping the discourse of the opposition. Though Joe Biden had been in politics for decades, Senator Obama was the clear superstar for the Democrats. Sarah Palin, on the other hand, came to eclipse McCain in media coverage and popular interest, achieving the kind of celebrity for which McCain had earlier ridiculed his Democratic opponent. (For example, a July 2008 McCain television ad referred to Obama as "the biggest celebrity in the world"—drawing attention to both his wild popularity and to the international, and therefore presumably anti-American, dimensions of his appeal. See Mooney, "McCain Ad Compares Obama to Britney Spears, Paris Hilton," 2008.) Following the election, McCain quickly faded from the headlines, but Sarah Palin's star continued to rise. In 2009/2010, she launched a very successful tour for her book *Going Rogue*, became a regular commentator on Fox News, gave a full-hour interview on the *Oprah Winfrey Show*, and delivered the keynote speech at the Tea Party national convention. This was due in large part to the appeal of the white populist vision of nation that she so vigorously championed.

3. Samuel Joseph Wurzelbacher (aka "Joe the Plumber") grabbed the national spotlight after challenging Barack Obama during a videotaped campaign stop in Ohio. Wurzelbacher, who declared an intent to open his own plumbing business, disputed the benefits of Obama's tax proposal for small business owners, arguing that he would in fact lose money under the Democratic candidate's plan. Capitalizing on the exchange, McCain and Palin began to invoke Wurzelbacher's name to bolster their claim that Obama did not represent the interests of "average Americans." During the October 15, 2008, presidential debate, John McCain mentioned "Joe the Plumber" more than 20 times. See "Complete Final Debate Transcript," 2008.

4. See list of more than six dozen related terms used in the 2008 campaign cycle on the blog *We Are Respectable Negroes*, Zora, DeVega, & Gartrelle, "Euphemisms for Naming White Folk," 2008.

5. Discussion of populism as an element of conservative discourse found in Brooks, "Class War before Palin," 2008; Frank, "Let's Talk Class Again," 2002.

6. The list of cultural symbols found in Huntington, "The Insider," 2003. As Sarah Palin said of the GOP candidate Scott Brown following his January 2010 victory for the Massachusetts U.S. Senate seat, "He was just a guy with a truck and a passion to serve our country." See "Sarah Palin Speaks at Tea Party Convention," 2010. For discussion of the racial coding of country music, see Mann, "Why Does Country Music Sound White?," 2008.

7. Silver, "'Real' America Looks Different to Palin, Obama," 2008; Taylor, "Race and the Election," 2008. See McCain's references to the United States as a Christian, or Judeo-Christian, nation in Canellos, "McCain's 'Judeo-Christian Values' Reference Puzzles," 2008; Mooney, Dalla, & Anderson, "Groups Criticize McCain for Calling U.S. 'Christian Nation,'" 2007; Pearson, "McCain in Michigan," 2008.

8. Barone, "49 Percent Nation," 2001; Huntington, "The Insider," 2003; Rogers and Teixeira, "America's Forgotten Majority," 2000; Frank, *What's the Matter with Kansas?*, 2004.

9. Benjamin, *Searching for Whitopia*, 2009, p. 5.

10. Tope, "Othering Obama," 2008.

11. Schildkraut, "The More Things Change," 2002; Higham, *Strangers in the Land*, 2002; Spencer, "Multiculturalism," 1994; Li and Brewer, "What Does It Mean to Be an American?," 2004.

12. Higham, *Strangers in the Land*, 2002.

13. Spencer, "Multiculturalism," 1994, pp. 551–552.

14. Barrett and Roediger, "How White People Became White," 2005, p. 36.

15. Citrin et al., "Multiculturalism in American Public Opinion," 2001; Bell & Hartmann, "Diversity in Everyday Discourse," 2007. As these authors point out, "diversity" and "multiculturalism" mean different things to different people. There is a general belief among many Americans at this time, however, that *some* degree of either, or both, is good for the United States.

16. Schildkraut, "The More Things Change," 2002; Gallagher, "Miscounting Race," 2003; Benjamin, *Searching for Whitopia*, 2009.

17. That is, maybe all religions and cultures are not morally equally after all. Maybe it is smart, and not racist, to suspect that the Muslims boarding your airplane are carrying a bomb. Perhaps they do hate us because we are white, Christian, and free. Steyn quote from the jacket of his 2006 book *America Alone: The End of the World as We Know It*. Reference to hating us for our freedom from President George W. Bush's September 20, 2001, address to Congress: "On September the 11th, enemies of freedom committed an act of war against our country. . . . Americans are asking, why do they hate us? . . . They hate our freedoms—our freedom of religion, our freedom of speech, our freedom to vote and assemble and disagree with each other." See Bush, "Freedom and Fear at War," 2001.

18. Spencer, "Multiculturalism," 1994, p. 550.

19. The relevant titles published by those on this list include Brimelow, *Alien Nation*, 1996; Coulter, *Godless*, 2006; and *Guilty*, 2009; Hanson, *Mexifornia*, 2003; Huntington, *Who Are We?*, 2004; Tancredo, *In Mortal Danger*, 2006. Huntington died in 2008, and Beck joined Fox in January 2009 after leaving CNN's Headline News, where he hosted a show from 2006 to 2008.

20. Buchanan, *Death of the West*, 2002, pp. 1, 5.

21. McLaughlin, "McLaughlin Group," 2007.

22. Buchanan, *Death of the West*, 2002, pp. 42, 24, 27.

23. Buchanan, *State of Emergency*, 2007, p. 13.

24. Ibid., pp. 5–7.

25. Brimelow, *Alien Nation*, 1996, p. xvii (emphasis mine).

26. Ibid., p. 56.

27. Buchanan, "Brief for Whitey," 2008.

28. Carrillo Rowe, "Whose 'America'?," 2004, p. 125.

29. Limbaugh, "From Kids on Bus to Kanye West," 2009; and "It's Payback Time," 2010.

30. O'Reilly, "GOP Presidential Hopeful John McCain Sits Down with Bill O'Reilly," 2007. Earlier quotes from Buchanan, "Brief for Whitey," 2008; Huff, "Pundit Glenn Beck Calls President Barack Obama a 'Racist,'" 2009.

31. Brimelow, *Alien Nation*, 1996; Buchanan, "Cultural War from the Soul of America," 1992; *Death of the West*, 2002; *State of Emergency*, 2007; Coulter, *Godless*, 2006; and *Guilty*, 2009; Farah, *Taking America Back*, 2010; Gibson, *War on Christmas*, 2006; *How the Left Swiftboated America*, 2009; Hanson, *Mexifornia*, 2003; Huntington, *Clash of Civilizations*, 1996; and *Who Are We?*, 2004; O'Reilly, *Culture Warrior*, 2006; and "GOP Presidential Hopeful John McCain Sits Down with Bill O'Reilly," 2007; Stanton & Maier, *Marriage on Trial*, 2004; Tancredo, *In Mortal Danger*, 2006.

32. O'Reilly, *Culture Warrior*, 2006, pp. 1–2. O'Reilly, Gibson, and other conservatives have also decried the "war on Christmas" brought about by the "cult of multiculturalism." See O'Reilly, *Culture Warrior*, 2006; Gibson, *War on Christmas*, 2006. Patrick Buchanan and the former Republican presidential hopeful Mike Huckabee have likened abortion to the Holocaust and to genocide. See Buchanan, *Death of the West*, 2002, p. 24; Crawford, "Huckabee Likens Abortion to a Holocaust," 2007.

33. Jacobs & Tope, "Politics of Resentment," 2007; Jerit, "Survival of the Fittest," 2004; Mendelberg, *Race Card*, 2001.

34. Nagourney, "New McCain," 2008.

35. Brooks, "Class War before Palin," 2008.

36. Palin, "Palin's Speech at the Republican National Convention," 2008; Abcarian, "Heels On, Gloves Off, Palin Says," 2008.

37. It would be inaccurate to say, however, that Palin fully embraced "traditional" gender norms. As she constantly reminded us, she was a wife and mother of five. But Palin was also very much a career woman, the governor of Alaska, and a very ambitious politician. And she did not achieve her success by riding the coattails of her husband, Todd ("Alaska's first dude"). Further, while many conservative screeds have been written about the evils of feminism, Palin has embraced the term, seeking to wrest it from its left-wing moorings. It is possible then that over the next several years, Sarah Palin will continue to lay out the contours of a kind of "right-wing feminism"—a notion that is alternately oxymoronic, appalling, and frankly confusing to many women on the left. For further discussion of Palin as a feminist (or not), see Goldberg, "Flirting Her Way to Victory," 2008; Goodman, "Sarah Zamboni Clears the Ice on Working Mothers," 2008; Luscombe, "Why Some Women Hate Sarah Palin," 2008; Muskal, "Steinem Criticizes Palin for Using Feminist Brand," 2010; Riley, "Sarah Palin Feminism," 2008; Rohter, "Palin Criticizes Obama as a Faux Feminist," 2008; Steinem, "Wrong Woman, Wrong Message," 2008; Traister, "Zombie Feminists of the RNC," 2008; Valenti, "Sarah Palin's 'Feminism' Is Irrelevant to Her Irresponsible Record," 2008; and "GOP Pinheads," 2008; Young, "Why Feminists Hate Sarah Palin," 2008.

38. Higham, *Strangers in the Land*, 2002, p. 4.

39. On widespread challenges to Obama's patriotism, see Parker, Sawyer, & Towler, "A Black Man in the White House?," 2009. Bachmann quoted in Matthews, "Hardball with Chris Matthews," 2008.

40. See further discussion of the Wright controversy in chapters 2 and 3.

41. Michelle Obama quoted in Oinounou and Kapp, "Michelle Obama Takes Heat," 2008. For criticism of the statement, see Berry, "If Michelle Obama Isn't Racist, What *Is* She?," 2008; Limbaugh, "Michelle Obama Slams America," 2008; Malkin, "Michelle Obama's America—and Mine," 2008; Massie, "Michelle Obama," 2008.

42. Blow, "Obama's Race War," 2010.

43. O'Reilly, "O'Reilly: 'I Don't Want to Go on a Lynching Party against Michelle Obama,'" 2008 (emphasis added).

44. The idea to forward this notion had been proposed in early 2007 by Hillary Clinton's chief campaign strategist, Mark Penn. In a memo dated March 19, Penn wrote:

> All of these articles about his boyhood in Indonesia and his life in Hawaii are geared towards showing his background is diverse, multicultural and putting that in a new light. Save it for 2050. It also exposes a very strong weakness for him—his roots to basic American values and culture are at best limited. Every speech should contain the line you were born in the middle of America to the middle class in the middle of the last century. Let's explicitly own 'American' in our programs, the speeches and the values. He doesn't. ("Penn Strategy Memo," 2008)

Clinton chose to ignore Penn's advice (Green, "Front-Runner's Fall," 2008), but Obama's conservative detractors pursued the argument aggressively.

45. "Another Obama-Osama Mix-Up on Fox," 2008; "Fox Identifies Osama bin Laden as Obama," 2008.

46. Brown, "Commentary: Race-Baiting Wrong, but So Is Over-Reaction," 2008; Elliot, "McCain Rally Speaker Refers to Obama's Middle Name," 2008; "Coulter Explains Why She Is 'Trying to Associate [Obama] with Saddam Hussein?,'" 2008; Hannity & Colmes, "Exclusive: Bill Cunningham on Obama Comments," 2008.

47. Hannity & Colmes, "Exclusive: Bill Cunningham on Obama Comments," 2008.

48. Martin & Smith, "Obama's Apple Pie Campaign," 2007; Macdonald, "Neil Macdonald on the Anatomy of a Smear Job," 2007.

49. CNN later reported that Obama in fact attended secular public school in Indonesia from 1969 to 1971. See "CNN Debunks False Report," 2007.

50. Allen, "We Scream, We Swoon, How Dumb Can We Get?," 2008.

51. Shear, "McCain Plans Fiercer Strategy against Obama," 2008. As it became apparent that the United States was facing one of the most severe economic recessions in its history, the tide turned distinctly in Obama's favor. McCain stumbled badly in his response to the financial meltdown, which ironically made him seem totally out of touch with the concerns of the "Middle Americans" his ticket claimed to champion. At this juncture, Obama's intellectual mastery and propensity to forward big ideas worked to his advantage and gave him a clear lead in the race. Balz & Cohen, "Economic Fears Give Obama Clear Lead over McCain in Poll," 2008. The Republicans in turn intensified their attacks, desperately attempting to move the conversation away from the economy and back to all that was wrong with Obama.

52. Cooper, "McCain: 'Who Is the Real Barack Obama?,'" 2008.

53. Ayers, now a college professor, was a member of a militant leftist group called the Weather Underground in the 1960s and 1970s. This group carried out several

domestic bombings in protest of the Vietnam War and other aspects of U.S. international policy. Obama and Ayers served together on the board of a Chicago nonprofit from 1999 to 2002, though they were not close associates. In August 2008, a group called the American Issues Project spent nearly $3 million on a television ad tying Obama to Ayers. The group was funded by the Texas billionaire Harold Simmons—the man responsible for the "swift boat" ads that had helped to destroy the 2004 Democratic presidential candidate John Kerry's political chances by undermining his credibility on his war record. See Fusco & Pallasch, "Who Is Bill Ayers?," 2008; Kuhnhenn, "Obama Seeks to Silence Ad Tying Him to 60s Radical," 2008; Keen, "Obama Dogged by Links to 1960s Radical," 2008.

54. Orr, "Palin: Obama 'Palling around with Terrorists,'" 2008; Conroy, "Palin: Obama Began His Political Career in Terrorist's Living Room," 2008.

55. See Bash, Hamby, & King, "Palin's 'Going Rogue,' McCain Aide Says," 2008; Clift, "Palin Reignites the Culture War," 2008; Sullivan, "Dangerous Panic on the Far Right," 2008.

56. Examples from rallies found, in turn, in Milbank, "In Fla., Palin Goes for the Rough Stuff as Audience Boos Obama," 2008; Jouvenal, "McCain-Palin Rallies Turning Ugly," 2008; Shear & Bacon, "Anger Is Crowd's Overarching Emotion at McCain Rally," 2008; Aigner, "McCain's 'Fellow Prisoners'?," 2008; McCaffrey, "Candidates Face Rowdy Crowd," 2008.

57. See Meckler, "McCain Asks Supporters to Show Obama Respect," 2008; Spetalnick, "Republican Anger Bubbles Up at McCain Rally," 2008. After the rally, two NBC reporters interviewed the woman, Gayle Quinnell from Shakopee, Minnesota. After informing Quinnell that Obama professes to be Christian, she responded, "He's still got Muslim in him. So that's still part of him. I got all the stuff from the library and I could send you all kinds of stuff on him." See "McCain Responds to 'Arab' Epithet at Rally," 2008.

58. In an article first published in the *Baltimore Sun*, the former McCain adviser Frank Schaeffer wrote, "John McCain and Sarah Palin, you are playing with fire, and you know it. You are unleashing the monster of American hatred and prejudice, to the peril of all of us. You are doing this in wartime. You are doing this as our economy collapses. You are doing this in a country with a history of assassinations.... Make your case. But stop stirring up the lunatic fringe of haters, or risk suffering the judgment of history and the loathing of the American people—forever." See "Open Letter to John McCain," 2008. See also Carpenter, "Just Say It," 2008; Murray, "John Lewis Condemns GOP Campaign Tactics," 2008; Sargent, "Note to News Orgs," 2008; Sullivan, "Dangerous Panic on the Far Right," 2008.

59. The idea of Obama as dangerous and foreign discussed in Tope, "Othering Obama," 2008. For discussion of disparate forms of racialization, see Kim, "Racial Triangulation of Asian Americans," 1999; Collins, "Like One of the Family," 2001; and the previous chapter of this book.

60. See Moraga, "What's Race Gotta Do with It?," 2009; Martin, "Election 2008," 2008; Wingfield & Feagin, *Yes We Can?*, 2010; Chang, "Asian Americans and the Road to the White House," 2009/2010; Fang, "Anderson Cooper 360," 2008.

61. See "CNN Election Center," 2008; Noah, "What We Didn't Overcome," 2008.

NOTES TO CHAPTER 8

1. Smith, "Culture of Conspiracy," 2009.
2. Koppelman, "Why the Stories about Obama's Birth Certificate Will Never Die," 2008. Quote from "Quest for Obama's Birth Doctor," 2009.
3. See archive on *WorldNetDaily* at http://www.wnd.com/?pageId=98546 (accessed April 12, 2011).
4. Smith, "Culture of Conspiracy," 2009.
5. Gordon, "Soldier Balks at Deploying," 2009.
6. Travis, "CNN Poll: Quarter Doubt Obama Was Born in U.S.," 2010.
7. Quote from Eldridge, "Trump Rides Issue of Obama's Birth Certificate," 2011. See also Blodget, "Trump," 2011; Carpenter, "GOP Congressman Introduces Birth Certificate Bill," 2009; Schelzig, "Tennessee: GOP's Ramsey Says He's Unsure of Obama's Citizenship," 2010; Evans, "Republican Senator Says He Backs Birther Lawsuits," 2010.
8. Hulse, "McCain's Canal Zone Birth Prompts Queries about Whether That Rules Him Out," 2008.
9. Holland, "Tea Party Candidates Could Damage Republicans," 2010; Newport, "Tea Party Supporters Overlap Republican Base," 2010. For discussion of points of conflict between the Tea Party and GOP leaders, see Zernike, "Tea Party Activists Angry at G.O.P.," 2011; Cohen, "Tea Party," 2011.
10. Bachmann, "Members of the Tea Party Caucus," 2010.
11. Zernike, "Tea Party Activists Angry at G.O.P.," 2011; "Republicans Win House Majority," 2010.
12. Palin delivered the last message via Twitter. Other quotes from Farber, "Palin," 2010; and Zernike, "Palin Assails Obama," 2010. See also Vogel, "Face of the Tea Party Is Female," 2010; Gardner, "Palin Fires Up GOP on Obama," 2010.
13. Tancredo quoted in Berger, "Tea Party Launches 'Counter-Revolution,'" 2010.
14. Cooper, "Patrick Swayze Dies; Rising Anger in America," 2009. Williams is also a radio talk show host.
15. "'Tea Partier' Mark Williams Writes 'Letter to Abe Lincoln' . . . from the 'Coloreds,'" 2010.
16. The 13th Amendment abolished slavery in 1865, and the 14th, adopted in 1868, guaranteed equal rights to all native-born or naturalized citizens. Quote from ibid.
17. "Tea Party Tension Flares," 2010.
18. Jonsson, "Are 'Tea Party' Rallies Given Preferential Treatment by Police?," 2010.
19. See collections of Tea Party signs at Kelly, "Tea Party and Racism," 2010; PG, "Tit for Tat," 2010; "Ten Most Offensive Tea Party Signs," 2010.
20. The Joker image first appeared on walls and utility posts throughout Los Angeles. It soon after appeared on dozens of conservative websites and at Tea Party rallies across the country. See Praetorius, "Obama Joker Poster Causes Stir on Web," 2009. The Republican National Committee even produced a fund-raising video featuring the image, which it later withdrew. See Memmot, "GOP Chairman Steele Repudiates 'Joker' Image of Obama in RNC Presentation," 2010.

21. Bradley, "Why Is the National Press Ignoring Small-Town Racism?," 2008; "Election Spurs 'Hundreds' of Race Threats, Crimes," 2008. Many of these crimes had strong anti-black overtones, while others referred to Obama as a terrorist and a Muslim. Wingfield and Feagin also discuss the use of Obama's election as a recruiting tool for white supremacist groups after November 4; see *Yes We Can?*, 2010, pp. 214–217.

22. See Reed, "Obama No," 2008; Bonilla-Silva and Ray, "When Whites Love a Black Leader," 2009; Street, *Barack Obama and the Future of American Politics*, 2009; Harlow, "Barack Obama and the (In)significance of His Presidential Campaign," 2009.

23. See Ford, "Church of the Ascending Obama," 2008, "Obama Insults Half a Race," 2008; "Obama '08 Phenomenon," 2008; and "Pandering to Racists," 2008; Ehrenstein, "Obama the 'Magic Negro,'" 2007; Gray, "Obama Mustn't Use People of Color as Props," 2008.

24. Tilove, "Obama Presents Dilemma for Scholars of Race," 2008.

25. Alterman, "Kabuki Democracy," 2010; Krugman, "President Is Missing," 2011. See also Beinart, "Why Obama Disappoints the Left," 2010.

26. The "beer summit" was an "informal" televised meeting, over beer, between President Obama, the Harvard professor Henry Louis Gates, Jr., and the police officer who had arrested Gates after he attempted to "break into" his own house. The "Gates incident" and its aftermath are discussed in Robinson, "Pique and the Professor," 2009; Pew Research Center, *Obama's Ratings Slide across the Board*, 2009; Erbe, "Obama's Henry Louis Gates Arrest Comment Is His Second Race Mistake," 2009; Calderone, "Fox's Beck," 2009; Caddell and Schoen, "Our Divisive President," 2010; Loury, "Obama, Gates, and the American Black Man," 2009; and chapter 3 of this book.

27. Quote from the National Urban League found in Hall, "Obama Urges a Dialogue on Race after Sherrod Case," 2010.

28. West entered into a lengthy, heated exchange with the civil rights leader Al Sharpton during the April 10, 2011, MSNBC special *The Black Agenda*, hosted by Ed Shultz. Sharpton is the prototypical outsider, long known for his street protests, marches, strident critiques of mainstream politicians, and outspoken condemnations of racial inequality; yet he has ironically become an informal adviser to and defender of the Obama administration. As West said to Sharpton during the forum, "I *worry* about you, brother, because you could be easily *manipulated* by those in the White House." Discussion of the West/Sharpton exchange found in Watkins, "Cornel West, Al Sharpton Argue about President Obama," 2011; Schneider, "Wild Shoutfest," 2011; and Harris, "Sharpton and West's MSNBC Shouting Match," 2011. Video of West's equally critical April 4, 2011, comments on President Obama, taped during an interview with *Russia Today*, found on YouTube at "Dr. Cornel West: 'Obama Becoming Puppet of Wall St. Oligarchs,'" http://www.youtube.com/watch?v=s4M4uBdrI_s (accessed April 11, 2011). For other African American critiques of the president, see Grove, "Are Blacks Abandoning Obama?," 2009; Washington, "What Has Barack Obama Done for Black America?," 2010; Kimberly, "Freedom Rider," 2011. Discussion of Sharpton as an administration insider found in Wallsten, "Obama's New Partner," 2010; Washington, "Obama Carefully Courts Black Votes with Sharpton," 2011.

29. See Rodriguez, "Obama and Immigration Reform," 2009; Lovato, "Act Now to Stop the Obama's Administration's Racist 287G Immigration Policy," 2009; Treviño, "Obama Explains Why He Used the Term 'Illegal Immigrant,'" 2009; Falcón, "Latinos Left out of Obama's State of the Union Speech," 2010; "Hispanics Left out of the State of the Union Speech!," 2010; "Enough with Empty Words," 2010; Navarrette, "Did Obama Break Promise to Latinos?," 2010; Schumacher-Matos, "Democrats Must Seize the Immigration Issue," 2010; Navarrette, "Dear Mr. President," 2010. Quote from Treviño, "Are Latinos Really Wanted by Either Party?," 2010.

30. Cesa, "Fooled Again by Breitbart and the Wingnut Right," 2010.

References

"AALDEF Exit Poll of over 16,000 Asian American Voters Shows Strong Support for Barack Obama in Historic 2008 Presidential Election." 2009. *Asian American Legal Defense and Education Fund.* January 5. Accessed March 17, 2009. http://aaldef. org/press-releases/press-release/aaldef-exit-poll-of-over-16000-asian-american-voters-shows-strong-support-for-barack-obama-in-histor.html#.

Abcarian, Robin. 2008. "Heels On, Gloves Off, Palin Says." *Los Angeles Times.* October 5. Accessed October 5, 2008. http://articles.latimes.com/2008/oct/05/nation/na-palin5.

Achenbach, Joel. 2008. "End of the Clinton Era?" *Washington Post.* January 6. Accessed January 6, 2008. http://voices.washingtonpost.com/achenblog/2008/01/end_of_the_clinton_era.html.

Aigner, Adam. 2008. "McCain's 'Fellow Prisoners'?" NBC News. October 8. Accessed October 8, 2008. http://firstread.msnbc.msn.com/_news/2008/10/08/4428842-mccains-fellow-prisoners-.

Allen, Charlotte. 2008. "We Scream, We Swoon, How Dumb Can We Get?" *Washington Post.* March 2. Accessed March 2, 2008. http://www.washingtonpost.com/wp-dyn/content/article/2008/02/29/AR2008022902992.html.

Alterman, Eric. 2010. "Kabuki Democracy: Why a Progressive Presidency Is Impossible, for Now." *The Nation.* July 7. Accessed July 8, 2010. http://www.thenation.com/article/37165/kabuki-democracy-why-progressive-presidency-impossible-now.

Amira, Dan. 2008. "Obama's Tough Talk on African-American Fathers Wins Big Points with Pundits." *New York Magazine.* June 16. Accessed June 20, 2008. http://nymag.com/daily/intel/2008/06/obamas_tough_talk_on_african-american_fathers_wins_big_points_with_pundits.html.

Anderson, Benedict. *Imagined Communities: Reflections on the Origin and Spread of Nationalism.* London: Verso, 1991.

Andrews, David. 1996. "The Fact(s) of Michael Jordan's Blackness: Excavating a Floating Racial Signifier." *Sociology of Sport Journal* 13, no. 2: 122–158.

"Another Obama-Osama Mix-Up on FOX 'News.'" 2008. *News Hounds.* July 10. Accessed May 3, 2009. http://www.newshounds.us/2008/07/10/another_obamaosama_mixup_on_fox_news.php.

Ansell, Amy E. 1997. *New Right, New Racism: Race and Reaction in the United States and Britain.* New York: NYU Press.

———. 2006. "Casting a Blind Eye: The Ironic Consequences of Color-Blindness in South Africa and the United States." *Critical Sociology* 32, nos. 2/3 (March): 333–356.

Appelbaum, Nancy P., Anne S. Macpherson, and Karin Alejandra Rosenblatt, eds. 2003. *Race and Nation in Modern Latin America*. Chapel Hill: University of North Carolina Press.

Arrillaga, Pauline. 2008. "Hispanics' Reluctance on Obama Highlights Black-Brown Divide," *New York Sun*. February 11. Accessed August 2, 2008. http://www.nysun. com/national/hispanics-reluctance-on-obama-highlights-black/71050/#.

Ashley. 2008. "This Just In! Feminism Must Focus on White Ladies." *Change Happens: The SAFER Blog*. June 10. Accessed June 15, 2008. http://www.safercampus.org/ blog/?p=466.

Asian American Legal Defense and Education Fund. 2008. "Asian American Voters Favor Clinton and McCain in Northeast." *New America Media*. February 6. Accessed February 14, 2008. http://news.ncmonline.com/news/view_article. html?article_id=2c7b71365dec50879d45ab3669a09161.

Asians Vote. 2008. "Fang, Obama, and Expanding the Definition of 'Asian American.'" *Asians Vote*. February 1. Accessed February 5, 2008. http://www.asiansvote.com/ entries/000202.shtml.

Asian Week Staff. 2008. "Endorsements." *Asian Week*. February 1. Accessed February 5, 2008. http://www.asianweek.com/2008/02/01/endorsements-2/.

Babington, Charles. 2008. "Might Obama's Success Undercut Affirmative Action?" *USA Today*. June 28. Accessed June 30, 2008. http://www.usatoday.com/news/ politics/2008-06-28-3426171631_x.htm.

Baca Zinn, Maxine, and Bonnie Thornton Dill. 1996. "Theorizing Difference from Multiracial Feminism." *Feminist Studies* 22, no. 2 (Summer): 321–331.

Bachmann, Michele. 2010. "Members of the Tea Party Caucus." *Congresswoman Michele Bachman*. July 21. Accessed August 1, 2010. http://bachmann.house.gov/ News/DocumentSingle.aspx?DocumentID=199440.

Bacon, James A. 2008. "Election Underscores New Hope for a Colorblind Society." *Richmond Times-Dispatch*. November 13. Accessed November 27, 2008. http:// www.inrich.com/cva/ric/opinion.apx.-content-articles-RTD-2008-11-13-0021. html.

Bacon, Perry. 2007. "Can Obama Count on the Black Vote?" *Time*. January 23. Accessed January 31, 2007. http://www.time.com/time/nation/article/0,8599,1581666,00.html.

Bai, Matt. 2008. "Is Obama the End of Black Politics?" *New York Times Magazine*. August 10. Accessed August 10, 2008. http://www.nytimes.com/2008/08/10/ magazine/10politics-t.html.

Balibar, Etienne. 1991. "Racism and Nationalism." Pp. 37–67 in *Race, Nation, Class: Ambiguous Identities*, by Etienne Balibar and Immanuel Wallerstein. New York: Verso.

Ballave, Marcelo. 2008. "Where Do Latinos Go Now?" *Latino Times* 7, no. 6 (June). Accessed July 22, 2008. http://www.latinotimes.org/june.pdf.

Balz, Dan, and Jon Cohen. 2008. "Economic Fears Give Obama Clear Lead Over McCain in Poll." *Washington Post*. September 24. Accessed September 24, 2008. http://www.washingtonpost.com/wp-dyn/content/article/2008/09/23/ AR2008092303667.html.

del Barco, Mandalit. 2008. "Uneasy Black-Latino Ties a Factor in Calif. Primary." National Public Radio. January 24. Accessed January 24, 2008. http://www.npr.org/templates/story/story.php?storyId=18375165.

Barone, Michael. 2001. "The 49 Percent Nation." *National Journal*. June 8. Accessed September 15, 2009. http://www.nationaljournal.com/about/njweekly/stories/2001/0608nj1.htm.

Barras, Jonetta Rose. 2008. "He Leapt the Tallest Barrier: What Does It Mean for Black America?" *Washington Post*. November 9. Accessed November 9, 2008. http://www.washingtonpost.com/wp-dyn/content/article/2008/11/07/AR2008110702894.html.

Barreto, Matt A., and Ricardo Ramírez. 2008. "The Latino Vote Is Pro-Clinton, Not Anti-Obama." *Los Angeles Times*. February 7. Accessed February 16, 2008. http://www.latimes.com/news/opinion/la-oew-barreto7feb07,0,6253659.story.

Barrett, James E., and David Roediger. 2005. "How White People Became White." Pp. 35–40 in *White Privilege: Essential Readings on the Other Side of Racism*, edited by Paula S. Rothenberg, 2nd ed. New York: Worth Publishers.

Barsky, Robert, John Bound, Kerwin Kofi Charles, and Joseph P. Lupton. 2002. "Accounting for the Black-White Wealth Gap: A Nonparametric Approach." *Journal of the American Statistical Association* 97, no. 459 (September): 663–673.

Bash, Dana, Peter Hamby, and John King. 2008. "Palin's 'Going Rogue,' McCain Aide Says." CNN. October 25. Accessed October 26, 2008. http://www.cnn.com/2008/POLITICS/10/25/palin.tension/.

Beck, Glenn. 2003. *The Real America: Messages from the Heart and Heartland*. New York: Pocket Books.

Beinart, Peter. 2007. "Black Like Me: Why White People Like Barack Obama." *New Republic*. February 5. Accessed February 7, 2007. http://www.tnr.com/article/politics/black-me.

———. 2010. "Why Obama Disappoints the Left." *Daily Beast*. July 12. Accessed July 30, 2010. http://www.thedailybeast.com/blogs-and-stories/2010-07-12/peter-beinart-on-why-liberals-are-down-on-obama/.

Bell, Joyce M., and Douglas Hartmann. 2007. "Diversity in Everyday Discourse: The Cultural Ambiguities and Consequences of 'Happy Talk.'" *American Sociological Review* 72, no. 6 (December): 895–914.

Benjamin, Rich. 2009. *Searching for Whitopia: An Improbable Journey to the Heart of White America*. New York: Hyperion Books.

Berger, Judd. 2010. "Tea Party Launches 'Counter-Revolution.'" Fox News. February 4. Accessed February 4, 2010. http://liveshots.blogs.foxnews.com/2010/02/04/tea-party-launches-counter-revolution/.

Berry, Katherine. 2008. "If Michelle Obama Isn't Racist, What *Is* She?" *Pajamas Media*. June 12. Accessed August 1, 2008. http://pajamasmedia.com/blog/if-michelle-obama-isnt-racist-what-is-she/.

Bevan, Tom. 2009. "Ballentine's Racist Attack on Juan Williams." *RealClearPolitics*. October 16. Accessed October 16, 2009. http://realclearpolitics.blogs.time.com/2009/10/16/ballentines-racist-attack-on-juan-williams/.

Bhavnani, Kum-Kum, ed. 2001. *Feminism and "Race."* Oxford: Oxford University Press.

Bialik, Carl. 2009. "Did Race Win the Election for Obama?" *Wall Street Journal.* January 7. Accessed April 24, 2009. http://blogs.wsj.com/numbersguy/did-race-win-the-election-for-obama-487.

Blauner, Robert. 1992. "Talking Past One Another: Black and White Languages of Race." *American Prospect.* June 23. Accessed March 5, 2009. http://www.prospect.org/cs/articles?article=talking_past_each_other.

Blodget, Henry. 2011. "Trump: Obama's Presidency May Be the Greatest Scam in the History of the United States." *Business Insider.* April 10. Accessed April 12, 2011. http://www.businessinsider.com/trump-obama-birth-certificate-2011-4.

Blow, Charles M. 2009. "No More Excuses?" *New York Times.* January 24. Accessed January 24, 2009. http://www.nytimes.com/2009/01/24/opinion/24blow.html.

———. 2010. "Obama's Race War." *New York Times.* July 30. Accessed July 30, 2010. http://www.nytimes.com/2010/07/31/opinion/31blow.html.

Bobo, Lawrence. 1999. "The Color Line, the Dilemma, and the Dream." Pp. 33–55 in *Civil Rights and Social Wrongs: Black-White Relations since World War II*, edited by John Higham. University Park: Pennsylvania State University Press.

———. 2004. "Inequalities That Endure? Racial Ideology, American Politics, and the Peculiar Role of the Social Sciences." Pp. 13–42 in *The Changing Terrain of Race and Ethnicity*, edited by Maria Krysan and Amanda E. Lewis. New York: Russell Sage Foundation.

Boger, John Charles, and Gary Orfield, eds. 2005. *School Resegregation: Must the South Turn Back?* Chapel Hill: University of North Carolina Press.

Bond, Carolyn, and Richard Williams. 2007. "Residential Segregation and the Transformation of Home Mortgage Lending." *Social Forces* 86, no. 2 (December): 671–698.

Bonilla-Silva, Eduardo. 1997. "Rethinking Racism: Toward a Structural Interpretation." *American Sociological Review* 62, no. 3 (June): 465–480.

———. 2001. *White Supremacy and Racism in the Post–Civil Rights Era.* Boulder, CO: Lynne Rienner.

———. 2002. "We Are All Americans! The Latin Americanization of Racial Stratification in the USA." *Race and Society* 5, no. 1: 3–17.

———. 2003. "'New Racism,' Color-Blind Racism, and the Future of Whiteness in America." Pp. 271–284 in *White Out: The Continuing Significance of Racism*, edited by Ashley W. Doane and Eduardo Bonilla-Silva. New York: Routledge.

———. 2004. "From Bi-racial to Tri-racial: Towards a New System of Racial Stratification in the USA." *Ethnic and Racial Studies* 27, no. 6 (November): 931–950.

———. 2008. "The 2008 Elections and the Future of Anti-racism in 21st-Century Amerika or How We Got Drunk with Obama's Hope Liquor and Failed to See Reality." Lecture delivered at the Association for Humanist Sociologists Meeting, Boston. *Black and Progressive Sociologists for Obama.* November 7. Accessed December 17, 2008. http://sociologistsforobama.blogspot.com/2008/11/eduardo-bonilla-silva-problem-with.html.

———. 2009. "Are the Americas 'Sick with Racism' or Is It a Problem at the Poles? A Reply to Christina A. Sue." *Ethnic and Racial Studies* 32, no. 6 (July): 1071–1082.

———. 2010. *Racism without Racists: Color-Blind Racism and the Persistence of Racial Inequality in the United States*, 3rd ed. Lanham, MD: Rowman and Littlefield.

Bonilla-Silva, Eduardo, and Victor Ray. 2009. "When Whites Love a Black Leader: Race Matters in Obamerica." *Journal of African American Studies* 13, no. 2 (June): 176–183.

Bosman, Julie. 2008. "Obama Sharply Assails Absent Black Fathers." *New York Times*. June 16. Accessed July 16, 2008. http://www.nytimes.com/2008/06/16/us/politics/15cnd-obama.html.

Boyer, Peter J. 2008. "The Color of Politics: A Mayor of the Post-racial Generation." *New Yorker*. February 4. Accessed March 20, 2008. http://www.newyorker.com/reporting/2008/02/04/080204fa_fact_boyer.

Bradley, Bill. 2008. "Why Is the National Press Ignoring Small-Town Racism?" *Vanity Fair*. November 12. Accessed January 22, 2009. http://www.vanityfair.com/online/daily/2008/11/why-is-the-national-press-ignoring-smalltown-racism.html.

Branch-Brioso, Karen, and Ronald Roach. 2009. "With Nation's New President, Promise and 'No Excuses' for Black Students." *Diverse: Issues in Higher Education*. January 21. Accessed May 2, 2009. http://diverseeducation.com/artman/publish/article_12199.shtml.

Bravo, Ellen. 2008. "Why So Many Feminists Are Deciding to Vote for Barack Obama." *Huffington Post*. February 1. Accessed February 1, 2008. http://www.huffingtonpost.com/ellen-bravo/why-so-many-feminists-are_b_84482.html.

Breines, Winifred. 2007. "Struggling to Connect: White and Black Feminism in the Movement Years." *Contexts* 6, no. 1 (February): 18–24.

Breslau, Karen. 2008. "Hillary Tears Up: A Muskie Moment, or a Helpful Glimpse of 'the Real Hillary'?" *Newsweek*. January 7. Accessed January 7, 2008. http://www.newsweek.com/2008/01/06/hillary-tears-up.html.

Brimelow, Peter. 1996. *Alien Nation: Common Sense about America's Immigration Disaster*. New York: Harper Perennial.

Brookhiser, Rick. 2008. "Let Us Not Forget." *National Review Online*. January 3. Accessed January 9, 2009. http://www.nationalreview.com/corner/155284/let-us-not-forget/rick-brookhiser.

Brooks, David. 2008. "The Class War before Palin." *New York Times*. October 9. Accessed October 9, 2008. http://www.nytimes.com/2008/10/10/opinion/10brooks.html.

Brown, Campbell. 2008. "Commentary: Race-Baiting Wrong, but So Is Over-Reaction." CNN. October 8. Accessed October 15, 2009. http://articles.cnn.com/2008-10-08/politics/campbell.brown.that.one_1_race-baiting-mccain-obama-supporters?_s=PM:POLITICS.

Brown, Carrie Budoff. 2010. "Hispanic Media Turn on President Obama." Politico.com. August 11. Accessed August 11, 2010. http://www.politico.com/news/stories/0810/40927.html.

Brown, Michael K., Martin Carnoy, Elliott Currie, and Troy Duster. 2003. *Whitewashing Race: The Myth of a Color-Blind Society*. Berkeley: University of California Press.

Brownfemipower. 2008. "OOOh, Look a Thoughtful Intelligent Analysis of Intersectionality!" *La Chola*. June 9. Accessed June 9, 2008. http://brownfemipower.com/.

Brunsma, David, ed. 2006. *Mixed Messages: Multiracial Identities in the "Color-Blind" Era*. Boulder, CO: Lynne Rienner.

Buchanan, Patrick. 1992. "The Cultural War for the Soul of America." *Patrick J. Buchanan: Official Website*. September 14. Accessed June 10 2008. http://buchanan.org/blog/the-cultural-war-for-the-soul-of-america-149.

———. 2002. *The Death of the West: How Dying Populations and Immigrant Invasions Imperil Our Country and Civilization*. New York: Thomas Dunne.

———. 2007. *State of Emergency: The Third World Invasion and Conquest of America*. New York: St. Martin's Griffin.

———. 2008. "A Brief for Whitey." Townhall.com. March 21. Accessed March 22, 2008. http://townhall.com/columnists/PatBuchanan/2008/03/21/a_brief_for_whitey.

Burns, Quiana. 2007. "Black Vote Support Not Sure Thing for Obama." ABC News. February 5. Accessed February 5, 2007. http://abcnews.go.com/Politics/story?id=2849517&page=1.

Bush, George W. 2001. "Freedom and Fear at War: Address to a Joint Session of Congress and the American People." *National Review*. September 20. Accessed November 6, 2008. http://old.nationalreview.com/document/document092101.shtml.

Butterfield, Sherri-Ann P. 2004. "'We're Just Black': The Racial and Ethnic Identities of Second-Generation West Indians in New York." Pp. 288–312 in *Becoming New Yorkers: Ethnographies of the New Second Generation*, edited by Philip Kasinitz, John H. Mollenkopf, and Mary C. Waters. New York: Russell Sage Foundation.

Bykofsky, Stu. 2008. "My First Post-racial Column: America Is on the Ascent." *Philadelphia Daily News*. November 6. Accessed November 20, 2008. http://www.philly.com/philly/news/politics/elections/20081106_Stu_Bykofsky__My_first_post-racial_column__America_is_on_the_ascent.html.

Byrne, Dennis. 2008. "Time to Give Race a Respite." *Chicago Tribune*. November 11. Accessed November 16, 2008. http://www.chicagotribune.com/news/nationworld/chi-oped1111byrnenov11,0,521148.story.

Caddell, Patrick H., and Douglas E. Schoen. 2010. "Our Divisive President." *Wall Street Journal*. July 28. Accessed July 28, 2010. http://online.wsj.com/article/NA_WSJ_PUB:SB10001424052748703700904575391553798363586.html.

Cain, Bruce E. 2008. "How Long Will the GOP Be in the Cold?" *Los Angeles Times*. November 5. Accessed November 5, 2008. http://www.latimes.com/news/opinion/la-oew-schnur-cain5-2008nov05,0,7982924.story.

Calabresi, Massimo. 2008. "Obama's 'Electability' Code for Race?" *Time*. May 6. Accessed June 3, 2008. http://www.time.com/time/politics/article/0,8599,1737725,00.html.

Calderone, Michael. 2009. "Fox's Beck: Obama Is 'a Racist.'" Politico.com. July 28. Accessed July 28, 2009. http://www.politico.com/blogs/michaelcalderone/0709/Foxs_Beck_Obama_is_a_racist.html.

Caldwell, Wilber W. 2006. *American Narcissism: The Myth of National Superiority*. New York: Algora Publishing.

Canellos, Peter. 2008. "McCain's 'Judeo-Christian Values' Reference Puzzles." *Boston Globe*. August 19. Accessed August 19, 2008. http://www.boston.com/news/nation/articles/2008/08/19/mccains_judeo_christian_values_reference_puzzles.

Carlsen, Laura. 2008. "Obama and the Minority Majority." *Americas Policy Program.* November 14. Accessed November 20, 2008. http://americas.irc-online.org/am/5672.

Carpenter, Amanda. 2009. "GOP Congressman Introduces Birth Certificate Bill." *Washington Times.* March 16. Accessed March 27, 2009. http://www.washingtontimes.com/weblogs/back-story/2009/Mar/16/gop-congressman-introduces-birth-certificate-bill/.

Carpentier, Megan. 2008. "Just Say It: The Race-Baiting Tactics of John McCain and Sarah Palin Are Reprehensible." *Jezebel.* October 10. Accessed October 13, 2008. http://jezebel.com/5061902/just-say-it-the-race+baiting-tactics-of-john-mccain-and-sarah-palin-are-reprehensible.

Carr, Leslie G. 1997. *"Color-Blind" Racism.* Thousand Oaks, CA: Sage Publications.

Carrillo Rowe, Aimee. 2004. "Whose 'America'? The Politics of Rhetoric and Space in the Formation of U.S. Nationalism." *Radical History Review* 89, no. 1 (Spring): 115–134.

Carroll, Jason. 2008. "Behind the Scenes: Is Barack Obama Black or Biracial?" CNN. June 9. Accessed June 9, 2008. http://www.cnn.com/2008/POLITICS/06/09/btsc.obama.race/index.html.

Cesa, Bob. 2010. "Fooled Again by Breitbart and the Wingnut Right." *Huffington Post.* July 21. Accessed July 21, 2010. http://www.huffingtonpost.com/bob-cesca/fooled-again-by-breitbart_b_654594.html.

Chang, Jeff. 2008. "Why Latinos and Asians Went for Hillary." *Huffington Post.* February 6. Accessed February 6, 2008. http://www.huffingtonpost.com/jeff-chang/why-latinos-and-asian-ame_b_85359.html.

Chang, Robert S. 2009/2010. "Asian Americans and the Road to the White House: Musings on Being Invisible." *Asian American Law Journal* 16:205–213.

Chen, Nancy, Ann Lata Kalayil, and Stanley M. Toy Jr. 2008. "Response to 80–20 from Obama AAPI Leaders." *Asian Americans for Obama.* January 17. Accessed February 5, 2008. http://www.asianamericansforobama.com/response-to-80-20-from-obama-aapi-leaders.

Chen, Thomas. 2009. "Why Asian Americans Voted for Obama." *Perspective Magazine.* February 26. Accessed April 10, 2009. http://www.perspy.com/?p=74.

Chiareli, Antonio. n.d. "Muslims and Arab Americans: A New 'Crisis of Visibility.'" Accessed September 10, 2010. http://www.uu.edu/institutes/henry/resources/article.cfm?ID=12.

Chideya, Farai. 1999. "A Nation of Minorities: America in 2050." *Civil Rights Journal* 4, no. 1 (Fall): 34.

Chin, Maytak. 2008. "Identity Politics: Where Do You Fit In?" *Asian American Action Fund.* January 30. Accessed February 12, 2008. http://www.aaa-fund.com/?p=165.

Chotiner, Isaac. 2008. "Asian Alienation: Why Did Asian Americans Vote So Overwhelmingly Against Barack Obama?" *New Republic.* February 7. Accessed February 7, 2008. http://www.tnr.com/article/politics/asian-alienation.

"Chris Matthews: 'I Felt This Thrill Going Up My Leg' as Obama Spoke." 2008. *Huffington Post.* February 13. Accessed February 13, 2008. http://www.huffingtonpost.com/2008/02/13/chris-matthews-i-felt-thi_n_86449.html.

Chuang, Angie. 2008. "Racial Rifts: Obama's Candidacy a Rorschach Test for Nation's Minorities." *Seattle Times*. July 16. Accessed July 20, 2008. http://seattletimes. nwsource.com/html/opinion/2008053408_raceriffop16.html.

Chude-Sokei, Louis. 2007. "Shades of Black." *Los Angeles Times*. February 18. Accessed February 18, 2008. http://articles.latimes.com/2007/feb/18/opinion/op-chude-sokei18.

Citrin, Jack, David O. Sears, Christopher Muste, and Cara Wong. 2001. "Multiculturalism in American Public Opinion." *British Journal of Political Science* 31, no. 2: 247–275.

Clift, Eleanor. 2008. "Palin Reignites the Culture War." *Newsweek*. October 3. Accessed October 3, 2008. http://www.newsweek.com/2008/10/02/palin-reignites-the-culture-war.html.

"CNN Debunks False Report about Obama." 2007. CNN. January 22. Accessed January 23, 2007. http://www.cnn.com/2007/POLITICS/01/22/obama.madrassa/.

"CNN Election Center." 2008. Accessed January 5, 2009. http://www.cnn.com/ELECTION/2008/results/president/.

Coates, Ta-Nehisi. 2007. "Is Obama Black Enough?" *Time*. February 1. Accessed February 1, 2007. http://www.time.com/time/nation/article/0,8599,1584736,00.html.

———. 2008. "A Deeper Black." *The Nation*. May 1. Accessed May 1, 2008. http://www.thenation.com/article/deeper-black.

———. 2008. "More Dumb Questions about Barack Obama and Black Folks." *Talking Points Memo*. June 9. Accessed June 11, 2008. http://tpmcafe.talkingpointsmemo.com/2008/06/09/more_dumb_race_questions_about/.

———. 2008. "'This Is How We Lost to the White Man': The Audacity of Bill Cosby's Black Conservatism." *The Atlantic*. May. Accessed May 15, 2008. http://www.theatlantic.com/magazine/archive/2008/05/-8216–this-is-how-we-lost-to-the-white-man-8217/6774/.

———. 2009. "Especially the Blacks and the Latinos." *The Atlantic*. May 28. Accessed May 28, 2009. http://www.theatlantic.com/culture/archive/2009/05/especially-the-blacks-and-the-latinos/18402/.

Cochran, David. 1999. *The Color of Freedom: Race and Contemporary American Liberalism*. Albany: SUNY Press.

Cohen, Sharon. 2007. "Obama's Path to Power Typical of New Generation of Black Political Leaders." *USA Today*. February 9. Accessed March 20, 2008. http://www.usatoday.com/news/washington/2007-02-09-newgeneration_x.htm.

Cohen, Tom. 2011. "Tea Party: Bring on a Government Shutdown." CNN. April 6. Accessed April 12, 2011. http://articles.cnn.com/2011-04-06/politics/tea.party.shut.down_1_government-shutdown-spending-cuts-republican-pledge?_s=PM:POLITICS.

Cohn, Jonathan. 2008. "Why Obama Should Ignore Ferraro." *New Republic*. March 12. Accessed March 18, 2008. http://www.tnr.com/blog/the-plank/why-obama-should-ignore-ferraro.

Collins, Patricia Hill. 1990. *Black Feminist Thought: Knowledge, Consciousness, and the Politics of Empowerment*. Boston: Unwin Hyman.

———. 1993. "Toward a New Vision: Race, Class, and Gender as Categories of Analysis and Connection." *Race, Sex, and Class* 1, no. 1 (Fall): 25–45.

———. 2001. "Like One of the Family: Race, Ethnicity, and the Paradox of American National Identity." *Ethnic and Racial Studies* 24, no. 1 (January): 3–28.

"Complete Final Debate Transcript: John McCain and Barack Obama." 2008. *Los Angeles Times.* October 15. Accessed October 16, 2008. http://latimesblogs.latimes.com/washington/2008/10/debate-transcri.html.

Conan, Neil. 2007. "Can Barack Obama Win the Black Vote?" National Public Radio. February 14. Accessed February 15, 2007. http://www.npr.org/templates/transcript/transcript.php?storyId=7402914.

Conason, Joe. 2008. "Was Hillary Channeling George Wallace?" Salon.com. May 9. Accessed May 12, 2008. http://www.salon.com/news/opinion/joe_conason/2008/05/09/clinton_remarks.

Condon, Stephanie. 2010. "Obama: My 'Biggest Disappointment' Is Not Passing DREAM Act." CBS News. December 22. Accessed April 14, 2011. http://www.cbsnews.com/8301-503544_162-20026460-503544.html.

———. 2011. "Obama's Challenge: Convince Latinos He's More Than the Anti-GOP Vote." CBS News. March 30. Accessed April 11, 2011. http://www.cbsnews.com/8301-503544_162-20048080-503544.html.

Conley, Dalton. 2009. *Being Black, Living in the Red: Race, Wealth, and Social Policy in America*, rev. ed. Berkeley: University of California Press.

Connerly, Ward. 2008. "A Triumph of Principle over Color." *Sacramento Bee.* November 16. Accessed November 16, 2008. http://www.sacbee.com/1190.

Conniff, Ruth. 2008. "Jeremiah Wright's Bombshell." *The Progressive.* April 28. Accessed May 5, 2008. http://www.progressive.org/mag_rc042808.

Conroy, Scott. 2008. "Palin: Obama Began His Political Career in Terrorist's Living Room." CBS News. October 5. Accessed October 5, 2008. http://www.cbsnews.com/8301-502443_162-4502414-502443.html.

Contreras, Raoul Lowery. 2008. "The Bradley Effect Is Still in Effect." *Los Angeles Times.* February 5. Accessed February 16, 2008. http://www.latimes.com/news/opinion/la-oew-contreras5feb05,0,5145379.story.

"A Conversation about Asian Pacific America and President Barack Obama. Interview with Dr. Konrad Ng." 2009/2010. *Asian American Law Journal* 16: 197–204. Accessed July 1, 2010. http://www.boalt.org/aalj/downloads/articles/a-conversation-about-asian-pacific-america-and-president-barack-obama-interview-with-dr-konrad-ng.pdf.

Cooper, Anderson. 2009. "Patrick Swayze Dies; Rising Anger in America; Yale Murder Mystery." Television transcript. *Anderson Cooper 360.* September 14. Accessed October 3, 2009. http://transcripts.cnn.com/TRANSCRIPTS/0909/14/acd.02.html.

Cooper, Helene. 2009. "Attorney General Chided for Language on Race." *New York Times.* March 7. Accessed March 7, 2009. http://www.nytimes.com/2009/03/08/us/politics/08race.html.

Cooper, Michael. 2008. "McCain: 'Who Is the Real Barack Obama?'" *Washington Post.* October 6. Accessed October 6. http://thecaucus.blogs.nytimes.com/2008/10/06/mccain-who-is-the-real-barack-obama/.

Corley, Cheryl. 2008. "Writer: Whites See Obama as a Black Exception." National Public Radio. August 27. Accessed August 28, 2008. http://www.npr.org/templates/story/story.php?storyId=94014535#.

———. 2010. "NAACP, Tea Party Volley over Racism Claims." National Public Radio. July 14. Accessed July 14, 2010. http://www.npr.org/templates/story/story. php?storyId=128505089.

Cornyetz, Nina. 1994. "Fetishized Blackness: Hip-Hop and Racial Desire in Contemporary Japan." *Social Text* 41 (Winter): 113–139.

Cose, Ellis. 1995. *The Rage of a Privileged Class: Why Do Prosperous Blacks Still Have the Blues?* New York: Harper Perennial.

Coulter, Ann. 2006. *Godless: The Church of Liberalism.* New York: Crown Forum.

———. 2009. *Guilty: Liberal "Victims" and Their Assault on America.* New York: Three Rivers Press.

"Coulter Explains Why She Is 'Trying to Associate [Obama] with Saddam Hussein?': 'Because I Think It's Funny.'" 2008. *Media Matters.* February 15. Accessed February 15, 2008. http://mediamatters.org/research/200802150002.

Coyne, Andrew. 2007. "The Blackness of Barack Obama." *National Post.* February 14. Accessed February 20, 2007. http://www.freerepublic.com/focus/f-news/1784870/posts.

Crawford, Jamie. 2007. "Huckabee Likens Abortion to a Holocaust." CNN. October 21. Accessed July 3, 2010. http://politicalticker.blogs.cnn.com/2007/10/21/huckabee-likens-abortion-to-holocaust/.

Crouch, Stanley. 2006. "What Obama Isn't: Black Like Me on Race." *New York Daily News.* November 2. Accessed January 15, 2007. http://www.nydailynews.com/archives/opinions/2006/11/02/2006-11-02_what_obama_isn_t__black_like.html.

Crowley, Candy, and Sasha Johnson. 2007. "Is Black America Ready to Embrace Obama?" CNN. February 28. Accessed February 28, 2007. http://articles.cnn.com/2007-02-28/politics/obama.black.vote_1_black-voters-obama-camp-obama-in-south-carolina?_s=PM:POLITICS.

Cubias, Daniel. 2008. "What Does an Obama Administration Mean for Latinos?" *Huffington Post.* November 12. Accessed November 12, 2008. http://www.huffingtonpost.com/daniel-cubias/what-does-an-obama-admini_b_143156.html#.

Cullen, Lisa Takeuchi. 2008. "Does Obama Have an Asian Problem?" *Time.* February 18. Accessed February 28, 2008. http://www.time.com/time/politics/article/0,8599,1714292,00.html.

———. 2008. "Does Obama Have an Asian Problem? We're Still Debating." *Time.* February 28. Accessed February 28, 2008. http://workinprogress.blogs.time.com/2008/02/28/does_obama_have_an_asian_probl_1/.

Curtis, Mary C. 2008. "The Loud Silence of Feminists." *Washington Post.* June 21. Accessed June 21, 2008. http://www.washingtonpost.com/wp-dyn/content/article/2008/06/20/AR2008062002209.html.

D. G. 2008. "Does 'Postracial' Just Mean Light-Skinned?" *PostBourgie.* February 26. Accessed February 28, 2008. http://www.postbourgie.com/2008/02/26/does-post-racial-just-mean-light-skinned/.

Dalmage, Heather. 2000. *Tripping on the Color Line: Black-White Multiracial Families in a Racially Divided World.* New Brunswick, NJ: Rutgers University Press.

Daniel, Reginald G. 2002. *More Than Black? Multiracial Identity and the New Racial Order.* Philadelphia: Temple University Press.

Darko, Donna. 2008. "The Race Trumps Gender Theme." *Donna Darko.* July 30. Accessed September 4, 2008. http://donnadarko.wordpress.com/2008/07/30/working-my-last-nerve/.

Davis, Tiffany Yvonne. 2007. "The American Dream Deferred: The Effects of Racialization on the Assimilation of First-Generation Mexican Migrants in the Twin Cities." PhD diss., University of Minnesota.

Dawson, Michael. 1994. *Behind the Mule: Race and Class in African-American Politics.* Princeton: Princeton University Press.

———. 2001. *Black Visions: The Roots of Contemporary African-American Political Ideologies.* Chicago: University of Chicago Press.

Dedman, Bill. 2008. "Historians Write 1st Draft on Obama Victory." MSNBC. November 5. Accessed April 20, 2011. http://www.msnbc.msn.com/id/27539416/ns/politics-decision_08/.

Dee. 2011. "Advice to President Obama on Winning the Hispanic Vote in 2012." *Immigration Talk with a Mexican American.* April 3. Accessed April 11, 2011. http://immigrationmexicanamerican.blogspot.com/2011/04/advice-to-president-obama-on-winning.html.

"Deportations by Fiscal Year." 2010. *America's Voice Online.* May 20. Accessed July 26, 2010. http://amvoice.3cdn.net/9d1585d0ce20801cf5_ghm6b5oub.jpg.

Dickerson, Debra. 2007. "Colorblind." Salon.com. January 22. Accessed January 22, 2007. http://www.salon.com/news/opinion/feature/2007/01/22/obama.

Dickerson, Niki T., and Jerry A. Jacobs. 2006. "Race Differentials in College Selectivity, 1981–2000." *Journal of African American Studies* 10, no. 1 (Summer): 3–18.

DiMaggio, Anthony. 2008. "Transcending Race?" *Counterpunch.* November 14/16. Accessed June 24, 2011. http://www.counterpunch.org/dimaggio11142008.html.

Donna. 2008. "White Women Feminism—There They Go Again." *Silence of Our Friends.* March 6. Accessed August 2, 2008. http://the-silence-of-our-friends.blogspot.com/2008/03/white-women-feminism-there-they-go.html.

Douglass, Susan. 2008. "Why Women Hate Hillary." *In These Times.* April 27. Accessed May 13, 2008. http://www.inthesetimes.com/article/3129/why_women_hate_hillary/.

D'Souza, Dinesh. 1995. *The End of Racism: Principles for a Multiracial Society.* New York: Free Press.

Dutta, Gautam. 2008. "Divide and Dishonor." *Asian American Action Fund.* January 30. Accessed February 5, 2008. http://www.aaa-fund.com/?p=164.

Dyson, Michael Eric. 2008. "Race, Post Race." *Los Angeles Times.* November 5. Accessed November 5, 2008. http://articles.latimes.com/2008/nov/05/opinion/oe-dyson5.

Edelman, Peter, Harry J. Holzer, and Paul Offner. 2006. *Reconnecting Disadvantaged Young Men.* Washington, DC: Urban Institute Press.

Edney, Hazel Trice. 2010. "Obama Needs Race Staff in the White House, Say Some Civil Rights Leaders." *Black Voice News.* August 2. Accessed September 20, 2010. http://www.blackvoicenews.com/news/news-wire/44791-obama-needs-race-staff-in-the-white-house-say-some-civil-rights-leaders.html.

Ehrenstein, David. 2007. "Obama the 'Magic Negro.'" *Los Angeles Times.* March 19. Accessed April 5, 2008. http://www.latimes.com/news/opinion/commentary/la-oe-ehrenstein19mar19,0,3391015.story.

Eilperin, Juliet. 2008. "Palin's 'Pro-America Areas' Remark: Extended Version." *Washington Post*. October 17. Accessed October 17, 2008. http://voices.washingtonpost. com/44/2008/10/palin-clarifies-her-pro-americ.html.

Elder, Larry. 2000. *The Ten Things You Can't Say in America*. New York: St. Martin's Press.

——. 2008. "Obama or Not, America Still a 'Racist Nation.'" Townhall.com. April 10. Accessed April 12, 2008. http://townhall.com/Columnists/Larry-Elder/2008/04/10/obama_or_not,_america_still_a_racist_nation.

Eldridge, David. 2011. "Trump Rides Issue of Obama's Birth Certificate: GOP Poll Puts Him at No. 2." *Washington Times*. April 10. Accessed April 12, 2011. http:// www.washingtontimes.com/news/2011/apr/10/trump-rides-issue-of-presidents-birth/.

"Election Spurs 'Hundreds' of Race Threats, Crimes." 2008. *USA Today*. November 15. Accessed November 15, 2008. http://www.usatoday.com/news/politics/2008-11-15-obama-election-race_N.htm.

Elliot, Philip. 2008. "McCain Rally Speaker Refers to Obama's Middle Name." Newsvine.com. October 8. Accessed December 12, 2008. http://www.newsvine. com/_news/2008/10/08/1971287-mccain-rally-speaker-refers-to-obamas-middle-name.

English, Bella. 2008. "The Diversity Bloc Is Divided." *Boston Globe*. February 15. Accessed February 18, 2008. http://www.boston.com/news/local/articles/2008/02/15/the_diversity_bloc_is_divided/.

"Enough with Empty Words." 2010. *La Opinión*. February 16. Accessed August 2, 2010. http://www.impre.com/laopinion/opinion/2010/2/16/enough-with-empty-words-173556-1.html.

Erbe, Bonnie. 2009. "Obama's Henry Louis Gates Arrest Comment Is His Second Race Mistake." *US News & World Report*. July 24. Accessed July 27, 2008. http:// www.usnews.com/opinion/blogs/erbe/2009/07/24/obamas-henry-louis-gates-arrest-comment-is-his-second-race-mistake.

Essed, Philomena. 1991. *Understanding Everyday Racism: An Interdisciplinary Theory*. Newbury Park, CA: Sage Publications.

Eubanks, W. Ralph. 2009. "Affirmative Action and After." *American Scholar*. Winter. http://www.theamericanscholar.org/affirmative-action-and-after/.

Evans, Ben. 2010. "Republican Senator Says He Backs Birther Lawsuits." ABC News. July 12. Accessed July 12, 2010. http://abcnews.go.com/Politics/ wireStory?id=11147438.

Falcón, Angelo. 2010. "Latinos Left out of Obama's State of the Union Speech." *Orlando Sentinel*. January 28. Accessed February 15, 2010. http://blogs.orlandosentinel.com/news_hispanicaffairs/2010/01/latinos-left-out-of-obamas-state-of-the-union-speech.html.

Fang, Jennifer. 2008. "Anderson Cooper 360: The Asian American Vote." *Racialicious*. February 12. Accessed February 13, 2008. http://www.racialicious. com/2008/02/12/anderson-cooper-360-the-asian-american-vote/.

——. 2008. "One Asian Passionate about Obama." *New America Media*. January 22. Accessed February 5, 2008. http://blogs.newamericamedia.org/andrew-lam/972/ one-asian-passionate-about-obama.

———. 2008. "Pitting Race against Gender in Election '08: Why the Battle of Electoral Identity Politics Is Bad for All of Us." *Reappropriate.* January 8. Accessed January 12, 2008. http://www.reappropriate.com/?p=949.

Farah, Joseph. 2010. *Taking America Back: A Radical Plan to Revive Freedom, Morality, and Justice,* 2nd ed. Washington, DC: WorldNetDaily News.

Farber, Dan. 2010. "Palin: 'America Is Ready for Another Revolution.'" CBS News. February 6. Accessed February 6, 2010. http://www.cbsnews.com/8301-503544_162-6181906-503544.html.

Feagin, Joe. 2000. *Racist America: Roots, Current Realities, and Future Reparations.* New York: Routledge.

———. 2006. *Systemic Racism: A Theory of Oppression.* New York: Routledge.

———. 2010. "Which Voters Had the Most Impact?: The Election of President Obama." *Racism Review.* August 22. Accessed August 24, 2010. http://www.racismreview.com/blog/2010/08/22/which-voters-had-the-most-impact-the-election-of-president-obama/.

Feagin, Joe, and Melvin P. Sikes. 1994. *Living with Racism: The Black Middle-Class Experience.* Boston: Beacon Press.

Feldt, Gloria. 2008. "Why Women Need to Learn History's Election Power Lesson." *Huffington Post.* February 18. Accessed March 11, 2008. http://www.huffington-post.com/gloria-feldt/why-women-need-to-learn-h_b_87218.html.

Fernandes, Sujatha. 2003. "Fear of a Black Nation: Local Rappers, Transnational Crossings, and State Power in Contemporary Cuba." *Anthropological Quarterly* 76, no. 4 (Fall): 575–608.

Foner, Nancy, ed. 2001. *Islands in the City: West Indian Migration to New York.* Berkeley: University of California Press.

Ford, Glen. 2008. "Church of the Ascending Obama." *Black Agenda Report.* August 13. Accessed August 22, 2008. http://www.blackagendareport.com/?q=node/10739.

———. 2008. "The Obama '08 Phenomenon: What Have We Learned?" *Black Agenda Report.* November 4. Accessed November 5, 2008. http://www.blackagendareport.com/?q=node/10873.

———. 2008. "Obama Insults Half a Race." *Black Agenda Report.* June 18. Accessed June 18, 2008. http://blackagendareport.com/?q=node/10661.

———. 2008. "Pandering to Racists." *Black Agenda Report.* October 28. Accessed November 5, 2008. http://blackagendareport.com/?q=content/pandering-racists.

Forrest, Kim, and Brooke Lea Foster. 2006. "25 Beautiful People: Barack Obama." *Washingtonian Magazine.* March 1. Accessed January 5, 2008. http://www.washingtonian.com/articles/people/2295.html.

Fortini, Amanda. 2008. "The Feminist Reawakening: Hillary Clinton and the Fourth Wave." *New York Magazine.* April 13. Accessed April 13, 2008. http://nymag.com/news/features/46011/.

"Fox Identifies Osama bin Laden as Obama—again." 2008. *News Hounds.* July 30. Accessed August 2, 2008. http://www.newshounds.us/2008/07/30/fox_identifies_osama_bin_laden_as_obama_again.php.

Fram, Alan. "Poll: Public Cool to Michelle, Doesn't Know Cindy." 2008. *RealClearPolitics.* July 2. Accessed July 2, 2008. http://www.realclearpolitics.com/news/ap/politics/2008/Jul/02/poll__public_cool_to_michelle__doesn_t_know_cindy.html.

Frank, Thomas. 2002. "Let's Talk Class Again." *London Review of Books* 24, no. 6 (March). Accessed July 2, 2008. http://www.lrb.co.uk/v24/n06/thomas-frank/lets-talk-class-again.

———. 2004. *What's the Matter with Kansas? How Conservatives Won the Heart of America*. New York: Metropolitan Books.

Frankenberg, Ruth. 2001. "The Mirage of Unmarked Whiteness." Pp. 72–96 in *The Making and Unmaking of Whiteness*, edited by Birgit Brander Rasmussen, Eric Klinenberg, Irene J. Nexica, and Matt Wray. Durham, NC: Duke University Press.

Frederick, Don. 2008. "Put Michelle Obama in the Bacon Camp." *Los Angeles Times*. June 18. Accessed June 18, 2008. http://latimesblogs.latimes.com/washington/2008/06/put-the-obamas.html.

Frederickson, George M. 2001. "Beyond Race? Ideological Color Blindness in the United States, Brazil, and South Africa." Pp. 59–71 in *Race in 21st-Century America*, edited by Curtis Stokes, Theresa Meléndez, and Genice Rhodes-Reed. East Lansing: Michigan State University Press.

Freedland, Jonathan. 2008. "America Has Not Lost Its Talent for Renewal—Even Redemption." *Guardian*. November 8. Accessed November 9, 2008. http://www.guardian.co.uk/commentisfree/2008/nov/08/us-elections2008-barack-obama.

Freedman, Samuel J. 2008. "After Obama Victory, Test for the Black Clergy." *New York Times*. November 15. Accessed November 25, 2008. http://www.nytimes.com/2008/11/15/us/15religion.html.

de la Fuente, Alejandro. 2001. *A Nation for All: Race, Inequality, and Politics in Twentieth-Century Cuba*. Chapel Hill: University of North Carolina Press.

Fusco, Chris, and Abdon M. Pallasch. 2008. "Who Is Bill Ayers?" *Chicago Sun-Times*. April 18. Accessed April 18, 2008. http://www.suntimes.com/news/politics/obama/902213,CST-NWS-ayers18.article.

Gallagher, Charles. 2003. "Color-Blind Privilege: The Social and Political Functions of Erasing the Color Line in Post-race America." *Race, Gender, and Class* 10, no. 4: 23–37.

———. 2003. "Miscounting Race: Explaining Whites' Misperceptions of Racial Group Size." *Sociological Perspectives* 46, no. 3: 381–396.

———. 2008. "Introduction." Pp. ix–xv in *Racism in Post-race America: New Theories, New Directions*, edited by Charles Gallagher. Chapel Hill, NC: Social Forces Publishing.

Gamboa, Suzanne. 2011. "Obama Woos Hispanic Vote on Education." MSNBC. March 31. Accessed April 11, 2011. http://www.msnbc.msn.com/id/42357769/ns/politics-white_house/.

Gandelman, Joe. 2008. "Rasmussen Poll: More Voters Think Obama Played Race Card Than McCain in Recent Political Mini-Firestorms." *Moderate Voice*. August 3. Accessed August 3, 2008. http://themoderatevoice.com/21531/rasmussen-poll-more-voters-think-obama-played-race-card-than-mccain-in-recent-political-mini-firestorms/.

Gane-McCalla, Casey. 2009. "Is Obama's Inauguration MLK's Dream? Yes and No." *Huffington Post*. January 17. Accessed January 17, 2009. http://www.huffingtonpost.com/casey-ganemccalla/is-obamas-inauguration-ml_b_158630.html#.

Gans, Herbert. 1999. "The Possibility of a New Racial Hierarchy in the 21st-Century United States." Pp. 371–390 in *The Cultural Territories of Race: Black and White Boundaries*, edited by Michèle Lamont. Chicago: University of Chicago Press.

Gardner, Amy. 2010. "Palin Fires Up GOP on Obama, Midterm Elections at Annual Conference." *Washington Post*. April 10. Accessed April 10, 2010. http://www. washingtonpost.com/wp-dyn/content/article/2010/04/09/AR2010040905445. html.

Gerstle, Gary. 2001. *American Crucible: Race and Nation in the Twentieth Century*. Princeton, NJ: Princeton University Press.

Gibson, Campbell, and Kay Jung. 2002. "Table 1: United States—Race and Hispanic Origin: 1790 to 1990." In *Historical Census Statistics on Population Totals by Race, 1790 to 1990, and by Hispanic Origin, 1970 to 1990, for the United States, Regions, Divisions, and States*. Washington, DC: U.S. Census Bureau. Accessed May 1, 2010. http://www.census.gov/population/www/documentation/twps0056/tab01.pdf.

Gibson, John. 2006. *The War on Christmas: How the Liberal Plot to Ban the Sacred Christian Holiday Is Worse Than You Thought*. New York: Sentinel.

———. 2009. *How the Left Swiftboated America: The Liberal Media Conspiracy to Make You Think George Bush Was the Worst President in History*. New York: HarperCollins.

Gillespie, Andra, ed. 2010. *Whose Black Politics? Cases in Post-racial Black Leadership*. New York: Routledge.

Giroux, Henry. 2009. "Judge Sonia Sotomayor and the New Racism: Getting beyond the Politics of Denial." *Truthout*. June 4. Accessed June 4, 2009. http://www.truthout.org/060409A.

Gitell, Seth. 2008. "Is Obama Like King?" *New York Sun*. January 8. Accessed January 9, 2008. http://www.nysun.com/opinion/is-obama-like-king/69072/.

Givhan, Robin. 2007. "Hillary Clinton's Tentative Dip into New Neckline Territory." *Washington Post*. July 20. Accessed July 20, 2007. http://www.washingtonpost. com/wp-dyn/content/article/2007/07/19/AR2007071902668.html.

Glenn, Evelyn Nakano. 2002. *Unequal Freedom: How Race and Gender Shaped American Citizenship and Labor*. Cambridge, MA: Harvard University Press.

Glod, Maria. 2007. "U.S. Teens Trail Peers Around World on Math-Science Test." *Washington Post*. December 5. Accessed December 5, 2008. http://www.washingtonpost.com/wp-dyn/content/article/2007/12/04/AR2007120400730.html.

Goldberg, Michelle. 2008. "3 A.M. for Feminism: Clinton Dead-Enders and the Crisis in the Women's Movement." *New Republic*. June 6. Accessed June 13, 2008. http://www.tnr.com/article/politics/3-am-feminism.

———. 2008. "Flirting Her Way to Victory: Sarah Palin's Farcical Debate Performance Lowered the Standards for Both Female Candidates and U.S. Political Discourse." *Guardian*. October 3. Accessed October 3, 2008. http://www.guardian.co.uk/commentisfree/cifamerica/2008/oct/03/sarah.palin.debate.feminism.

Gonzalez, Juan. 2009. "Day of Pride for Latinos as Obama Nominates Sonia Sotomayor for Supreme Court." *New York Daily News*. May 26. Accessed May 28, 2009. http://www.nydailynews.com/news/politics/2009/05/26/2009-05-26_day_of_pride_for_latinos_across_us.html.

Gonzalez, Matt. 2008. "The Obama Craze: Count Me Out." *Counterpunch.* February 29. Accessed March 8, 2008. http://www.counterpunch.org/gonzalez02292008. html.

Goodman, Ellen. 2008. "Sarah Zamboni Clears the Ice on Working Mothers." *Boston Globe.* September 12. Accessed September 12, 2008. http://www.boston.com/bostonglobe/editorial_opinion/oped/articles/2008/09/12/sarah_zamboni_clears_the_ ice_on_working_mothers/.

Gordon, Lily. 2009. "Soldier Balks at Deploying; Says Obama Isn't President." *Columbus (GA) Ledger-Enquirer.* July 14. Accessed July 14, 2009. http://www.ledger-enquirer.com/2009/07/14/776335/soldier-balks-at-deploying-says.html.

Graves, Earl G., Sr. 2008. "No More Excuses." *Black Enterprise.* December 19. Accessed January 5, 2008. http://findarticles.com/p/articles/mi_m1365/is_6_39/ ai_n31196880/?tag=content;col1.

Gray, Kevin Alexander. 2008. "Obama Mustn't Use People of Color as Props." *The Progressive.* June 24. Accessed July 11, 2008. http://www.progressive.org/mp/ grey062408.

———. 2008. "Why Does Barack Obama Hate My Family? Vilifying Black Men to Win Favor with the Man." *Counterpunch.* July 11. Accessed July 11, 2008. http:// www.counterpunch.org/gray07112008.html.

Green, Joshua. 2008. "The Front-Runner's Fall." *The Atlantic.* September. Accessed September 15, 2008. http://www.theatlantic.com/magazine/archive/2008/09/the-front-runner-8217-s-fall/6944/.

Greenberg, David. 2008. "Why Obamamania? Because He Runs as the Great White Hope." *Washington Post.* January 13. Accessed January 13, 2008. http://www.washingtonpost.com/wp-dyn/content/article/2008/01/11/AR2008011101414.html.

Grieco, Elizabeth. 2010. *Race and Hispanic Origin of the Foreign-Born Population in the United States: 2007.* Washington, DC: U.S. Census Bureau. Accessed May 13, 2010. http://www.census.gov/prod/2010pubs/acs-11.pdf.

Grieve, Timothy. 2008. "We Are Ready to Believe Again." Salon.com. January 3. Accessed January 3, 2008. http://www.salon.com/news/politics/war_ room/2008/01/03/speeches.

Grove, Lloyd. 2009. "Are Blacks Abandoning Obama?" *Daily Beast.* December 15. Accessed December 16, 2009. http://www.thedailybeast.com/blogs-and-stories/2009-12-15/has-obama-abandoned-blacks/.

Guillermo, Emil. 2008. "Obama's Colorblind Ambition." *Asian Week.* June 6. Accessed November 2, 2008. http://www.asianweek.com/2008/06/06/%EF%BB%BFobama% E2%80%99s-colorblind-ambition/.

———. 2008. "Why Is Obama Snubbing Asian Americans?" *Asian Week.* January 13. Accessed February 10, 2008. http://www.asianweek.com/2008/01/13/why-is-obama-snubbing-asian-americans/#.

Guinier, Lani, and Gerald Torres. 2003. *The Miner's Canary: Enlisting Race, Resisting Power, Transforming Democracy.* Cambridge, MA: Harvard University Press.

Hall, Mimi. 2010. "Obama Urges a Dialogue on Race after Sherrod Case." *USA Today.* July 29. Accessed July 29, 2010. http://www.usatoday.com/news/washington/2010-07-30-obama30_ST_N.htm?csp=34.

Hannity, Sean, and Alan Colmes. 2008. "Exclusive: Bill Cunningham on Obama Comments." Television transcript. *Hannity & Colmes.* February 27. Accessed February 28, 2008. http://www.foxnews.com/story/0,2933,333054,00.html.

Hanson, Victor Davis. 2003. *Mexifornia: A State of Becoming.* San Francisco: Encounter Books.

Harlow, Roxanna. 2009. "Barack Obama and the (In)significance of His Presidential Campaign." *Journal of African American Studies* 13, no. 2: 1559–1646.

Harris, Angel L., Monica Trujillo, and Kenneth Jamison. 2008. "Academic Outcomes among Latino/a and Asian Americans: An Assessment of the Immigration Effect." *Annals of the American Academy of Political and Social Science* 620, no. 1 (November): 90–114.

Harris, Jenee Desmond. 2011. "Sharpton and West's MSNBC Shouting Match." *The Root.* April 11. Accessed April 11, 2011. http://www.theroot.com/buzz/sharpton-and-wests-msnbc-shouting-match.

Harris, Paul. 2008. "Young, Gifted, Black . . . and Leading America." *The Observer.* August 10. Accessed August 10, 2008. http://www.guardian.co.uk/world/2008/aug/10/race.politics.

Harshaw, Tobin. 2009. "Sotomayor, Race, and the Right." *New York Times.* May 29. Accessed June 2, 2009. http://opinionator.blogs.nytimes.com/2009/05/29/weekend-opinionator-sotomayor-race-and-the-right/.

Hart, Peter. 2007. "Obamamania: How Loving Barack Obama Helps Pundits Love Themselves." *Extra!* March/April. Accessed April 3, 2007. http://www.fair.org/index.php?page=3094.

Hartmann, Douglas. 2006. "Bound by Blackness or Above It? Michael Jordan and the Paradoxes of Post–Civil Rights American Race Relations." Pp. 301–324 in *Sport and the Racial Mountain: A Biographical History of the African American Athlete,* edited by David K. Wiggins. Fayetteville: University of Arkansas Press.

Hartmann, Douglas, Joseph Gerteis, and Paul R. Croll. 2009. "An Empirical Assessment of Whiteness Theory: Hidden from How Many?" *Social Problems* 56, no. 3 (August): 403–424.

Hausmann, Leslie R. M., Feifei Ye, Janet Ward Schofield, and Rochelle L. Woods. 2009. "Sense of Belonging and Persistence in White and African American First-Year Students." *Research in Higher Education* 50, no. 7 (November): 649–669.

Hechtkopf, Kevin. 2010. "Tom Tancredo Tea Party Speech Slams 'Cult of Multiculturalism.'" CBS News. February 5. Accessed February 6, 2010. http://www.cbsnews.com/8301-503544_162-6177125-503544.html.

Heileman, John. 2008. "The Evita Factor: Is Hillary Clinton's Popularity with Hispanics the Key to Super Tuesday?" *New York Magazine.* February 1, 2008. Accessed February 16, 208. http://nymag.com/news/politics/powergrid/43587/#.

Herbert, Bob. 2010. "Neglecting the Base." *New York Times.* September 20. Accessed September 20, 2010. http://www.nytimes.com/2010/09/21/opinion/21herbert.html?_r=1&adxnnl=1&ref=opinion&adxnnlx=1285070637-zHpOnUtSC4yX9N9gNLjIuQ.

Herring, Cedric. 2002. "Is Job Discrimination Dead?" *Contexts* 1, no. 2 (Summer): 13–18.

Higham, John. 2002. *Strangers in the Land: Patterns of American Nativism, 1860–1925*, 2nd ed. New Brunswick, NJ: Rutgers University Press.

Hirshman, Linda. 2008. "Looking Forward, Feminism Needs to Focus." *Washington Post*. June 8. Accessed January 12, 2011. https://www.washingtonpost.com/wp-dyn/content/article/2008/06/06/AR2008060603494.html.

"Hispanics Left out of the State of the Union Speech!" 2010. *La Prensa San Diego*. January 29. Accessed March 3, 2010. http://laprensa-sandiego.org/editorial-and-commentary/editorial/hispanics-left-out-of-the-state-of-the-union-speech/#.

Hochschild, Jennifer L., and Vesla Weaver. 2007. "The Skin Color Paradox and the American Racial Order." *Social Forces* 86, no. 2 (December): 643–670.

Holcomb, Lori. 2009. "Smith: Obama Sets Bar High." *Battle Creek (MI) Enquirer*. February 11. Accessed February 11, 2009. http://www.battlecreekenquirer.com/.

Holland, Steven. 2010. "Tea Party Candidates Could Damage Republicans." Reuters. March 24. Accessed May 5, 2010. http://www.reuters.com/article/idUSTR-E62N5H620100324.

hooks, bell. 1981. *Ain't I a Woman? Black Women and Feminism*. Boston: South End Press.

Hornick, Ed. 2008. "Poll: 'Sharp Reversal' for Obama with Latino Voters." CNN. July 24. Accessed July 24, 2008. http://articles.cnn.com/2008-07-24/politics/pew.latino.poll_1_obama-latino-voters-full-poll?_s=PM:POLITICS.

Hsu, Hua. 2009. "The End of White America?" *The Atlantic*. January/February. Accessed March 20, 2009. http://www.theatlantic.com/magazine/archive/2009/01/the-end-of-white-america/7208/.

Hu-DeHart, Evelyn. 2001. "21st-Century America: Black and White and Beyond." Pp. 79–95 in *Race in 21st-Century America*, edited by Curtis Stokes, Theresa Meléndez, and Genice Rhodes-Reed. East Lansing: Michigan State University Press.

Huddy, Leonie, and Nayda Terkildsen. 1993. "The Consequences of Gender Stereotypes for Women Candidates at Different Levels and Types of Office." *Political Research Quarterly* 46, no. 3 (September): 503–525.

Huff, Richard. 2009. "Pundit Glenn Beck Calls President Barack Obama a 'Racist', Fox News Channel Execs Downplay Comments." *New York Daily News*. July 29. Accessed August 1, 2009. http://www.nydailynews.com/news/politics/2009/07/29/2009-07-29_fox_news_glenn_beck_president_barack_obama_is_racist_with_deepseated_hatred_of_w.html.

Hull, Gloria T., Patricia Bell Scott, and Barbara Smith, eds. 1982. *All the Women Are White, All the Blacks Are Men, but Some of Us Are Brave: Black Women's Studies*. Old Westbury, NY: Feminist Press.

Hulse, Carl. 2008. "McCain's Canal Zone Birth Prompts Queries about Whether That Rules Him Out." *New York Times*. February 28. Accessed February 28, 2008. http://www.nytimes.com/2008/02/28/us/politics/28mccain.html.

Huntington, Roy. 2003. "The Insider." *American Handgunner*. January/February 2003. Accessed February 28, 2008. http://findarticles.com/p/articles/mi_m0BTT/is_161_27/ai_95907835/?tag=content;col1.

Huntington, Samuel P. 1996. *The Clash of Civilizations and the Remaking of World Order*. New York: Simon & Schuster.

———. 2004. *Who Are We? The Challenges to America's Identity.* New York: Simon & Schuster.

Huston, Warner Todd. 2008. "AP Finds Race Hustler to Say Obama Isn't the Cure." NewsBusters.org. November 25. Accessed January 3, 2009. http://newsbusters. org/blogs/warner-todd-huston/2008/11/25/ap-finds-race-hustler-say-obama-isnt-cure.

Hutchinson, Earl Ofari. 2010. "Defecting Black Vote Spells Big Trouble for Democrats." *New America Media.* September 5. Accessed September 7, 2010. http:// newamericamedia.org/2010/09/defecting-black-vote-spells-big-trouble-for-democrats.php.

"Is Barack Obama Black Enough?" 2007. *Walk Taken.* July 13. Accessed July 13, 2007. http://walktaken.com/2007/07/13/is-barack-obama-black-enough/.

Jacobs, David, and Daniel Tope. 2007. "The Politics of Resentment in the Post–Civil Rights Era: Minority Threat, Homicide, and Ideological Voting in Congress." *American Journal of Sociology* 112 (March): 1458–1494.

Jerit, Jennifer. 2004. "Survival of the Fittest: Rhetoric during the Course of a Presidential Campaign." *Political Psychology* 25, no. 4 (July): 563–575.

Jill. 2008. "Has Feminism Lost Its Focus?" *Feministe.* June 9. Accessed June 9, 2008. http://www.feministe.us/blog/archives/2008/06/09/has-feminism-lost-its-focus/.

Johnson, Allan. 1997. *The Gender Knot: Unraveling Our Patriarchal Legacy.* Philadelphia: Temple University Press.

Johnson, Heather Beth. 2006. *The American Dream and the Power of Wealth: Choosing Schools and Inheriting Inequality in the Land of Opportunity.* New York: Routledge.

Jones, Jeffrey M. 2011. "Obama Approval Slips among Blacks, Hispanics in March." Gallup.com. April 7. Accessed April 11, 2011. http://www.gallup.com/poll/146981/ obama-approval-slips-among-blacks-hispanics-march.aspx.

Jonsson, Patrik. 2010. "Are 'Tea Party' Rallies Given Preferential Treatment by Police?" *Christian Science Monitor.* April 19. Accessed April 22, 2010. http://www. csmonitor.com/USA/Politics/2010/0419/Are-tea-party-rallies-given-preferential-treatment-by-police.

Jordan, Miriam, and Leslie Eaton. 2008. "Big Turnout of Latino Voters Boosted Obama." *Wall Street Journal.* November 6. Accessed November 6, 2008. http:// online.wsj.com/article/SB122593469349803755.html.

Joseph, Ralina. 2009. "'Tyra Banks Is Fat': Reading Post-racism and Post-feminism in the New Millennium." *Critical Studies in Media Communication* 26, no. 3 (August): 237–254.

Jouvenal, Justin. 2008. "McCain-Palin Rallies Turning Ugly." Salon.com. October 7. Accessed January 18, 2011. http://www.salon.com/news/politics/war_ room/2008/10/07/rallies.

Judis, John B. 2007. "Hillary Clinton's Firewall: Will Barack Obama's Anemic Standing among Latinos Be His Undoing?" *New Republic.* December 18. Accessed January 4, 2008. http://www.tnr.com/article/politics/hillary-clintons-firewall.

Kahlenberg, Richard. 2008. "Barack Obama and Affirmative Action." *Inside Higher Ed.* May 12. Accessed November 29, 2008. http://www.insidehighered.com/ views/2008/05/12/kahlenberg.

———. 2008. "What's Next for Affirmative Action?" *The Atlantic*. November 6. Accessed November 29, 2008. http://www.theatlantic.com/magazine/ archive/2008/11/what-s-next-for-affirmative-action/7122/.

Kamiya, Gary. 2007. "Is Race Dying?" Salon.com. November 27. Accessed November 27, 2007. http://www.salon.com/news/opinion/kamiya/2007/11/27/race.

———. 2008. "It's OK to Vote for Obama Because He's Black." Salon.com. February 26. Accessed February 27, 2008. http://www.salon.com/news/opinion/ kamiya/2008/02/26/obama.

Kang, Eugene. 2007. "Obama Announces Asian Americans and Pacific Islanders National Leadership Council." *Organizing for America*. October 26. Accessed February 17, 2008. http://my.barackobama.com/page/community/post/eugenekang/ CS3r.

Kasinitz, Philip. 1992. *Caribbean New York: Black Immigrants and the Politics of Race*. Ithaca, NY: Cornell University Press.

Kaufman, Jonathan. 2007. "Whites' Great Hope?: Barack Obama and the Dream of a Color-Blind America." *Wall Street Journal*. November 10. Accessed January 4, 2008. http://www.jonathankaufman.org/PDF/Whites%20Great%20Hope_ JKaufman.pdf.

Kaufman, Jonathan, and Gary Fields. 2008. "Election of Obama Recasts National Conversation on Race." *Wall Street Journal*. November 10. Accessed April 20, 2011. http://online.wsj.com/article/SB122627584403012071.html.

Keen, Judy. 2008. "Obama Dogged by Links to 1960s Radical." *USA Today*. August 25. Accessed July 3, 2010. http://www.usatoday.com/news/politics/ election2008/2008-08-25-ayers_N.htm.

Keillor, Garrison. 2008. "Wow! America Is Cool." Salon.com. November 12. Accessed November 12, 2008. http://www.salon.com/news/opinion/garrison_keillor/2008/11/12/obama_victory.

Keith, Verna M., and Cedric Herring. 1991. "Skin Tone and Stratification in the Black Community." *American Journal of Sociology* 97, no. 3 (November): 760–778.

Kellner, Douglas. 2004. "The Sports Spectacle, Michael Jordan, and Nike." Pp. 358–382 in *Sport and the Color Line: Black Athletes and Race Relations in Twentieth-Century America*, edited by Patrick B. Miller and David Kenneth Wiggins. New York: Routledge.

Kelly, Mo. 2010. "Tea Party and Racism—Lovers and Friends, Part II." *Mo Kelly Report*. April 21. Accessed May 5, 2010. http://mokellyreport.wordpress. com/2010/04/21/tea-party-and-racism-lovers-and-friends-part-ii/.

Kelly, Rita Mae, and Georgia Duerst-Lahti. 1995. "The Study of Gender Power and Its Link to Governance and Leadership." Pp. 39–64 in *Gender Power, Leadership, and Governance*, edited by Georgia Duerst-Lahti and Rita Mae Kelly. Ann Arbor: University of Michigan Press.

Kessler, Ronald. 2008. "Obama Encourages Black Victimhood." NewsMax.com. March 26. Accessed March 26, 2008. http://www.newsmax.com/RonaldKessler/ obama-wright/2008/03/26/id/323301.

Khimm, Suzy. 2010. "Why Have Hispanics Soured on Obama?" *Mother Jones*. August 11. Accessed August 11, 2010. http://motherjones.com/mojo/2010/08/hispanics-media-voters-disappointed-obama.

Kim, Claire Jean. 1999. "The Racial Triangulation of Asian Americans." *Politics and Society* 27, no. 1 (March): 105–138.

———. 2004. "Imagining Race and Nation in Multiculturalist America." *Ethnic and Racial Studies* 27, no. 6 (November): 987–1005.

Kim, Janine Young. 1999. "Are Asians Black? The Asian American Civil Rights Agenda and the Contemporary Significance of the Black/White Paradigm." *Yale Law Journal* 108, no. 8 (June): 2385–2412.

Kim, Kenneth. 2008. "Did Asian Americans Swing California for Clinton?" *New America Media*. February 7. Accessed February 14, 2008. http://news.newamericamedia.org/news/view_article.html?article_id=d7a4a2a86575f4bfbc4e0e32a87a448d.

Kimberly, Margaret. 2011. "Freedom Rider: Thinking Post-Obama." *Black Agenda Report*. April 5. Accessed April 11, 2011. http://www.blackagendareport.com/content/freedom-rider-thinking-post-obama.

King-Meadows, Tyson. 2010. "The 'Steele Problem' and the New Republican Battle for Black Votes: Legacy, Loyalty, and Lexicon in Maryland's 2006 Senator Contest." Pp. 241–270 in *Whose Black Politics? Cases in Post-racial Black Leadership*, edited by Andra Gillespie. New York: Routledge.

Kirsanow, Peter. 2009. "Obama and the Aspirations of Black Kids." *National Review Online*. January 9. Accessed October 4, 2009. http://www.nationalreview.com/corner/176104/obama-and-aspirations-black-kids/peter-kirsanow.

Kissling, Frances. 2008. "Why I'm Still Not for Hillary Clinton." Salon.com. January 10. Accessed March 18, 2008. http://www.salon.com/news/opinion/feature/2008/01/10/kissling_clinton.

Klein, Joe. 2006. "The Fresh Face." *Time*. October 15. Accessed October 15, 2006. http://www.time.com/time/magazine/article/0,9171,1546362,00.html.

Klein, Rick, and Joseph Williams. 2007. "Obama's Silence on Imus Alarms Some Blacks." *Boston Globe*. April 11. Accessed April 17, 2007. http://www.boston.com/news/nation/articles/2007/04/11/obamas_silence_on_imus_alarms_some_blacks/.

Koffler, Daniel. 2008. "And Now Hillary Clinton Wants to Sue OPEC." *Jewcy*. May 1. Accessed May 1, 2008. http://www.jewcy.com/post/and_now_she_wants_sue_opec.

Koppelman, Alex. 2008. "Bill Bennett Knows Black People." Salon.com. January 4. Accessed January 4, 2008. http://www.salon.com/news/politics/war_room/2008/01/04/bennett#.

———. 2008. "Why the Stories about Obama's Birth Certificate Will Never Die." Salon.com. December 5. Accessed May 5, 2010. http://www.salon.com/news/feature/2008/12/05/birth_certificate.

Kozol, Jonathan. 2005. *The Shame of the Nation: The Restoration of Apartheid Schooling in America*. New York: Crown.

Krugman, Paul. 2011. "The President Is Missing." *New York Times*. April 10. Accessed April 11, 2011. http://www.nytimes.com/2011/04/11/opinion/11krugman.html.

Krysan, Maria, and Michael Bader. 2008. "Perceiving the Metropolis: Seeing the City through a Prism of Race." Pp. 227–246 in *Racism in Post-race America: New Theories, New Directions*, edited by Charles Gallagher. Chapel Hill: Social Forces Publishing.

Kuhn, David Paul. 2008. "Obama Shifts Affirmative Action Rhetoric." Politico. com. August 10. Accessed August 10, 2008. http://www.politico.com/news/stories/0808/12421.html.

Kuhnhenn, Jim. 2008. "Obama Seeks to Silence Ad Tying Him to 60s Radical." Associated Press. August 25. Accessed August 25, 2008. http://www.breitbart.com/article.php?id=D92PL7400.

Kurtz, Howard. 2008. "When Journalism Turns Personal." *Washington Post*. November 6. Accessed November 7, 2008. http://www.washingtonpost.com/wp-dyn/content/article/2008/11/06/AR2008110600674.html.

Kutzinski, Vera M. 1993. *Sugar's Secrets: Race and the Erotics of Cuban Nationalism*. Charlottesville: University of Virginia Press.

Lacy, Karyn. 2007. *Blue-Chip Black: Race, Class, and Status in the New Black Middle Class*. Berkeley: University of California Press.

Lam, Andrew. 2009. "Our Man Obama—The Post-imperial Presidency." *New America Media*. January 14. Accessed January 30, 2009. http://news.newamericamedia.org/news/view_article.html?article_id=e96674231b31155c9ae5adeca7c1ec08.

Lamont-Hill, Marc. 2008. "Not My Brand of Hope." *The Root*. February 5. Accessed February 5, 2008. http://www.theroot.com/views/not-my-brand-hope.

Layton, Azza Salama. 1997. "International Pressure and the U.S. Government's Response to Little Rock." *Arkansas Historical Quarterly* 56, no. 3 (Autumn): 257–272.

Lee, Carol D. 2009. "From Du Bois to Obama: The Education of Peoples of African Descent in the United States in the 21st Century." *Journal of Negro Education* 78, no. 4 (Fall): 367–384.

Lee, Erika. 2004. "American Gatekeeping: Race and Immigration Law in the 20th Century." Pp. 119–144 in *Not Just Black and White: Historical and Contemporary Perspectives on Immigration, Race, and Ethnicity in the United States*, edited by Nancy Foner and George M. Fredrickson. New York: Russell Sage Foundation.

Lee, Stacey J. 2009. *Unraveling the "Model Minority" Stereotype: Listening to Asian American Youth*, 2nd. ed. New York: Teachers College Press.

Leibovich, Mark. 2004. "The Other Man of the Hour." *Washington Post*. July 27. Accessed January 15, 2008. http://www.washingtonpost.com/wp-dyn/articles/A16606-2004Jul26.html.

Lewis, Amanda. 2001. "There Is No 'Race' in the Schoolyard: Color-Blind Ideology in an Almost All-White School." *American Educational Research Journal* 28, no. 4 (Winter): 781–811.

Li, Qiong, and Marilynn B. Brewer. 2004. "What Does It Mean to Be an American? Patriotism, Nationalism, and American Identity after 9/11." *Political Psychology* 25, no. 5: 727–739.

Liddle, Rod. 2008. "Hillary, They Just Don't Like You." *Sunday Times*. June 8. Accessed June 12, 2008. http://www.timesonline.co.uk/tol/comment/columnists/rod_liddle/article4087544.ece.

Lie, John. 2004. "The Black-Asian Conflict?" Pp. 301–314 in *Not Just Black and White: Historical and Contemporary Perspectives on Immigration, Race, and Ethnicity in the United States*, edited by Nancy Foner and George M. Fredrickson. New York: Russell Sage Foundation.

Lilpop, John. 2008. "Is Black Racism Obama's Greatest Advantage?" *Student Operated Press*. February 6. Accessed April 23, 2009. http://thesop.org/story/politics/2008/02/06/is-black-racism-obamas-greatest-advantage.php.

"Limbaugh: '[A] Lot of These Feminists and Women . . . Think They're Owed' a Clinton Win; 'They've Had Two or Three Abortions.'" 2008. *Media Matters*. April 1. Accessed July 14, 2008. http://mediamatters.org/mmtv/200804010009.

Limbaugh, Rush. 2007. "Does Our Looks-Obsessed Culture Want to Stare at an Aging Woman?" Radio transcript *Rush Limbaugh Show*. December 17. Accessed April 4, 2008. http://www.rushlimbaugh.com/home/daily/site_121707/content/01125114.guest.html.

———. 2008. "Michelle Obama Slams America, Says Husband Can Save Its Soul." Radio transcript *Rush Limbaugh Show*. February 19. Accessed February 19, 2008. http://www.rushlimbaugh.com/home/daily/site_021908/content/01125108.guest.html.

———. 2009. "From Kids on Bus to Kanye West: Race Rules All in Obama's America." Radio transcript. *Rush Limbaugh Show*. September 15. Accessed September 15, 2009. http://www.rushlimbaugh.com/home/daily/site_091509/content/01125106.guest.html.

———. 2010. "It's Payback Time: The Obama Economy Is Purposeful Disaster." Radio transcript. *Rush Limbaugh Show*. July 2. Accessed July 2, 2010. http://www.rushlimbaugh.com/home/daily/site_070210/content/01125106.guest.html.

Linkins, Jason. 2008. "MSNBC Hosts Founder of Anti-Hillary Group 'C.U.N.T.'" *Huffington Post*. February 19. Accessed February 19, 2008. http://www.huffingtonpost.com/2008/02/19/msnbc-hosts-founder-of-an_n_87356.html.

Liss, Sharon Kehnemui. 2007. "Report: Jesse Jackson Says Barack Obama 'Acting White' in Case of Six Blacks Accused in Assault Case." Fox News. September 19. Accessed September 19, 2007. http://www.foxnews.com/story/0,2933,297332,00.html.

Lithwick, Dahlia. 2008. "Shades of Gray: Barack Obama Has Gotten Past Affirmative Action. Have We?" Slate.com. March 31. Accessed March 31, 2008. http://www.slate.com/id/2187718.

Lizza, Ryan. 2008. "Minority Reports: After New Hampshire, a Hint of Racial Politics." *New Yorker*. January 21. Accessed January 21, 2008. http://www.newyorker.com/reporting/2008/01/21/080121fa_fact_lizza.

Lochhead, Carolyn. 2008. "Obama's Candidacy Shakes Up Racial Politics." *San Francisco Chronicle*. February 17. Accessed February 17, 2008. http://articles.sfgate.com/2008-02-17/news/17142943_1_black-candidate-black-man-21st-century.

———. 2008. "Obama Takes Big Risk on Driver's License Issue." *San Francisco Chronicle*. January 28. Accessed January 29, 2008. http://articles.sfgate.com/2008-01-28/news/17149619_1_driver-s-licenses-illegal-immigrants-immigration-overhaul.

Logan, Enid Lynette. 1999. "El apóstol y el comandante en jefe: Racial Discourses and Practices in Cuba, 1890–1999." Pp. 195–213 in *The Global Color Line: Racial and Ethnic Inequality and Struggle from a Global Perspective*, edited by Joe Feagin and Pinar Batur-VanderLippe. Stamford, CT: JAI Press.

———. 2010. "Each Sheep with Its Mate: Marking Race and Legitimacy in Cuban Ecclesiastical Archives, 1890–1940." *New West Indian Guide/Nieuwe West-Indische Gids* 84, nos. 1–2: 5–39.

Long, Lynette. 2008. "Obama Is a Megalomaniac." *Lynette Long: Truth, Justice, and the American Way.* July 25. Accessed August 4, 2008. http://www.lynettelong.com/my_weblog/2008/07/obama-is-a-mega.html.

———. 2008. "Painful Lessons: Primary Reveals Obstacles Facing Women in Politics." *Baltimore Sun.* May 18. Accessed May 18, 2008. http://articles.baltimoresun.com/2008-05-18/news/0805160266_1_obama-women-voters-white-women.

Lopez, Mark Hugo, and Paul Taylor. 2009. "Dissecting the 2008 Electorate: Most Diverse in U.S. History." *Pew Research Center.* April 30. Accessed May 7, 2009. http://pewresearch.org/pubs/1209/racial-ethnic-voters-presidential-election.

Lourde, Audre. 1984. *Sister Outsider.* Trumansburg, NY: Crossing Press.

Loury, Glenn. 2009. "Obama, Gates, and the American Black Man." *New York Times.* July 26. Accessed January 10, 2011. https://www.nytimes.com/2009/07/26/opinion/26loury.html.

Lovato, Roberto. 2008. "Clinton's Latino Advantage Decreases, Obama Surges as Latinos Vote beyond Black and White." *Huffington Post.* February 6. Accessed February 6, 2008. http://www.huffingtonpost.com/roberto-lovato/clintons-latino-advantage_b_85243.html.

———. 2008. "Everyone's an Expert on the Latino Vote, Except Latinos." *Huffington Post.* January 22. Accessed January 22, 2008. http://www.huffingtonpost.com/roberto-lovato/everyones-an-expert-on-th_b_82773.html#.

———. 2009. "Act Now to Stop the Obama Administration's Racist 287G Immigration Policy." *Of América.* July 24. Accessed September 9, 2009. http://ofamerica.wordpress.com/2009/07/24/act-now-to-stop-the-obama-administrations-racist-287g-policy/#.

———. 2009. "New Republic Attacks Judge Sotomayor with Sexist, Racist 'Angry Latina' Meme." *Of América.* May 4. Accessed May 7, 2009. http://ofamerica.wordpress.com/2009/05/04/new-republic-attacks-judge-sotomayor-with-sexist-racist-angry-latina-meme/#.

Lui, Meizhu. 2004. "Doubly Divided: The Racial Wealth Gap." Pp. 42–49 in *The Wealth Inequality Reader,* edited by Chuck Collins, Amy Gluckman, Betsy Leondar-Wright, Meizhu Lui, Amy Offner, and Adria Scharf. Cambridge, MA: Economic Affairs Bureau.

Lui, Meizhu, Barbara Robles, Betsy Leondar-Wright, Rose Brewer, and Rebecca Adamson. 2006. *The Color of Wealth: The Story behind the U.S. Racial Wealth Divide.* New York: New Press.

Luqman, Amina. 2007. "Obama's Tightrope." *Washington Post.* July 6. Accessed July 6, 2007. http://www.washingtonpost.com/wp-dyn/content/article/2007/07/05/AR2007070501828.html.

Luscombe, Belinda. 2008. "Why Some Women Hate Sarah Palin." *Time.* October 2. Accessed October 2, 2008. http://www.time.com/time/politics/article/0,8599,1846832,00.html.

Mabry, Marcus. 2008. "Color Test: Where Whites Draw the Line." *New York Times.* June 8. Accessed June 8, 2008. http://www.nytimes.com/2008/06/08/weekinreview/08mabry.html.

Mac Donald, Heather. 2009. "Promoting Racial Paranoia." *National Review Online.* July 24. Accessed July 24, 2009. http://www.nationalreview.com/articles/227946/promoting-racial-paranoia/heather-mac-donald.

Macdonald, Neil. 2007. "Neil MacDonald on the Anatomy of a Smear Job." CBC News. January 23. Accessed January 23, 2007. http://www.cbc.ca/news/reportsfromabroad/macdonald/20070123.html.

MacGillis, Alec, and Perry Bacon Jr. 2007. "Obama Rises in New Era of Black Politicians." *Washington Post.* July 29. Accessed January 15, 2008. http://www.washingtonpost.com/wp-dyn/content/article/2007/07/27/AR2007072702455.html.

Maira, Sunaina. 2008. "'We Ain't Missing': Palestinian Hip-Hop—A Transnational Youth Movement." *CR: The New Centennial Review* 8, no. 2 (Fall): 162–192.

Malkin, Michelle. 2008. "Michelle Obama's America—and Mine." *Michelle Malkin.* February 20. Accessed February 24, 2008. http://michellemalkin.com/2008/02/20/michelle-obamas-america-and-mine/.

Mann, Geoff. 2008. "Why Does Country Music Sound White? Race and the Voice of Nostalgia." *Ethnic and Racial Studies* 31, no. 1 (January): 73–100.

Manneh, Suzanne. 2010. "Census to Count Arabs as White, despite Write-In Campaign." *New America Media.* March 25. Accessed May 13, 2010. http://news.newamericamedia.org/news/view_article.html?article_id=87932e5f600086f93be8b029e4a6ff40.

Martin, Courtney. 2008. "Dear Hillary: A Letter from an Obama Feminist." *American Prospect.* June 9. Accessed June 10, 2008. http://www.prospect.org/cs/articles?article=dear_hillary.

———. 2008. "More Than a Mother-Daughter Debate." *American Prospect.* April 21. Accessed July 14, 2008. http://www.prospect.org/cs/articles?article=more_than_a_motherdaughter_debate.

Martin, Jonathan, and Ben Smith. 2008. "Obama's Apple Pie Campaign." Politico.com. July 7. Accessed July 7, 2008. http://www.politico.com/news/stories/0708/11550.html.

Martin, Renee. 2008. "Election 2008: Race Is More Than Black and White." *Global Comment.* August 25. Accessed September 19, 2008. http://globalcomment.com/2008/election-2008-race-is-more-than-black-and-white/.

Martin, Roland. 2007. "Sen. Clinton, Are You Black Enough to Be President?" CNN. August 9. Accessed August 10, 2007. http://politicalticker.blogs.cnn.com/2007/08/09/sen-clinton-are-you-black-enough-to-be-president/.

———. 2008. "The Full Story behind Wright's 'God Damn America' Sermon." *Anderson Cooper 360.* March 21. Accessed March 21, 2008. http://ac360.blogs.cnn.com/2008/03/21/the-full-story-behind-wright%E2%80%99s-%E2%80%9Cgod-damn-america%E2%80%9D-sermon/.

Marx, Anthony. 1998. *Making Race and Nation: A Comparison of South Africa, the United States, and Brazil.* Cambridge: Cambridge University Press, 1998.

Massey, Douglas S. 2000. "Residential Segregation and Neighborhood Conditions in U.S. Metropolitan Areas." Pp. 391–434 in *America Becoming: Racial Trends and Their Consequences*, edited by Neil J. Smelser, William J. Wilson, and Faith Mitchell. Washington, DC: National Academy Press.

McAuliff, Michael. 2008. "Hillary Clinton Tries to Bag Votes with Duck Tale." *New York Daily News.* February 19. Accessed February 19, 2008. http://www.nydailynews.com/news/politics/2008/02/19/2008-02-19_hillary_clinton_tries_to_bag_votes_with_.html.

McCaffrey, Shannon. 2008. "Candidates Face Rowdy Crowd: U.S. Senate Hopefuls Focus on Economy." *Athens (GA) Banner-Herald*. October 10. Accessed October 13, 2008. http://www.onlineathens.com/stories/101008/ele_342247649.shtml.

"McCain Responds to 'Arab' Epithet at Rally: 'Obama a Decent Family Man.'" 2008. *Huffington Post*. October 10. Accessed October 10, 2008. http://www.huffington-post.com/the-uptake/mccain-responds-to-arab-a_b_133820.html.

McCormick, Joseph P., and Charles E. Jones. 1993. "The Conceptualization of Deracialization: Thinking through the Dilemma." Pp. 66–84 in *Dilemmas of Black Politics: Issues of Leadership and Strategy*, edited by Georgia A. Persons. New York: HarperCollins.

McKinney, Dave, and Abdon Pallasch. 2008. "Obama Draws Parallels to Martin Luther King Jr." *Chicago Sun-Times*. August 29. Accessed September 3, 2008. http://www.suntimes.com/news/politics/obama/1134541,CST-NWS-dem29.article.

McLarin, Kim. 2008. "Family Fight." *XX Factor*. June 7. Accessed June 7, 2008. http://www.slate.com/blogs/blogs/xxfactor/archive/2008/06/07/family-fight.aspx.

McLaughlin, John. 2007. "The McLaughlin Group. Host: John McLaughlin. Panel: Patrick Buchanan, MCNBC; Eleanor Clift, Newsweek; Tony Blankley, The Washington Times; Kim Mance, Council of Women, World Leaders. Taped: Friday July 6, Broadcast: Weekend of July 7–8." Television transcript. *McLaughlin Group*. Accessed March 11, 2008. http://www.mclaughlin.com/transcript.htm?id=605.

McWhorter, John. 2000. *Losing the Race: Self-Sabotage in Black America*. New York: Free Press.

———. 2008. "ObamaKids: And the 10-Year-Olds Shall Lead Us." *New York Magazine*. August 10. Accessed August 22, 2008. http://nymag.com/news/features/49141/.

Meckler, Laura. 2008. "McCain Asks Supporters to Show Obama Respect." *Wall Street Journal*. October 12. Accessed October 15, 2008. http://online.wsj.com/article/NA_WSJ_PUB:SB122368132195924869.html.

Melber, Ari. 2008. "Obama, Race, and the Presidency." *The Nation*. January 3. Accessed January 3, 2008. http://www.thenation.com/article/obama-race-and-presidency.

Memmot, Mark. 2010. "GOP Chairman Steele Repudiates 'Joker' Image of Obama in RNC Presentation." National Public Radio. March 4. Accessed April 22, 2010. http://www.npr.org/blogs/thetwo-way/2010/03/obama_gop_fear_clown_images.html.

Mendelberg, Tali. 2001. *The Race Card: Campaign Strategy, Implicit Messages, and the Norm of Equality*. Princeton, NJ: Princeton University Press.

Merida, Kevin. 2008. "America's History Gives Way to Its Future." *Washington Post*. November 5. Accessed November 5, 2008. http://www.washingtonpost.com/wp-dyn/content/article/2008/11/05/AR2008110500148.html.

———. 2008. "Obama Wave Stuns Clinton's Black Supporters." *Washington Post*. February 19. Accessed March 18, 2008. http://www.washingtonpost.com/wp-dyn/content/article/2008/02/18/AR2008021802364.html.

Milbank, Dana. 2008. "In Fla., Palin Goes for the Rough Stuff as Audience Boos Obama." *Washington Post*. October 6. Accessed October 6, 2008. http://voices.washingtonpost.com/44/2008/10/in-fla-palin-goes-for-the-roug.html.

Milligan, Susan. 2008. "Clinton's Struggle Vexes Feminists." *Boston Globe.* February 9. Accessed February 12, 2008. http://www.boston.com/news/nation/articles/2008/02/19/clintons_struggle_vexes_feminists/.

Mills, Nicolaus, ed. 1994. *Arguing Immigration: The Debate over the Changing Face of America.* New York: Simon & Schuster.

Minushkin, Susan, and Mark Lopez. 2008. *The Hispanic Vote in the 2008 Democratic Presidential Primaries.* Washington, DC: Pew Hispanic Center. Accessed July 14, 2008. http://pewhispanic.org/files/reports/86.pdf.

Mitchell, Greg. 2008. "Full Transcript of Hillary Claiming Sexism Worse than Racism in Campaign." *Huffington Post.* May 20. Accessed May 20, 2008. http://www.huffingtonpost.com/greg-mitchell/full-transcript-of-hillar_b_102716.html.

Mitchell, Mary. 2008. "Facts Don't Back Black-Brown Divide in Texas." *Chicago Sun-Times.* March 4. Accessed July 14, 2008. http://www.suntimes.com/news/mitchell/823805,CST-NWS-mitch04.article#.

"MLK to Obama: A Dream Realized?" 2008. MSNBC. August 23. Accessed August 23, 2008. http://www.msnbc.msn.com/id/26271271/#.

Mooney, Alexander. 2008. "McCain Ad Compares Obama to Britney Spears, Paris Hilton." CNN. July 30. Accessed July 30, 2008. http://www.cnn.com/2008/POLITICS/07/30/mccain.ad/index.html.

Mooney, Alexander, Sareena Dalla, and Scott Anderson. 2007. "Groups Criticize McCain for Calling U.S. 'Christian Nation.'" CNN. October 1. Accessed October 1, 2007. http://www.cnn.com/2007/POLITICS/10/01/mccain.christian.nation/.

Moraga, Cherrie. 2009. "What's Race Gotta Do with It?—November 2008." *Meridians: Feminism, Race, Transnationalism* 9, no. 1: 163–173.

Morgan, Robin. 2008. "Goodbye To All That (#2)." *Women's Media Center.* February 2. Accessed March 18, 2008. http://www.womensmediacenter.com/ex/020108.html.

"Morning in America: A Letter from Feminists on the Election." 2008. *The Nation.* March 17. Accessed March 18, 2008. http://www.thenation.com/article/morning-america.

Morris, Dick. 2008. "How Clinton Will Win the Nomination by Losing S.C." *RealClearPolitics.* January 23. Accessed January 23, 2008. http://www.realclearpolitics.com/articles/2008/01/how_clinton_will_win_the_nomin.html.

Morris, Phillip. 2008. "America Begins Its Journey into a Post-racial Era." *Cleveland Plain Dealer.* November 5. Accessed November 10, 2008. http://www.cleveland.com/morris/index.ssf/2008/11/phillip_morris_america_begins.html.

Morrison, Toni. 1998. "Comment." *New Yorker.* October 5. Accessed April 26, 2008. http://www.newyorker.com/archive/1998/10/05/1998_10_05_031_TNY_LIBRY_000016504.

Moynihan, Michael C. 2008. "A Transformation on Race." *Reason Magazine.* November. Accessed November 20, 2008. http://reason.com/archives/2008/11/05/a-transformation-on-race.

"Mr. Obama and Rev. Wright." 2008. *New York Times.* April 30. Accessed April 30, 2008. http://www.nytimes.com/2008/04/30/opinion/30wed1.html.

Munoz, Rosalio. 2008. "McCain-Palin Attacks Fall Flat with Latinos." *LA Progressive.* September 22. Accessed November 14, 2008. http://www.laprogressive.com/election-reform-campaigns/mccain-palin-attacks-fall-flat-with-latinos/.

Murray, Shailagh. 2008. "John Lewis Condemns GOP Campaign Tactics." *Washington Post.* October 11. Accessed October 11, 2008. http://voices.washingtonpost.com/44/2008/10/john-lewis-condemns-gop-campai.html.

Muskal, Michael. 2010. "Steinem Criticizes Palin for Using Feminist Brand." *Los Angeles Times.* June 23. Accessed June 23 2010. http://latimesblogs.latimes.com/dcnow/2010/06/steinem-criticizes-palin-for-using-feminist-brand.html.

Nagourney, Adam. 2008. "The New McCain: More Aggressive and Scripted on the Campaign Trail." *New York Times.* September 18. Accessed September 18, 2008. http://www.nytimes.com/2008/09/19/us/politics/19mccain.html.

Nagourney, Adam, and Jennifer Steinhauer. 2008. "In Obama's Pursuit of Latinos, Race Plays Role." *Washington Post.* January 15. Accessed January 17, 2008. http://www.nytimes.com/2008/01/15/us/politics/15hispanic.html.

Nakoso, Dan. 2008. "Obama's Hawaii Trip: Family Comes First." *Time.* October 25, 2008. Accessed October 25, 2008. http://www.time.com/time/nation/article/0,8599,1853792,00.html.

Narcisse, Jonathan. 2008. "New Agenda for Black America?" *Des Moines Register.* November 15. Accessed November 20, 2008. http://www.desmoinesregister.com/article/20081115/OPINION01/811150316/1036/OPINION.

Nash, Manning. 1962. "Race and the Ideology of Race." *Current Anthropology* 3, no. 3 (June): 285–288.

"National Exit Polls Table." 2008. *New York Times.* November 5. Accessed November 5, 2008. http://elections.nytimes.com/2008/results/president/national-exit-polls.html.

National Urban League. 2005. *Empowering Communities, Changing Lives: 2005 Annual Report.* New York: National Urban League. Accessed January 11, 2011. http://www.nul.org/sites/default/files/2005AnnualRpt.pdf.

Navarrette, Ruben, Jr. 2008. "Commentary: Latinos Will Vote for Obama." CNN. June 8. Accessed July 14, 2008. http://articles.cnn.com/2008-06-08/politics/navarrette_1_latino-voters-illinois-senator-barack-obama?_s=PM:POLITICS#.

———. 2010. "Dear Mr. President." *Latino Magazine.* Summer. Accessed August 15, 2010. http://www.latinomagazine.com/summer_10/features/obama.htm.

———. 2010. "Did Obama Break Promise to Latinos?" CNN. July 8. Accessed July 8, 2010. http://articles.cnn.com/2010-07-08/opinion/navarrette.obama.promise_1_immigration-bill-immigration-reform-latino-support?_s=PM:OPINION.

Neiwert, David. 2008. "Bill Bennett: Obama's Win Means 'You Don't Take Excuses Anymore' from Minorities." *Crooks and Liars.* November 5. Accessed January 4, 2009. http://crooksandliars.com/david-neiwert/bill-bennett-obama-wins-means-no-mor.

———. 2008. "Blowing the Dog Whistle." *Firedoglake.* April 14. Accessed May 8, 2008. http://firedoglake.com/2008/04/14/blowing-the-dog-whistle/.

Newport, Frank. 2010. "Tea Party Supporters Overlap Republican Base: Eight out of 10 Tea Party Supporters Are Republicans." Gallup.com. July 2. Accessed July 2, 2010. http://www.gallup.com/poll/141098/Tea-Party-Supporters-Overlap-Republican-Base.aspx?.

Newton-Small, Jay. 2008. "Obama's Flag Pin Flip-Flop?" *Time.* May 14. Accessed May 15, 2008. http://www.time.com/time/politics/article/0,8599,1779544,00.html.

Nezua. 2008. "Latinos [and Allies] Want Specifics, Not Soundbytes." *The Unapologetic Mexican.* July 11. Accessed August 3, 2008. http://www.theunapologeticmexican. org/elgrito/2008/07/latinos_and_allies_want_specifics_not_soundbytes.html.

Ngai, Mae M. 2004. *Impossible Subjects: Illegal Aliens and the Making of Modern America.* Princeton: Princeton University Press.

Nicholas, Peter. 2008. "Meet the Guy Next Door: Barack Obama." *Los Angeles Times.* May 6. Accessed May 7, 2008. http://articles.latimes.com/2008/may/06/nation/ na-campaign6.

Noah, Timothy. 2008. "What We Didn't Overcome." Slate.com. November 10. Accessed November 10, 2008. http://www.slate.com/id/2204251/.

Novak, Robert D. 2008. "Clinton's Risky Gamble." *Washington Post.* January 28. Accessed September 6, 2010. http://www.washingtonpost.com/wp-dyn/content/ article/2008/01/27/AR2008012701612.html.

Obama, Barack. 2004. "Keynote Address at the 2004 Democratic National Convention." *Organizing for America.* July 27. Accessed March 13, 2008. http://www. barackobama.com/2004/07/27/keynote_address_at_the_2004_de.php.

———. 2007. "Full Text of Senator Barack Obama's Announcement for President." Delivered in Springfield, IL. *Organizing for America.* February 10. Accessed February 12, 2007. http://www.barackobama.com/2007/02/10/remarks_of_senator_barack_obam_11.php.

———. 2007. "Selma Voting Rights March Commemoration." Delivered in Selma, AL. *Organizing for America.* March 4. Accessed March 5, 2007. http://www.barackobama.com/2007/03/04/selma_voting_rights_march_comm.php.

———. 2008. "The America We Love: Remarks of Senator Obama." Delivered in Independence, MO. *Organizing for America.* June 30. Accessed June 30, 2008. http://www.barackobama.com/2008/06/30/remarks_of_senator_barack_obam_83.php.

———. 2008. "Election Night: Remarks of President-Elect Barack Obama." Delivered in Chicago. *Organizing for America.* November 4. Accessed November 8, 2008. http://www.barackobama.com/2008/11/04/remarks_of_presidentelect_bara.php.

———. 2008. "A More Perfect Union." Delivered in Philadelphia. *Organizing for America.* March 18. Accessed March 18, 2008. http://www.barackobama. com/2008/03/18/remarks_of_senator_barack_obam_53.php.

———. 2008. "Text of Obama's Fatherhood Speech." Delivered in Chicago. Politico. com. June 15. Accessed June 16, 2008. http://www.politico.com/news/stories/0608/11094.html.

"The Obama Card." 2007. *Los Angeles Times.* February 13. Accessed February 15, 2007. http://articles.latimes.com/2007/feb/13/opinion/ed-obama13#.

"Obama Love 3.0." 2008. John McCain campaign television ad. July 22. Accessed August 5, 2008. http://www.youtube.com/watch?v=u6CSix3Dyo4.

O'Brien, Eileen. 2003. "The Personal Is Political: The Influence of White Supremacy on White Antiracists' Personal Relationships." Pp. 253–270 in *White Out: The Continuing Significance of Racism,* edited by Ashley W. Doane and Eduardo Bonilla-Silva. New York: Routledge.

———. 2008. *The Racial Middle: Latinos and Asian Americans Living Beyond the Racial Divide.* New York: NYU Press.

Oinounou, Mosheh, and Bonney Kapp. 2008. "Michelle Obama Takes Heat for Saying She's 'Proud of My Country' for the First Time." Fox News. February 19. Accessed August 10, 2008 http://www.foxnews.com/story/0,2933,331288,00.html.

Okihiro, Gary. 1994. *Margins and Mainstreams: Asians in American History and Culture*. Seattle: University of Washington Press.

Olbermann, Keith. 2008. "Clinton, You Invoked a Political Nightmare: Referencing RFK's Assassination as a Reason for Staying in the Race Is Unforgiveable." *Countdown with Keith Olbermann*. May 23. Accessed May 24, 2008. http://www.msnbc.msn.com/id/24797758/.

Oliver, Melvin, and Thomas Shapiro. 2006. *Black Wealth/White Wealth: A New Perspective on Racial Inequality*. New York: Routledge.

Olopade, Dayo. 2008. "The Father 'Hood." *New Republic*. June 15. Accessed June 15, 2008. http://www.tnr.com/blog/the-plank/the-father-hood.

Omi, Michael A. 2001. "The Changing Meaning of Race." Pp. 243–263 in *America Becoming: Racial Trends and Their Consequences*, vol. 1, edited by Neil J. Smelser, William J. Wilson, and Faith Mitchell. Washington, DC: National Academy Press.

Omi, Michael, and Howard Winant. 1994. *Racial Formation in the United States: From the 1960s and the 1990s*, 2nd ed. New York: Routledge.

"O'Reilly: 'I Don't Want to Go on a Lynching Party against Michelle Obama Unless There's Evidence, Hard Facts, That Say This Is How the Woman Really Feels.'" 2008. *Media Matters*. February 20. Accessed February 21, 2008. http://mediamatters.org/research/200802200001?f=h_latest.

"O'Reilly to 'Race Hustlers' and 'Race-Baiters': '[T]he Gloves Are Off.'" 2008. *Media Matters for America*. April 8. Accessed January 4, 2009. http://mediamatters.org/research/200804080006.

O'Reilly, Bill. 2006. *Culture Warrior*. New York: Broadway Books.

———. 2007. "GOP Presidential Hopeful John McCain Sits Down with Bill O'Reilly." Television transcript. *O'Reilly Factor*. Fox News. May 30. Accessed May 30, 2007. http://www.foxnews.com/story/0,2933,276732,00.html.

Orey, Byron D. 2006. "Deracialization or Racialization: The Making of a Black Mayor in Jackson, Mississippi." Department of Political Science, Faculty Publications, University of Nebraska–Lincoln. Accessed July 28, 2010. http://digitalcommons.unl.edu/cgi/viewcontent.cgi?article=1018&context=poliscifacpub.

O'Rourke, Megan. 2008. "Death of a Saleswoman: How Hillary Clinton Lost Me— and a Generation of Young Voters." Salon.com. June 5. Accessed July 18, 2008. http://www.slate.com/id/2192827.

Orr, Jimmy. 2008. "Palin: Obama 'Palling around with Terrorists.'" *Christian Science Monitor*. October 5. Accessed October 5, 2008. http://www.csmonitor.com/USA/Politics/The-Vote/2008/1005/palin-obama-palling-around-with-terrorists.

———. 2009. "Jimmy Carter Racism Charge: Obama Doesn't Agree Says Gibbs." *Christian Science Monitor*. September 16. Accessed November 20, 2009. http://www.csmonitor.com/USA/Politics/The-Vote/2009/0916/jimmy-carter-racism-charge-obama-doesnt-agree-says-gibbs.

Padgett, Tim. 2009. "Picking Sotomayor: Bridging the Black-Latino Divide." *Time*. May 27, 2009. Accessed May 27, 2009. http://www.time.com/time/nation/article/0,8599,1901249,00.html.

Page, Clarence. 2008. "Jackson's Eloquent Tears." *Chicago Tribune*. November 9. Accessed November 9, 2008. http://articles.chicagotribune.com/2008-11-09/news/0811080277_1_election-night-barack-obama-exit-polls.

Page, Susan. 2008. "Obama to NAACP: Blacks Must Seize Responsibility." *USA Today*. July 15. Accessed July 15, 2008. http://www.usatoday.com/news/politics/election2008/2008-07-14-obama-naacp_N.htm.

Pager, Devah. 2003. "The Mark of a Criminal Record." *American Journal of Sociology* 108, no. 5: 937–975.

Palin, Sarah. 2008. "Palin's Speech at the Republican National Convention." *New York Times*. September 3. Accessed September 3, 2008. http://elections.nytimes.com/2008/president/conventions/videos/transcripts/20080903_PALIN_SPEECH.html.

———. 2009. *Going Rogue: An American Life*. New York: HarperCollins.

Parker, Christopher S., Mark Q. Sawyer, and Christopher Towler. 2009. "A Black Man in the White House?" *Du Bois Review* 6, no. 1 (March): 193–217.

Passel, Jeffrey, and D'Vera Cohn. 2008. "Immigration to Play Lead Role in Future U.S. Growth." *Pew Research Center*. February 11. Accessed May 13, 2010. http://pewresearch.org/pubs/729/united-states-population-projections#.

Pearson, Rick. 2007. "McCain in Michigan: 'We Are Judeo-Christian' Nation." *Chicago Tribune*. January 14. Accessed January 14, 2007. http://www.swamppolitics.com/news/politics/blog/2008/01/mccain_in_michigan_we_are_jude.html.

Pedraza, Silvia. 2005. "Assimilation or Transnationalism? Conceptual Models of the Immigrant Experience in America." Pp. 419–428 in *Cuba in Transition*. Vol. 15. *Papers and Proceedings of the Fifteenth Annual Meeting of the Association for the Study of the Cuban Economy (ASCE)*. Washington, DC: Association for the Study of the Cuban Economy. Accessed May 29, 2010.

"Penn Strategy Memo, March 19, 2007." 2008. *The Atlantic*. August 11. Accessed September 15, 2008. http://www.theatlantic.com/politics/archive/2008/11/penn-strategy-memo-march-19-2008/37952.

Perea, Juan. 1997. "The Black/White Binary Paradigm of Race: The 'Normal Science' of American Racial Thought." *California Law Review* 85, no. 5: 1213–1258.

Peretz, Martin. 2008. "Barack Obama: Putting Race Hustlers Out of Work." *New Republic*. April 29. Accessed May 5, 2008. http://www.tnr.com/blog/the-spine/barack-obama-putting-race-hustlers-out-work.

Perry, Huey. 1995. *Blacks and the American Political System*. Gainesville: University of Florida Press.

———. 1996. *Race, Governance, and Politics in the United States*. Gainesville: University of Florida Press.

Persons, Georgia A., ed. 1993. *Dilemmas of Black Politics: Issues of Leadership and Strategy*. New York: HarperCollins.

Pew Hispanic Center. 2009. "Table 1: Population, by Race and Ethnicity: 2000 and 2007." In *Statistical Portrait of Hispanics in the United States, 2007*. Washington, DC: Pew Hispanic Center. Accessed May 13, 2010. http://pewhispanic.org/files/factsheets/hispanics2007/Table-1.pdf.

Pew Research Center. 2007. *Blacks See Growing Values Gap between Poor and Middle Class: Optimism about Black Progress Declines*. Washington, DC: Pew Research Center. Accessed November 16, 2007. http://pewsocialtrends.org/assets/pdf/Race.pdf.

————. 2009. *Obama's Ratings Slide across the Board: The Economy, Health Care Reform, and Gates Grease the Skids.* Washington, DC: Pew Research Center. Accessed August 10, 2008. http://people-press.org/reports/pdf/532.pdf.

PG Your Humble Messenger. 2010. "Tit for Tat." *Constitution Club.* March 31. Accessed April 22, 2010. http://constitutionclub.org/2010/03/31/tit-for-tat/.

Picca, Leslie Houts, and Joe. R. Feagin. 2007. *Two-Faced Racism: Whites in the Backstage and Frontstage.* New York: Routledge.

Pickler, Nedra. 2007. "Democrats Face Off in 'YouTube' Debate." MSNBC. July 23. Accessed July 27, 2007. http://www.msnbc.msn.com/id/19914962/#.

Pimentel, Benjamin. 2008. "Barack Obama through Filipino-American Eyes." *Philippine Star.* November 2, 2008. Accessed November 13, 2008. http://www.philstar. com/Article.aspx?articleid=412073.

————. 2008. "Obama, First Pinoy President?" *Inquirer Global Nation.* January 29. Accessed February 14, 2008. http://globalnation.inquirer.net/mindfeeds/mindfeeds/view/20080129-115469/Obama-first-Pinoy-US-President.

————. 2008. *Pareng Barack: Filipinos in Obama's America.* Pasig City, Philippines: Anvil Publishing.

Powell, John A. 2009. "Post-racialism or Targeted Universalism?" *Denver University Law Review* 86, no. 1 (February): 785–806.

Powell, Michael. 2008. "Embracing His Moment, Obama Preaches Hope in New Hampshire." *New York Times.* January 5. Accessed January 5, 2008. http://www. nytimes.com/2008/01/05/us/politics/05obama.html.

Powell, Michael, and Jodi Cantor. 2008. "Michelle Obama Looks for a New Introduction." *New York Times.* June 18. Accessed June 18, 2008. http://www.msnbc.msn. com/id/25234989.

Praetorius, Dean. 2009. "Obama Joker Poster Causes Stir on Web." ABC News. August 3. Accessed August 3, 2009. http://abcnews.go.com/Politics/President44/ story?id=8239870&page=1.

Prelutsky, Burt. 2007. "Black Racism." Townhall.com. January 22. Accessed January 15, 2008. http://townhall.com/columnists/BurtPrelutsky/2007/01/22/ black_racism.

————. 2008. "Obama: Guilty by Association." Townhall.com. June 23. Accessed June 24, 2008. http://townhall.com/columnists/BurtPrelutsky/2008/06/23/obama_ guilty_by_association.

"President-Elect Obama: The Voters Rebuke Republicans for Economic Failure." 2008. *Wall Street Journal.* November 5. Accessed November 5, 2009. http://online. wsj.com/article/NA_WSJ_PUB:SB122586244657800863.html.

Preston, Julia. 2010. "Deportations from U.S. Hit a Record High." *New York Times.* October 6. Accessed April 11, 2011. http://www.nytimes.com/2010/10/07/ us/07immig.html.

Price, Hugh B. 2008. "The Obama Victory: Giving Affirmative Action Its Due." *Brookings.* June 24. Accessed June 26, 2008. http://www.brookings.edu/opinions/2008/0624_affirmative_action_price.aspx.

el Profe. 2008. "Hispanics and Barack Obama: Racism without shame." *Latino Insurgent.* March 5. Accessed May 15, 2008. http://latinoinsurgent.blogspot. com/2008/03/hispanics-and-barack-obama-racism.html.

"Quest for Obama's Birth Doctor." 2009. *The Birthers: Dedicated to the Rebirth of Our Constitutional Republic*. Accessed April 10, 2011. http://www.birthers.org/misc/ ObamaDr.htm.

Ramirez, Jessica. 2008. "McCain's Immigration Dilemma." *Newsweek*. July 19. Accessed July 23, 2008. http://www.newsweek.com/2008/07/18/why-won-t-juan-come-to-the-phone.html.

Rasmussen Reports. 2008. "Only 22% Say McCain Ad Racist, but Over Half (53%) See Obama Dollar-Bill Comment That Way." *Rasmussen Reports*. August 3. Accessed August 10, 2008. http://www.rasmussenreports.com/public_content/politics/ elections/election_2008/2008_presidential_election/only_22_say_mccain_ad_rac-ist_but_over_half_53_see_obama_dollar_bill_comment_that_way.

Raspberry, William. 2008. "A Path beyond Grievance." *Washington Post*. November 11. Accessed November 11, 2008. http://www.washingtonpost.com/wp-dyn/content/ article/2008/11/10/AR2008111001544.html.

Reagan, Bianca. 2008. "Fried Chicken Tacos." *BlogHer*. January 21. Accessed February 15, 2008. http://www.blogher.com/fried-chicken-tacos#.

Redenbaugh, Russell. 2008. "Barack Obama: Only in America." *RealClearMarkets*. November 11. Accessed November 13, 2008. http://www.realclearmarkets.com/ articles/2008/11/barack_obama_and_only_in_ameri.html.

Reed, Adolph. 2008. "Obama No." *The Progressive*. May. Accessed August 10, 2008. http://www.progressive.org/mag_reed0508.

Reed, Betsy. 2008. "Race to the Bottom." *The Nation*. May 1. Accessed May 2, 2008. http://www.thenation.com/article/race-bottom-0.

Remnick, David. 2008. "The Joshua Generation: Race and the Campaign of Barack Obama." *New Yorker*. November 17. Accessed January 15, 2009. http://www.newy-orker.com/reporting/2008/11/17/081117fa_fact_remnick.

Reno, Jamie. 2008. "Black-Brown Divide." *Newsweek*. January 26. Accessed January 26, 2008. http://www.newsweek.com/2008/01/25/black-brown-divide.

"Republicans Win House Majority, Make Senate Gains in Wave Election." 2010. Fox News. November 2. Accessed April 12, 2011. http://www.foxnews.com/poli-tics/2010/11/02/poll-closing-key-east-coast-races-balance-power-line/.

Reynolds, Dean. 2007. "Obama's Racial Identity Still an Issue." CBS News. November 27. Accessed November 28, 2007. http://www.cbsnews.com/stories/2007/11/27/ eveningnews/main3546210.shtml.

Rich, Frank. 2010. "The Rage Is Not about Health Care." *New York Times*. March 28. Accessed March 28, 2010. http://www.nytimes.com/2010/03/28/opinion/28rich. html.

Riley, Naomi Schaefer. 2008. "Sarah Palin Feminism." *Wall Street Journal*. September 5. Accessed September 5, 2008. http://online.wsj.com/article/ SB122058255216602625.html?mod=googlenews_wsj.

Rikyrah. 2008. "When It Comes to Michelle Obama, Where Are the Feminists?" *Jack & Jill Politics*. June 23. Accessed June 23, 2008. http://www.jackandjillpolitics. com/2008/06/when-it-comes-to-michelle-obama-where-are-the-feminists/.

Rivas, Ana. 2008. "Latino Bloggers React to Candidates' Outreach Efforts." *Wall Street Journal*. July 14. Accessed July 14, 2008. http://blogs.wsj.com/wash-wire/2008/07/14/latino-bloggers-react-to-candidates-outreach-efforts/.

Roberts, Dorothy. 2002. *Shattered Bonds: The Color of Child Welfare*. New York: Basic Books.

Robinson, Eugene. 2007. "Obama Opens Debate on Affirmative Action." *Washington Post*. May 15. Accessed May 15, 2007. http://articles.sfgate.com/2007-05-15/opinion/17243226_1_affirmative-action-obama-s-remarks-fifth-or-sixth-generation-college.

———. 2009. "Pique and the Professor." *Washington Post*. July 28. Accessed July 28. http://www.washingtonpost.com/wp-dyn/content/article/2009/07/27/AR2009072701907.html.

Robinson, Sara. 2008. "Standing at the Nexus of Change." *Ornicus*. July 10. Accessed July 15, 2008. http://www.dneiwert.blogspot.com/2008_07_06_archive.html.

Rockquemore, Kerry Ann, and David L. Brunsma. 2002. *Beyond Black: Biracial Identity in America*. Thousand Oaks, CA: Sage Publications.

Rodriguez, Gregory. 2007. "The Fantasy of L.A.'s 'Race War': Why Is Everyone So Anxious to Elevate Latino-black Violence to Historic Levels?" *Los Angeles Times*. October 1. Accessed January 4, 2008. http://www.latimes.com/news/printedition/asection/la-oe-rodriguez1oct01,0,7276088.column.

———. 2008. "The Black-Brown Divide." *Time*. January 26. Accessed January 31, 2008. http://www.time.com/time/magazine/article/0,9171,1707221,00.html#.

———. 2008. "Dialogue Isn't the Last Word." *Los Angeles Times*. May 5. Accessed May 17, 2008. http://articles.latimes.com/2008/may/05/opinion/oe-rodriguez5.

———. 2009. "Obama and Immigration Reform." *Los Angeles Times*. March 23. Accessed March 28, 2009. http://www.latimes.com/news/opinion/commentary/la-oe-rodriguez23-2009mar23,0,6724063,print.column.

Rodriguez, Jason. 2006. "Color-Blind Ideology and the Cultural Appropriation of Hip-Hop." *Journal of Contemporary Ethnography* 23, no. 6 (December): 645–668.

Rodriguez, Richard. 2008. "Obama Is More Brown Than Black." *Newsweek*. May 24. Accessed May 24, 2008. http://www.newsweek.com/2008/05/24/see-the-brown-in-us.html.

Roebuck, Rolando. 2008. "Hispanics, Racism, and Obama." *Metro Latino USA*. February 7. Accessed May 15, 2008. http://www.metrolatinousa.com/article.cfm?articleID=29548.

Roediger, David R. 2008. *How Race Survived U.S. History: From Settlement and Slavery to the Obama Phenomenon*. New York: Verso.

Rogers, Joel, and Ruy Teixeira. 2000. "America's Forgotten Majority." *The Atlantic*. Accessed June 20, 2008. http://www.theatlantic.com/past/docs/issues/2000/06/rogers.htm.

Rohter, Larry. 2008. "Palin Criticizes Obama as a Faux Feminist." *New York Times*. October 21. Accessed October 21, 2008. http://thecaucus.blogs.nytimes.com/2008/10/21/palin-criticizes-obama-as-faux-feminist/.

Root, Maria P. 1992. *Racially Mixed People in America*. Newbury Park, CA: Sage Publications.

Ross, Brian, and Rehag El-Buri. 2008. "Obama's Pastor: God Damn America, U.S. to Blame for 9/11." *ABC News*. March 13. Accessed March 15, 2008. http://abcnews.go.com/Blotter/DemocraticDebate/story?id=4443788&page=1.

Roth, Bennett. 2008. "Latino Vote Is the Winning Ticket for Super Tuesday." *Houston Chronicle*. February 3. Accessed February 14, 2008. http://www.chron.com/disp/story.mpl/politics/5510404.html#.

"Rove: Obama Is the Type of Guy Who Hangs Out at Country Clubs." 2008. *Talking Points Memo*. June 23. Accessed July 15, 2008. http://tpmelectioncentral.talking-pointsmemo.com/2008/06/rove_obama_is_the_type_of_guy.php.

Saad, Lydia. 2008. "Whites May Exaggerate Black-Hispanic Tensions." Gallup.com. July 17. Accessed May 4, 2009. http://www.gallup.com/poll/108868/whites-may-exaggerate-blackhispanic-tensions.aspx.

Sabater, Liza. 2008. "Divide and Conquer: Obama and the Latino Vote in the NY Times." *Culture Kitchen*. January 17. Accessed January 22, 2008. http://www.culturekitchen.com/liza/blog/divide_and_conquer_obama_and_the_latino_vote_in_th#.

Salant, Jonathan D. 2008. "Jackson's 'Crude' Remarks May Give Boost to Obama." *Bloomberg*. July 10. Accessed August 4, 2008 http://www.bloomberg.com/apps/news?pid=newsarchive&sid=aatOueE_l3MI.

Samuel, Terence. 2007. "Young, Black, and Post–Civil Rights." *American Prospect*. September 4. Accessed September 4, 2007. http://www.prospect.org/cs/articles?article=young_black_and_postcivil_rights.

———. 2008. "On the 2008 Primary and Black Anger." *American Prospect*. April 25. Accessed April 25, 2008. http://www.prospect.org/cs/articles?article=on_the_2008_primary_and_black_anger.

Sanneh, Kelefa. 2008. "What He Knows for Sure: Tavis Smiley Confronts the Obama Candidacy." *New Yorker*. August 4. Accessed August 8, 2008. http://www.newyorker.com/reporting/2008/08/04/080804fa_fact_sanneh.

"Sarah Palin Speaks at Tea Party Convention." 2010. CNN. February 6. Accessed February 7, 2010. http://archives.cnn.com/TRANSCRIPTS/1002/06/cnr.09.html.

Sargent, Greg. 2008. "Note To News Orgs: McCain and Palin Are Largely Responsible for Unhinged Tone at Their Rallies." *Talking Points Memo*. October 10. Accessed October 10, 2008. http://tpmelectioncentral.talkingpointsmemo.com/2008/10/note_to_news_orgs_mccain_and_p.php.

Sarmah, Satta. 2007. "Is Obama Black Enough?" *Columbia Journalism Review*. February 15. Accessed February 16, 2007. http://www.cjr.org/politics/is_obama_black_enough.php.

Saslow, Eli. 2008. "To Women, So Much More Than Just a Candidate." *Washington Post*. March 4. Accessed March 4, 2008. http://www.washingtonpost.com/wp-dyn/content/story/2008/03/03/ST2008030303087.html.

Schaeffer, Frank. 2008. "Jesse Jackson (with a Little Help From James Dobson) Just Handed the White House to Obama." *Huffington Post*. July 10. Accessed July 10, 2008. http://www.huffingtonpost.com/frank-schaeffer/jesse-jackson-with-a-litt_b_111917.html.

———. 2008. "An Open Letter to John McCain." *Huffington Post*. October 10. Accessed October 10, 2008 http://www.huffingtonpost.com/frank-schaeffer/an-open-letter-to-john-mc_b_133489.html.

Schaller, Thomas. 2008. "How Hillary Clinton Botched the Black Vote." Salon.com. May 5. Accessed February 10, 2010. http://www.salon.com/news/opinion/feature/2008/05/05/clinton_blackvote.

Scheiber, Noam. 2004. "Race against History: Barack Obama's Miraculous Campaign." *New Republic.* May 31. Accessed January 4, 2007. http://www.tnr.com/article/politics/race-against-history.

Schelzig, Erik. 2010. "Tennessee: GOP's Ramsey Says He's Unsure of Obama's Citizenship." *Chattanooga (TN) Times Free Press.* February 2. Accessed March 5, 2010. http://www.timesfreepress.com/news/2010/feb/02/tennessee-gops-ramsey-says-hes-unsure-obama-citize/?breakingnews.

Schildkraut, Deborah J. 2002. "The More Things Change . . . American Identity and Mass and Elite Responses to 9/11." *Political Psychology* 23, no. 3 (September): 511–535.

Schneider, Matt. 2011. "Wild Shoutfest between Al Sharpton and Cornel West on Obama and Race." Mediaite.com. April 11. Accessed April 11, 2011. http://www.mediaite.com/tv/wild-shoutfest-between-al-sharpton-and-cornel-west-on-obamas-leadership-on-racial-issues/.

Schorn, Daniel. 2007. "Transcript Excerpt: Sen. Barack Obama [with Steve Kroft]." CBS News. February 11. Accessed April 22, 2008. http://www.cbsnews.com/stories/2007/02/11/60minutes/main2458530_page3.shtml#.

Schott Foundation for Public Education. 2010. *Yes We Can: The Schott 50 State Report on Public Education and Black Males, 2010.* Cambridge, MA: Schott Foundation for Public Education. Accessed September 12, 2010. http://schottfoundation.org/publications/schott-2010-black-male-report.pdf.

Schumacher-Matos, Eduardo. 2010. "Democrats Must Seize the Immigration Issue." *Washington Post.* August 5. Accessed August 5, 2010. http://www.washingtonpost.com/wp-dyn/content/article/2010/08/05/AR2010080503750_pf.html.

Sears, David O., Colette van Laar, Mary Carrillo, and Rick Kosterman. 1997. "Is It Really Racism? The Origins of White Americans' Opposition to Race-Targeted Policies." *Public Opinion Quarterly* 61, no. 1: 16–53.

Seigel, Micol. 2009. *Uneven Encounters: Making Race and Nation in Brazil and the United States.* Durham, NC: Duke University Press.

Serwer, Adam. 2008. "He's Black, Get over it." *American Prospect.* December 5. Accessed January 12, 2011. http://www.prospect.org/cs/articles?article=hes_black_get_over_it.

———. 2008. "Obama's Racial Catch-22." *American Prospect.* August 4, 2008. Accessed August 4, 2008. http://www.prospect.org/cs/articles?article=obamas_racial_catch22.

Shapiro, Ari. 2008. "The Latino Vote: Pro-Clinton or Anti-Obama?" National Public Radio. March 3. Accessed August 2, 2008. http://www.npr.org/templates/story/story.php?storyId=87860383.

Shear, Michael D. 2008. "McCain Plans Fiercer Strategy against Obama." *Washington Post.* October 4. Accessed October 4, 2008. http://www.washingtonpost.com/wp-dyn/content/article/2008/10/03/AR2008100303738.html.

Shear, Michael D., and Perry Bacon Jr. 2008. "Anger Is Crowd's Overarching Emotion at McCain Rally." *Washington Post.* October 10. Accessed October 10, 2008. http://www.washingtonpost.com/wp-dyn/content/article/2008/10/09/AR2008100903169.html.

Shiver, Kyle-Anne. 2008. "Women Voters and the Obama Crush." *American Thinker.* March 11. Accessed April 25, 2008. http://www.americanthinker.com/2008/03/women_voters_and_the_obama_cru.html.

Silva, Mark. 2009. "Michelle Obama's Popularity Soars, Topping Recent First Ladies, Survey Finds." *Chicago Tribune.* April 24. Accessed April 24, 2009. http://www.chicagotribune.com/news/nationworld/chi-talk-michelle-popularapr24,0,7472730.story.

Silver, Nate. 2008. "'Real' America Looks Different to Palin, Obama." *FiveThirtyEight: Politics Done Right.* October 18. Accessed October 18, 2008. http://www.fivethirtyeight.com/2008/10/real-america-looks-different-to-palin.html.

Skurski, Julie. 1994. "The Ambiguities of Authenticity: Dona Barbara and the Construction of National Identity." *Poetics Today* 15, no. 4 (Winter): 605–642.

Slevin, Peter. 2010. "Deportation of Illegal Immigrants Increases under Obama Administration." *Washington Post.* July 26. Accessed July 26, 2010. http://www.washingtonpost.com/wp-dyn/content/article/2010/07/25/AR2010072501790.html.

Smith, Ben. 2008. "Hispanics Turn Cold Shoulder to McCain." Politico.com. October 9. Accessed October 9, 2008. http://www.politico.com/news/stories/1008/14444.html.

———. 2009. "Culture of Conspiracy: The Birthers." Politico.com. March 1. Accessed March 1, 2009. http://www.politico.com/news/stories/0209/19450.html.

Smith, Karen Sue. 2008. "Courting the Latino Vote." *America Magazine.* June 23. Accessed May 4, 2010. http://www.americamagazine.org/content/article.cfm?article_id=10886.

Smith, Tracy. 2008. "New Generation of Black Leaders Emerging." CBS News. January 21. Accessed January 21, 2008. http://www.cbsnews.com/stories/2008/01/21/earlyshow/contributors/tracysmith/main3734118.shtml.

Snell, Tracy. 2009. *Capital Punishment, 2008: Statistical Tables.* Washington, DC: U.S. Department of Justice, Bureau of Justice Statistics. Accessed September 13, 2010. http://bjs.ojp.usdoj.gov/content/pub/pdf/cp08st.pdf.

Sniderman, Paul, and Thomas Piazza. 1993. *The Scar of Race.* Cambridge, MA: Harvard University Press.

Solis-Marich, Mario. 2008. "McAuliffe: Obama Has a Hispanic Problem." *Huffington Post.* June 2. Accessed June 2, 2008. http://www.huffingtonpost.com/mario-solis-marich/mcauliffe-obama-has-a-his_b_104645.html#.

Solomon, Deborah. 2008. "All in the Family: Questions for Maya Soetoro-Ng." *New York Times.* January 20. Accessed January 20, 2008. http://www.nytimes.com/2008/01/20/magazine/20wwln-Q4-t.html.

Spaulding, Pam. 2008. "White Dog Whistles No More." *Pam's House Blend.* May 8. Accessed May 8, 2008. http://www.pamshouseblend.com/showDiary.do?diaryId=5311.

Spencer, Martin E. 1994. "Multiculturalism, 'Political Correctness,' and the Politics of Identity." *Sociological Forum* 9, no. 4: 547–567.

Spetalnick, Matt. 2008. "Republican Anger Bubbles Up at McCain Rally." Reuters. October 13. Accessed October 13, 2008. http://www.reuters.com/article/idUSTRE49A0P720081011.

Stan, Adele M. 2008. "The Feminist Case for Obama." *Washington Post.* March 4, 2008. Accessed March 4, 2008. http://www.washingtonpost.com/wp-dyn/content/article/2008/03/04/AR2008030401240.html.

Stanard, Alexa. 2008. "Michelle Obama, Radically Awesome." *Michigan Messenger.* July 16. Accessed August 8, 2008. http://michiganmessenger.com/1574/michelle-obama-radically-awesome.

Stanton, Glen T., and Bill Maier. 2004. *Marriage on Trial: The Case against Same-Sex Marriage and Parenting.* Downers Grove, IL: IVP Books.

Staples, Brent. 2007. "Decoding the Debate over the Blackness of Barack Obama." *New York Times.* February 11. Accessed February 11, 2007. http://www.nytimes.com/2007/02/11/opinion/11sun3.html.

Starr, Penny. 2009. "Obama Is 'First Hispanic President,' Geraldo Rivera Says." *CNS News.* March 29. Accessed May 13, 2009. http://www.cnsnews.com/news/article/45316.

St. Clair, Stacy. 2009. "Michelle Obama Image Makeover: First Lady's Approval Ratings Soar as She Embraces Traditional Role—with a Modern Twist." *Chicago Tribune.* April 29. Accessed April 29, 2009. http://www.chicagotribune.com/news/local/chi-michelle-obama-28-apr28,0,3727662.story.

Steele, Shelby. 2007. *A Bound Man: Why We Are Excited about Obama and Why He Can't Win.* New York: Free Press.

———. 2007. "The Identity Card." *Time.* November 30. Accessed January 15, 2008. http://www.time.com/time/magazine/article/0,9171,1689619,00.html.

———. 2008. "The Obama Bargain." *Wall Street Journal.* March 18. Accessed November 9, 2008. http://online.wsj.com/public/article/SB120579535818243439.html.

———. 2008. "Obama's Post-racial Promise." *Los Angeles Times.* November 5. Accessed November 9, 2008. http://articles.latimes.com/2008/nov/05/opinion/oe-steele5.

———. 2009. "Sotomayor and the Politics of Race." *Wall Street Journal.* June 9. Accessed June 20, 2009. http://online.wsj.com/article/NA_WSJ_PUB:SB124442662679393077.html.

Stein, Sam. 2008. "Palin Explains What Parts of Country Not 'Pro-America.'" *Huffington Post.* October 17. Accessed October 18, 2008. http://www.huffingtonpost.com/2008/10/17/palin-clarifies-what-part_n_135641.html.

———. 2010. "Robert Byrd: Obama Aides Recall the Symbolism of His Endorsement." *Huffington Post.* June 28. Accessed June 28, 2010. http://www.huffingtonpost.com/2010/06/28/robert-byrd-obama-aides-r_n_627579.html.

Steinberg, Stephen. 1995. *Turning Back: The Retreat from Racial Justice in American Thought and Policy.* Boston: Beacon Press.

Steinem, Gloria. 2008. "Women Are Never Front-Runners." *New York Times.* January 8. Accessed January 8, 2008. http://www.nytimes.com/2008/01/08/opinion/08steinem.html.

———. 2008. "Wrong Woman, Wrong Message." *Los Angeles Times.* September 4. Accessed September 4, 2008. http://articles.latimes.com/2008/sep/04/news/OE-STEINEM4.

Steinhorn, Leonard, and Barbara Diggs-Brown. 2000. *By the Color of Our Skin: The Illusion of Integration and the Reality of Race.* New York: Dutton.

Steyn, Mark. 2006. *America Alone: The End of the World as We Know It.* Washington, DC: Regnery Publishing.

———. 2008. "Post 'Post-Racial Candidate.'" *National Review Online.* March 22. Accessed January 4, 2009. http://article.nationalreview.com/352445/post-post-racial-candidate/mark-steyn.

Stoler, Ann, Laura. *Race and the Education of Desire: Foucault's History of Sexuality and the Colonial Order of Things.* Durham, NC: Duke University Press, 1995.

Street, Paul. 2009. *Barack Obama and the Future of American Politics.* Boulder, CO: Paradigm Publishers.

Suarez, Fernandez. 2008. "Bottoms Up: Just Another Saturday Night for Clinton? Shot of Whiskey, Beer, and Pizza." CBS News. April 12. Accessed April 12 2008. http://www.cbsnews.com/8301-502443_162-4011410-502443.html.

Sullivan, Andrew. 2007. "Jackson vs. Obama." *Daily Dish.* September 19. Accessed September 19, 2007. http://andrewsullivan.theatlantic.com/the_daily_dish/2007/09/jackson-vs-obam.html.

———. 2008. "The Dangerous Panic on the Far Right." *Daily Dish.* October 10. Accessed October 10, 2008. http://andrewsullivan.theatlantic.com/the_daily_dish/2008/10/the-dangerous-p.html.

Swarns, Rachel. 2008. "Delicate Obama Path on Class and Race Preferences." *New York Times.* August 3. Accessed August 10, 2008. http://www.nytimes.com/2008/08/03/us/politics/03affirmative.html.

Sweeney, Kathryn A., & Belisa González. 2008. "Affirmative Action Never Helped Me: Public Response to Ending Affirmative Action in Michigan." Pp. 135–148 in *Racism in Post-race America: New Theories, New Directions,* edited by Charles Gallagher. Chapel Hill: Social Forces Publishing.

Swift, Jon. 2008. "Iowa Caucus Results Explained." *Jon Swift.* January 4. Accessed January 16, 2008. http://jonswift.blogspot.com/2008/01/iowa-caucus-results-explained.html.

Takaki, Ronald. 1990. *Strangers from a Different Shore: A History of Asian Americans.* New York: Penguin Books.

Tancredo, Tom. 2006. *In Mortal Danger: The Battle for America's Border and Security.* Nashville: WND Books.

Tapper, Jake. 2008. "Wright Assails Media, Cheney, Obama at National Press Club." ABC News. April 28. Accessed May 3, 2008. http://blogs.abcnews.com/politicalpunch/2008/04/wright-assails.html.

Tapper, Jake, and Katie Hinman. 2007. "Obama Declares His Candidacy: Invoking Lincoln, Illinois, Senator Opens White House Bid." ABC News. February 10. Accessed February 10, 2007. http://abcnews.go.com/GMA/Politics/story?id=2865196&page=1.

Tate, Katherine. 2001. "The Political Representation of Blacks in Congress: Does Race Matter?" *Legislative Studies Quarterly* 26, no. 4 (November): 623–638.

Tatum, Beverly Daniel. 2003. *Why Are All the Black Kids Sitting Together in the Cafeteria? And Other Conversations about Race,* rev. ed. New York: Basic Books.

Taylor, Keeanga-Yamatta. 2008. "Race and the Election: When the 'Real America' Enters the Voting Booth." *Counterpunch.* October 22. Accessed October 22, 2008. http://www.counterpunch.org/taylor10222008.html.

Taylor, Stuart, Jr. 2007. "The Great Black-White Hope." *The Atlantic*. February 3. Accessed February 5, 2007. http://www.theatlantic.com/magazine/archive/2007/02/the-great-black-white-hope/5647/.

———. 2008. "Racism Marginalized—Even If Obama Loses." NationalJournal.com. October 25. Accessed November 29, 2008. http://www.nationaljournal.com/njmagazine/or_20081025_8927.php.

"'Tea Partier' Mark Williams Writes 'Letter to Abe Lincoln' . . . from the 'Coloreds.'" 2010. *Reid Report*. July 14. Accessed July 18, 2010. http://blog.reidreport.com/2010/07/tea-partier-mark-williams-writes-open-letter-to-lincoln-from-the-coloreds/.

"Tea Party Tension Flares as 'Federation' Gives Firebrand Activist the Boot." 2010. Fox News. July 19. Accessed July 19, 2010. http://www.foxnews.com/politics/2010/07/19/tea-party-tension-flares-federation-gives-firebrand-activist-boot/.

"Ten Most Offensive Tea Party Signs and Extensive Photo Coverage from Tax Day Protests." 2009. *Huffington Post*. December 29. Accessed December 29, 2009. http://www.huffingtonpost.com/2009/04/16/10-most-offensive-tea-par_n_187554.html.

Thernstrom, Abigail. 2008. "Subtle, Serious, Patriotic." *National Review Online*. March 20. Accessed March 31, 2008. http://www.nationalreview.com/articles/223972/subtle-serious-patriotic/abigail-thernstrom.

Thernstrom, Abigail, and Stephan Thernstrom, eds. 2002. *Beyond the Color Line: New Perspectives on Race and Ethnicity in America*. Stanford, CA: Hoover Institution Press.

Thompson, Krissah. 2010. "Activist Al Sharpton Takes on New Role as Administration Ally." *Washington Post*. April 17. Accessed April 17, 2010. http://www.washingtonpost.com/wp-dyn/content/article/2010/04/16/AR2010041602381.html.

Tilove, Jonathan. 2008. "Obama Presents Dilemma for Scholars of Race." *Chronicle of Higher Education*. August 13. Accessed August 16, 2008. http://chronicle.com/article/Obama-Presents-Dilemma-for-/43330/.

———. 2008. "'Pookie' Keeps Popping Up in Obama's Speeches." *Houston Chronicle*. January 30. Accessed August 16, 2008. http://www.chron.com/disp/story.mpl/life/main/5500250.html.

———. 2008. "The Third Labor of Obama—Hispanic and Asian Voters." *Jonathan Tilove*. January 31. Accessed March 24, 2010. http://jonathantilove.com/obamas-third-labor/.

Tope, Daniel. 2008. "Othering Obama." *Political Sociology: States, Power, and Societies* 14, no. 3 (Fall): 1, 4.

Traister, Rebecca. 2008. "Hey, Obama Boys: Back Off Already!" Salon.com. April 14. Accessed April 14, 2008. http://www.salon.com/life/feature/2008/04/14/obama_supporters.

———. 2008. "Zombie Feminists of the RNC." Salon.com. September 11. Accessed September 11, 2008. http://www.salon.com/life/feature/2008/09/11/zombie_feminism.

———. 2010. *Big Girls Don't Cry: The Election That Changed Everything for American Women*. New York: Free Press.

Traub, James. 2007. "Is (His) Biography (Our) Destiny?" *New York Times.* November 4. Accessed November 4, 2007. http://www.nytimes.com/2007/11/04/magazine/04obama-t.html.

———. 2008. "The Emerging Minority." *New York Times.* March 2. Accessed March 2, 2008. http://www.nytimes.com/2008/03/02/magazine/02wwln-lede-t.html.

Travis, Shannon. 2010. "CNN Poll: Quarter Doubt Obama Was Born in U.S." CNN. August 4. Accessed August 4, 2010. http://politicalticker.blogs.cnn.com/2010/08/04/cnn-poll-quarter-doubt-president-was-born-in-u-s/.

Trepagnier, Barbara. 2010. *Silent Racism: How Well-Meaning White People Perpetuate the Racial Divide,* 2nd ed. Boulder, CO: Paradigm Publishers.

Treviño, Marisa. 2009. "Obama Explains Why He Used the Term 'Illegal Immigrant.'" *Latina Lista.* September 24. Accessed October 18, 2009. http://www.latinalista.net/palabrafinal/2009/09/obama_explains_why_he_used_the_term_ille.html.

———. 2010. "Are Latinos Really Wanted by Either Party?" *Huffington Post.* September 17. Accessed September 17, 2010. http://www.huffingtonpost.com/marisa-trevi/are-latinos-really-wanted_b_686152.html.

———. 2011. "Some Latinos Wondering Why Vote for Obama in 2012." *Latina Lista.* April 4. Accessed April 11, 2011. http://www.latinalista.net/palabrafinal/2011/04/some_latinos_wondering_why_vote_for_obam.html.

Tubman, Jill. 2009. "The Rotting Racist Underbelly of the Tea Party Protests." *Jack & Jill Politics.* April 13. Accessed April 13, 2009. http://www.jackandjillpolitics.com/2009/04/the-rotting-racist-underbelly-of-the-tea-party-protests/.

Tuchman, Gary. 2008. "Anderson Cooper 360." CNN. February 8. Accessed February 16, 2008. http://archives.cnn.com/TRANSCRIPTS/0802/08/acd.02.html.

Twine, France Winddance. 1998. *Racism in a Racial Democracy: The Maintenance of White Supremacy in Brazil.* New Brunswick, NJ: Rutgers University Press.

Twine, France Winddance, and Charles A. Gallagher. 2008. "The Future of Whiteness: A Map of the Third Wave." *Ethnic and Racial Studies* 31, no. 1 (January): 4–24.

Umlauf, Simon. 2002. "Cuban Hip-Hop: The Rebellion within the Revolution." CNN. November 25. Accessed March 10, 2009. http://archives.cnn.com/2002/SHOWBIZ/Music/11/22/hln.hot.hit.cuban.hip.hop/.

"U.S. Deports Record Number of Migrants in 2010." 2010. Fox News Latino. December 29. Accessed April 11, 2011. http://latino.foxnews.com/latino/news/2010/12/29/deports-record-number-migrants/.

Valbrun, Marjorie. 2007. "Black Like Me? Those Asking If Barack Obama Is 'Black Enough' Are Asking the Wrong Question." *Washington Post.* February 15. Accessed February 15, 2007. http://www.washingtonpost.com/wp-dyn/content/article/2007/02/15/AR2007021501270.html.

Valdes-Rodriguez, Alisa. 2008. "Obama and the Latino Vote." *Alisa Valdes-Rodriguez Blog.* January 17. Accessed February 14, 2008. http://www.blogher.com/frame.php?url=http://www.feministe.us/blog/archives/2008/01/17/6666/.

Valenti, Jessica. 2008. "GOP Pinheads: Women Aren't 'Feminist' Unless They Vote for Sarah Palin." *Jezebel.* October 22. Accessed October 22, 2008. http://jezebel.com/5067066/gop-pinheads-women-arent-feminist-unless-they-vote-for-sarah-palin.

———. 2008. "Sarah Palin's 'Feminism' Is Irrelevant to Her Irresponsible Record." *Jezebel*. September 4. Accessed May 12, 2009. http://jezebel.com/5045409/sarah-palins-feminism-is-irrelevant-to-her-irresponsible-record.

Venezia, Todd. 2007. "Nut Buster: Wacky Hillary Gizmo Is a Real Easy Shell." *New York Post*. September 7. Accessed September 30, 2007. http://www.nypost.com/p/news/national/item_4eiLSEWHjAzDpC5vy7YTOJ;jsessionid=32B13AD893967D73 1268627A3CBE3AA8.

Vennochi, Joan. 2007. "That Clinton Cackle." *Boston Globe*. September 30. Accessed September 30, 2007. http://www.boston.com/news/nation/articles/2007/09/30/that_clinton_cackle/.

———. 2008. "Closing the Door on Victimhood." *Boston Globe*. November 6. Accessed November 6, 2008. http://www.boston.com/bostonglobe/editorial_opinion/oped/articles/2008/11/06/closing_the_door_on_victimhood/.

Vick, Karl, and Alec MacGillis. 2008. "Obama Confronts Ethnic Tensions in Bid for Votes." *Washington Post*. February 1. Accessed February 23, 2008. http://www.washingtonpost.com/wp-dyn/content/article/2008/01/31/AR2008013103726.html.

Vickerman, Milton. 2001. "Jamaicans: Balancing Race and Ethnicity." Pp. 201–228 in *New Immigrants in New York*, edited by Nancy Foner. New York: Columbia University Press.

Vogel, Kenneth. 2010. "Face of the Tea Party Is Female." Politico.com. March 26. Accessed March 26, 2010. http://www.politico.com/news/stories/0310/35094.html.

Wade, Peter. 1993. *Blackness and Race Mixture: The Dynamics of Racial Identity in Colombia*. Baltimore: Johns Hopkins University Press.

Wakeman, Jessica. 2008. "Misogyny's Greatest Hits: Sexism in Hillary Clinton Coverage." *Extra!* May/June. Accessed June 13, 2008. http://www.fair.org/index.php?page=3407.

Waldman, Paul. 2008. "Why Conservatives' Crush on Obama Is Doomed." *American Prospect*. January 9. Accessed January 31, 2008. http://www.prospect.org/cs/articles?article=why_conservatives_crush_on_obama_is_doomed.

Walker, Rob. 2003. "'Whassup, Barbie?' Marketers Are Embracing the Idea of a 'Post-racial' America." *Boston Globe*. January 12.

Wallace-Wells, Benjamin. 2006. "Is America Too Racist for Barack? Too Sexist for Hillary?" *Washington Post*. November 12. Accessed November 19, 2006. http://www.washingtonpost.com/wp-dyn/content/article/2006/11/10/AR2006111001387.html.

Wallsten, Peter. 2010. "Obama's New Partner: Al Sharpton." *Wall Street Journal*. March 17. Accessed April 12, 2011. http://online.wsj.com/article/SB10001424052748704588404575123404191464126.html.

Walsh, Joan. 2008. "Obama on Father's Day." Salon.com. June 16. Accessed June 16, 2008. http://www.salon.com/news/opinion/joan_walsh/feature/2008/06/16/obama_fathers_day.

Walters, Ronald W. 1999. *African American Leadership*. Albany: SUNY Press.

———. 2005. *Freedom Is Not Enough: Black Voters, Black Candidates, and American Presidential Politics*. Lanham, MD: Rowan and Littlefield.

Wang, Jimmy. 2009. "Now Hip-Hop, Too, Is Made in China." *New York Times*. January 23. Accessed January 23, 2009. http://www.nytimes.com/2009/01/24/arts/music/24hiphop.html.

Wang, Jun. 2008. "Asian Americans Outraged by CNN Election Report." *New America Media.* February 14. Accessed February 15, 2008. http://news.ncmonline.com/news/view_article.html?article_id=44cb40c466e5c8e91f4d0e557ef911bc.

Washington, Jesse. 2009. "Obama Takes a Stand on Race in a Divisive Case." CBS News. July 23. Accessed May 14, 2010. http://www.thefreelibrary.com/Obama+takes+a+stand+on+race+_+in+a+divisive+case-a01611945634.

———. 2011. "Obama Carefully Courts Black Votes with Sharpton." *New York Times.* April 5. Accessed April 12, 2011. http://www.nytimes.com/aponline/2011/04/05/us/AP-US-Obama-and-Sharpton.html.

Washington, Laura S. 2010. "What Has Barack Obama Done for Black America?" *In These Times.* March 24. Accessed March 24, 2010. http://www.inthesetimes.com/article/5733/what_has_barack_obama_done_for_black_america/.

Waters, Mary. 1990. *Ethnic Options.* Berkeley: University of California Press.

———. 1996. "The Intersection of Gender, Race, and Ethnicity in the Identity Development of Caribbean American Teens." Pp. 65–81 in *Urban Girls: Resisting Stereotypes, Creating Identities,* edited by Bonnie J. Ross Leadbeater and Niobe Way. New York: NYU Press.

———. 1999. *Black Identities: West Indian Immigrant Dreams and American Realities.* New York: Russell Sage Foundation.

Watkins, Boyce. 2011. "Cornel West, Al Sharpton Argue about President Obama." *Boyce Blog.* April 11. Accessed April 11, 2011. http://boycewatkins.wordpress.com/2011/04/11/cornel-west-al-sharpton-argue-about-president-obama/.

Webb, James. 2010. "Diversity and the Myth of White Privilege." *Wall Street Journal.* July 23. Accessed July 23, 2010. http://online.wsj.com/article/NA_WSJ_PUB:SB10001424052748703724104575379630952309408.html.

Weisman, Jonathan. 2008. "Obama, at Fundraiser, Pronounces Himself an 'Honorary AAPI.'" *Washington Post.* July 29. Accessed July 29, 2008. http://voices.washingtonpost.com/44/2008/07/obama-at-fundraiser-pronounces.html.

Weisman, Jonathan, and Laura Meckler. 2008. "Obama Sweeps to Historic Victory." *Wall Street Journal.* November 6. Accessed November 6, 2008. http://online.wsj.com/article/NA_WSJ_PUB:SB122581133077197035.html.

Wessler, Seth Freed. 2011. "Hostile State Battles Now Define Immigration Debate." *Colorlines.* January 6. Accessed April 11, 2011. http://colorlines.com/archives/2011/01/sparing_no_time_in_the.html.

Will, George. 2007. "Misreading Obama's Identity." *Washington Post.* December 30. Accessed December 30, 2007. http://www.washingtonpost.com/wp-dyn/content/article/2007/12/28/AR2007122802448.html.

Williams, Joseph, and Matt Negrin. 2008. "Affirmative Action Foes Point to Obama." *Boston Globe.* March 18. Accessed March 22, 2008. http://www.boston.com/news/nation/articles/2008/03/18/affirmative_action_foes_point_to_obama/.

Williams, Juan. 2007. "Black Voters Aren't Fully Sold On Obama." National Public Radio. February 9. Accessed February 15, 2008. http://www.npr.org/templates/story/story.php?storyId=7299432.

———. 2007. "Obama's Color Line." *New York Times.* November 30. Accessed November 30, 2007. http://www.nytimes.com/2007/11/30/opinion/30williams.html.

———. 2008. "What Obama's Victory Means for Racial Politics." *Wall Street Journal.* November 10. Accessed November 15, 2008. http://online.wsj.com/article/NA_ WSJ_PUB:SB122628263723412543.html.

Williams, Mike. 2009. "After Obama, No Excuses." *Raleigh (NC) News and Observer.* January 24. Accessed January 24, 2009. http://www.newsobserver.com/.

Williams, Patricia. 2007. "L'Étranger." *The Nation.* February 22. Accessed May 2, 2007. http://www.thenation.com/issue/march-5-2007.

Wilson, Marie C. 2008. "Commentary: Clinton Started a New Political Movement." CNN. June 6. Accessed June 15, 2008. http://www.cnn.com/2008/POLI-TICS/06/06/wilson/index.html.

Winant, Howard. 1994. *Racial Conditions: Politics, Theory, Comparisons.* Minneapolis: University of Minnesota Press.

———. 2001. *The World Is a Ghetto: Race and Democracy since World War II.* New York: Basic Books.

———. 2004. *The New Politics of Race: Globalism, Difference, Justice.* Minneapolis: University of Minnesota Press.

Wing, Bob. 2009. "Obama, Race, and the Future of US Politics." *Political Affairs Magazine.* March 31. Accessed March 31, 2009. http://www.politicalaffairs.net/ article/articleview/8092/.

Wingfield, Adia Harvey, and Joe R. Feagin. 2010. *Yes We Can? White Racial Framing and the 2008 Presidential Campaign.* New York: Routledge.

Wise, Tim. 2008. "Your Whiteness Is Showing: An Open Letter to Certain White Women Who Are Threatening to Withhold Support from Obama in November." *Counterpunch.* June 7–8. Accessed June 15, 2008. http://www.counterpunch.org/ wise06072008.html.

———. 2009. *Between Barack and a Hard Place: Racism and White Denial in the Age of Obama.* San Francisco: City Lights.

———. 2010. *Colorblind: The Rise of Post-racial Politics and the Retreat from Racial Equity.* San Francisco: City Lights.

Witt, Linda, Karen M. Paget, and Glenna Matthews. 1994. *Running as a Woman: Gender and Power in American Politics.* New York: Free Press.

Wong, Scott, and Shira Toeplitz. 2010. "Dream Act Dies in Senate." *Politico.* December 18. Accessed April 11, 2011. http://www.politico.com/news/stories/1210/46573. html.

Woods, Jewel. 2008. "Bringing Sexy Back: Barack Obama and the 'Triumph' of White-Collar Masculinity." *Jewel Woods.* July 18. Accessed July 18, 2008. http:// jewelwoods.com/node/8.

Wooten, Jim. 2008. "Obama and Race Preferences." *Atlanta Journal-Constitution.* June 16. Accessed June 16, 2008. http://www.ajc.com/opinion/content/shared-blogs/ajc/thinkingright/entries/2008/06/16/obama_and_race_preferences.html.

Yancey, George. 2003. *Who Is White? Latinos, Asians, and the New Black/Nonblack Divide.* Boulder, CO: Lynne Rienner.

Yang, Jeff. 2008. "American More Than a Birthright." *San Francisco Chronicle.* October 23. Accessed November 15, 2008. http://articles.sfgate.com/2008-10-23/ entertainment/17138893_1_asian-americans-chinese-exclusion-act-wong-kim-ark.

———. 2008. "Could Obama be the First Asian American President?" *San Francisco Chronicle*. July 30. Accessed August 2, 2008. http://articles.sfgate.com/2008-07-30/entertainment/17120479_1_asian-americans-first-black-president-african-american.

Yetman, Norman, ed. 1998. *Majority and Minority: The Dynamics of Race and Ethnicity in American Life*, 6th ed. Boston: Allyn and Bacon.

Yglesias, Matt. 2008. "The Rise of the Non-whites." *Think Progress*. November 5. Accessed November 8, 2008. http://yglesias.thinkprogress.org/2008/11/the_rise_of_the_non_whites/.

Young, Cathy. 2008. "Why Feminists Hate Sarah Palin." *Wall Street Journal*. September 15. Accessed September 15, 2008. http://online.wsj.com/article/SB122143727571134335.html?mod=opinion_main_commentaries.

Younge, Gary. 2007. "Is Obama Black Enough?" *Guardian*. March 1. Accessed March 4, 2007. http://www.guardian.co.uk/world/2007/mar/01/usa.uselections2008.

———. 2007. "The Obama Effect." *The Nation*. December 13. Accessed January 15, 2008 http://www.thenation.com/article/obama-effect.

———. 2008. "An Obama Victory Would Symbolise a Great Deal and Change Very Little." *Guardian*. January 7. Accessed January 10, 2008. http://www.guardian.co.uk/commentisfree/2008/jan/07/barackobama.uselections2008.

Zeitlin, Matt. 2008. "Barack Obama Is My Imaginary Hip Black Friend." *Matt Zeitlin*. January 12. Accessed August 26, 2009. http://whippersnapper.wordpress.com/2008/01/12/barack-obama-is-my-imaginary-hip-black-friend/.

Zeleny, Jeff. 2008. "Obama and Clinton Statements on Police Trial." *New York Times*. April 25. Accessed April 25, 2008. http://cityroom.blogs.nytimes.com/2008/04/25/obama-respect-the-verdict/.

Zernike, Kate. 2010. "Palin Assails Obama at Tea Party Meeting." *New York Times*. February 7. Accessed April 14, 2011. http://www.nytimes.com/2010/02/07/us/politics/08palin.html.

———. 2011. "Tea Party Activists Angry at G.O.P." *New York Times*. January 1. Accessed April 12, 2011. http://www.nytimes.com/2011/01/02/us/politics/02teaparty.html.

Zora, Lady, Chauncey DeVega, and Gordon Gartrelle. 2008. "Euphemisms for Naming White Folk." *We Are Respectable Negroes*. September 24. Accessed September 24, 2008. http://wearerespectablenegroes.blogspot.com/2008/09/euphemisms-for-naming-white-folk-and.html.

Index

Affirmative action: colorblind individualism and, 36–37; opposition to, 16–18, 43–44, 131nn6–7

African Americans, 1, 3; black immigrants compared to, 27; class and, 6, 22, 146n24; colorism and, 27; Conservative views of, 45, 47, 113–14; demographic and cultural importance of, 68; new politics of race, views of, 44, 100–101, 150n80. *See also* Blacks

Alien Nation (Brimelow), 112

Allen, Charlotte, 64

Alterman, Eric, 127

America Alone: The End of the World as We Know It (Steyn), 154n17

American Issues Project, 156n53

American Journal of Sociology, 27

American Prospect, 89

American Thinker, 64

Andrews, D. L., 136n42

Ansell, Amy, 131n7

Arab Americans, 85

Asian American Action Fund, 100

Asian American and Pacific Islander ties to Obama, B., 101–2

Asian American Law Review, 81

Asian Americans, 84, 147n41; anti-black racism and, 91; black/Asian conflict, 91, 93, 97; black/white racial politics related to, 11, 81; 80–20 Initiative for, 93, 148n47; nation, inclusion in, 85, 146n19; Obama, B., identification with, 101–2; relevance of election to, 81

Assimilation, 84, 115–16

The Atlantic, 19, 41, 98, 118

Ayers, William, 117–18, 156n53

Bachmann, Michele, 116, 123

Bacon, James, 18

Balibar, Etienne, 67

Baltimore Sun, 157n58

Banks, Tyra, 38, 136n35

Barco, Mandalit del, 91

Barras, Jonetta Rose, 42, 137n46

Barrett, James, 110

Beck, Glenn, 40–41, 107, 111, 114, 154n19

Beinart, Peter, 41

Bendixen, Sergio, 62

Benjamin, Rich, 109

Bennett, Bill, 44

Biden, Joe, 153n2

Birthers: McCain and, 122–23; racial politics of, 121–23; Trump and, 122

Blacks: black/Asian conflict, 91, 93, 97; black/Latino conflict, 91–92, 97–98, 150n69; culture as source of white racial authenticity and national identity, 46, 68; expectations of, 33–35, 37, 135n21; "good" and "bad," 41, 136n42; identities, 1–2, 6, 50, 88, 94–95, 126–27; lessons of election for, 13, 35; perception of selves as victims, 13, 15, 19, 26, 31, 37, 39, 43, 59, 113, 137n46; personal responsibility theme and, 21–22, 32, 41–43; poor, 37, 42–43, 137nn49, 54; as problematic public figures, 41–42, 137n49; as racially advantaged, 16. *See also* African Americans; Excuses

Black/Asian conflict, 91, 93, 97

Black electoral politics: bargainers compared to challengers in, 35–36; deracialization in, 34; political science on, 34

About the Author

ENID LOGAN is Associate Professor of Sociology at the University of Minnesota.